The Self in Its Worlds

Other Works by Troy Wilson Organ

An Index to Aristotle (1949)
The Examined Life (1956)
The Self in Indian Philosophy (1964)
The Art of Critical Thinking (1965)
The Hindu Quest for the Perfection of Man (1970, 1980)
Hinduism, Its Historical Development (1974)
Western Approaches to Eastern Philosophy (1975)
Third Eye Philosophy (1987)
Philosophy and the Self: East and West (1987)

The Self in Its Worlds

EAST AND WEST

Troy Wilson Organ

SELINSGROVE: SUSQUEHANNA UNIVERSITY PRESS
LONDON AND TORONTO: ASSOCIATED UNIVERSITY PRESSES

Associated University Presses
440 Forsgate Drive
Cranbury, NJ 08512

Associated University Presses
25 Sicilian Avenue
London WC1A 2QH, England

Associated University Presses
P.O. Box 488, Port Credit
Mississauga, Ontario
Canada L5G 4M2

The paper used in this publication meets the requirements of the American National Standard for Permanence of Paper for Printed Library Materials Z39.48–1984.

Library of Congress Cataloging-in-Publication Data

Organ, Troy Wilson.
The self in its worlds.

Bibliography: p.
Includes index.
1. Philosophy, Comparative. 2. Self (Philosophy) 3. East and West. I. Title.
B799.074 1988 126 87-42799
ISBN 0-941664-88-0 (alk. paper)

Printed in the United States of America

Contents

Preface 7

1 The Self in the Natural World—Theories of Reality 11
2 The Self in the Natural World—Causality 48
3 The Self in the Natural World—Time 77
4 The Self in the Social World 94
5 The Self and Values 129
6 The Self in the Aesthetic World 143
7 The Self in the Religious World 168

Postlude 200

Notes 213

Recommended Readings 235

Index 245

Preface

In *Philosophy and the Self: East and West* I compared how Eastern and Western philosophers understand the human being as thinker, as speaker, as knower, and as a self. In *The Self in Its Worlds: East and West* I compare the worlds that Eastern and Western human beings fashion. Human beings live in the same reality, but not in the same world. A *world*—as I use the term in this analysis—is a creative response to objective reality.

Śaṅkara, one of India's greatest philosophers, stressed *adhyāsa* as the factor that differentiates world and reality. This Sanskrit word is usually translated *superimposition.* Its basic feature is the transference of qualities, relationships, spatial and temporal locations, and other properties to things that do not in reality possess these characteristics. Śaṅkara's favorite illustration of *adhyāsa* was that of a traveler who thought a rope on the path was a snake, that is, the traveler superimposed a snake on the rope. Often the superimpositions are personal qualities, for example, "the *friendly* shade of a tree." Perhaps God is the ultimate *adhyāsa.*

This book is an examination of the four worlds that scientists, artists, politicians, poets, prophets, and priests superimpose on reality: the natural world, the social world, the aesthetic world, and the religious world. It is a consideration of ways in which Eastern and Western people construct a *Weltanschauung* (a world view) upon an *Umwelt*[1] (a perceptual world). My hope is that this study will encourage others to labor for a human community in which *Eastern* and *Western* are complementary, rather than contradictory, adjectives.

The Self in Its Worlds

1

The Self in the Natural World—Theories of Reality

The term *metaphysics* was coined by Andonicus of Rhodes in the first century B.C. to indicate additional Aristotelian materials he annexed to a treatise already written called *Physics*. *Metá* means "after", so all he intended by *Metaphysics* was "the material appended to the *Physics*" or "*Physics*, volume 2." Unfortunately, *metá* also means over and above or beyond. Therefore the word *metaphysics* has sometimes been used to mean that which transcends the commonplace, the usual, and in some circumstances, the normal. I shall not use the term in this prejudicial sense, nor shall I use it as Andonicus did. Metaphysics is not occult lore. Neither is it physics. Metaphysics is more general than physics. Physics studies spatial and temporal things. Metaphysics studies space and time. Physics asks what causes what. Metaphysics asks what is the meaning of the term *cause*. Physics discovers the physical universe. Metaphysics asks what makes it a universe. Metaphysics examines the assumptions of physics.

There are two types of metaphysics: qualitative and quantitative. Qualitative metaphysics asks what is the nature of ultimate reality, and answers that it must be like matter, or minds, or the objects of minds. Quantitative metaphysics asks how many irreducible realities are there, and answers that there may be one, or two, or many. Putting the two questions and the possible answers together indicates four fundamental types of metaphysical systems: *monistic idealism, pluralistic idealism, pluralistic materialism,* and *metaphysical dualism.* To these four systems must be added the view that ultimate reality is beyond knowing. Since, according to this position, ultimate reality transcends epistemological categories, perhaps the system can be called *metaphysical transcendentalism.*

Idealism, when used to designate a metaphysical system, means that which pertains to ideas, and, since ideas are commonly thought to be mind-dependent, the term also means that which is mental, although spiritual, personal, or psychical are possible implications. The notion of a norm that is a state of perfection is to be eschewed. Since idealism is contrary, if not contradictory, to materialism, the view that matter is the primordial constituent of the universe, a term like *spiritualism* might be preferable to idealism were it not for the fact that the term *spiritualism* has come to mean the belief that spirits of the dead communicate with the living. *Immaterialism* would be a good term for this type of metaphysical system, except for the negativity of the term. According to *Philosophie* (1958) of the *Fischer Lexikon*, "Fundamental to the idealist tradition is the insistence on spirit as an immaterial entity (whether a substance or unity) which is in some sense efficacious in guiding the body and in ordering the material world, whether from without it or within it. Fundamental to the materialist tradition is the denial of this claim and the interpretation of spiritual phenomena as natural events within the world of matter."[1] The claim of Wilbur Long in the *Dictionary of Philosophy* that "the history of philosophy broadly understood, is largely the history of Idealism"[2] does not do justice to a rich tradition of materialism both in the West and the East. The term *idealism* was first used in the seventeenth century for the Platonic theory of eternal, unchanging, archetypal, universal, and mind-independent objects of thought called *Ideas* or *Forms* and also for the theory of Descartes and Locke that the objects of thought are mind-dependent. The obvious confusion of this dual meaning is avoided by calling the former *objective idealism* and the latter *subjective idealism.* Subjective idealism, which is known also as psychological idealism or subjectivism, holds that all reality is ideas of knowers. To be is to be sensed or thought by an individual. In its extreme form this is known as *solipsism*, the view that nothing, not even another self, is more than an idea of the one holding the view. Solipsism is nonsense as a theory, since stating the theory assumes another mind to whom the theory is stated, and that is a violation of the theory.

Monistic Idealism

Berkeley

George Berkeley (1685–1753), the great idealist of the Western world, is often described as a subjective idealist on the grounds of his oft-propounded expression *esse est percipi* (to be is to be perceived). But this is not correct, since he held that being perceived implies a perceiver whose reality does not in turn depend upon being perceived by another perceiver. Anything that has reality is either a mind or an object of a mind. Berkeley stated the fundamentals of his metaphysics in two thin volumes: *The Principles of Human Knowledge* (1710) and *Three Dialogues between Hylas and Philonous* (1713). Both had the negative purpose of rejecting the abstract idea of matter and the positive purpose of making mind or spirit the fundamental reality.

Berkeley began his *Principles* in the following manner:

> It is evident to any one who takes a survey of the objects of human knowledge, that they are either ideas actually imprinted on the senses; or else such as are perceived by attending to the passions and operations of the mind; or lastly, ideas formed by help of memory and imagination—either compounding, dividing, or barely representing those originally perceived in the aforesaid ways. By sight I have the ideas of light and colours, with their several degrees and variations. By touch I perceive hard and soft, heat and cold, motion and resistance, and of all these more and less either as to quantity or degree. Smelling furnishes me with odours; the palate with tastes; and hearing conveys sounds to the mind in all their variety of tone and composition. And as several of these are observed to accompany each other, they come to be marked by one name, and so to be reputed as one thing. Thus, for example, a certain colour, taste, smell, figure and consistence having been observed to go together, are accounted one distinct thing, signified by the name *apple*; other collections of ideas constitute a stone, a tree, a book, and the like sensible things—which as they are pleasing, or disagreeable excite the passions of love, hatred, joy, grief, and so forth.

Then, having established that things—the objects of knowledge—are ideas received from sensations, or ideas perceived by examining the working of the mind, or ideas formed by the mind, he noted that there is obviously another reality, namely, the mind that perceives: "there is likewise something which knows or perceives them [the ideas], and exercises divers operations, as willing, imagining, remembering, about them. This perceiving, active being is what I call *mind*, *spirit*, *soul*, or *myself*. By which words I do not denote any of my ideas, but a thing entirely distinct from them, wherein, they exist, or, which is the same thing, whereby they are perceived—for the existence of an idea consists in being perceived."[3] Berkeley had only two things in his theory of reality: self-existent minds and mind-dependent ideas. Minds have reality in and of themselves. Ideas depend upon minds for their reality. So only minds have ultimate reality.

Berkeley made a distinction that he did not develop and that is often missed by students of Berkeley. He wrote, "I find I can *excite ideas in my mind* at pleasure, and vary and shift the scene as oft as I think fit. . . . But, whatever power I may have over my own thoughts, I find the *ideas actually perceived by sense* have not a like dependence on my will."[4] This implies there are two kinds of ideas: those that can be created, and those that cannot be created. The former would be the ideas of a rationalist and the latter the ideas of an empiricist. But Berkeley expressly denied the former: "Ideas imprinted on the senses are real things, or do really exist; this we do not deny, but we deny they can subsist without the minds which perceive them, or that they are resemblances of any archetypes existing without the mind."[5] The last clause is a rejection of Platonism. Berkeley ignored the ideas he can "vary and shift" as he turned to "the ideas actually presented by senses." He wrote, "When in broad daylight I open my eyes, it is not in my power to choose whether I shall see or no, or to determine what particular objects shall present themselves to my view; and so likewise as to the hearing and other senses; the ideas imprinted on them are not creatures of my will."[6] In the latter part of section 90 he drew no distinction between sensation and idea, writing that

> the very being of a sensation or idea consists in being perceived, and an idea can be like nothing but an idea. Again, the things perceived by sense may be termed external, with regard to their origin—in that they are not generated from within by the mind itself, but imprinted by a Spirit distinct from that which perceives them. Sensible objects may likewise be said to be "without the mind" in another sense, namely when they exist in some other mind; thus, when I shut my eyes, the things I saw may still exist, but it must be in another mind.

All ideas or sensations depend on minds. I as a mind am unable to create my own sensations. I have faith that the things I sense still exist when I no longer sense them. So there must be a mind that produces what I sense and that preserves what I sense when I no longer sense it. This "other mind" he referred to throughout the *Principles* as "some other Will or Spirit," "that Governing Spirit," "a Free Spirit," "Supreme Spirit," "Almighty Spirit," "Spirit, 'who works all in all,' and 'by whom all things consist,'" "that supreme and wise Spirit 'in whom we live, move, and have our being,'" "the Author of nature," "Creator," "Providence," "the Intelligence that sustains and rules the ordinary course of things," "a Superior Mind," "that Eternal Invisible Mind which produces and sustains all things," and—of course—"God." Berkeley, who rose to the rank of bishop in the Church of England, left no doubt as to which God he had in mind.

Berkeley at age twenty had formulated what he called the "immaterial hypothesis," the view that matter does not exist. "Matter" or "material substance," according to Berkeley, are words that do not stand for anything objective or subjective. Its defenders said "matter" names that which supports qualities. But Berkeley said "matter" is an empty noise. How can a thing be in the natural world if it cannot be seen, heard, tasted, smelled, or touched? How can a thing be in the spiritual world if it does not sense or think? Matter is an abstract idea with no roots in reality. "It neither acts, nor perceives, nor is perceived; for this is all that is meant by saying it is an inert, senseless, unknown substance; which is a definition entirely made up of negatives, excepting only the relative notion of its standing under or supporting."[7] The argument offered by its defenders is "the description of a nonentity."[8] Berkeley had thought that his rejection of matter and assignment of matter's reputed function to God would be well received. But that was not the case. He was laughed at, ridiculed, declared to be insane, and chastized for seeking notoriety by presenting an absurdly novel doctrine. Some said his philosophy was just what one might expect from an Irishman!

In response to the attacks, and to clarify his meaning, Berkeley wrote the *Three Dialogues between Hylas and Philonous. Hylas* is the Greek term for matter; *Philonous*, a word created from the Greek, means a lover of mind. The zenith of the conversation appears at the close of the first dialogue when Philonous offers the following challenge to Hylas: "I am content to put the whole upon this issue. If you can conceive it possible for any mixture or combination of qualities, or any sensible object whatever, to exist without the mind, then I will grant it actually to be so." Hylas confidently accepts the challenge: "If it comes to that the point will soon be decided. What more easy than to conceive a tree or house existing by itself, independent of, and unperceived by, any mind whatsoever? I do at this present time conceive them existing after that manner."[9] Philonous then attempts a coup de grace by reminding Hylas that one cannot see an unseen object or think an unthought-of thought, so how can he contend that he is able to conceive "a house or tree existing independent and out of all minds whatsoever?"[10] And Hylas admits, "As I was thinking of a tree in a solitary place where no one was present to see it, methought that was to conceive a tree as existing unperceived or unthought of, not considering that I myself conceived it all the while."[11]

What Hylas should have done was to point out to Philonous that there is a difference between the *object* of thought and the *conditions* of thought. Of course, one cannot think without thinking, but it is possible to have as the object of one's thought an-existing-tree-about-which-one-hundred-people-are-thinking, an-existing-tree-about-which-ten-people-are-thinking, an-existing-tree-about-which-one-person-is-thinking, and an-existing-tree-about-which-no-one-is-thinking. To counter that in every case the thinker of the thought is thinking, and therefore the tree cannot exist unthought of, is to confuse the epistemological condition and the epistemological object. The object of thought that Hylas proposed was a-tree-existing-unthought-of-by-anyone, and the fact that Hylas was entertaining this object of thought did not affect the unthought-of-by-anyone-aspect of the object of thought. He might have replied, "The fact that I am thinking of a-tree-existing-unthought-of-by-me cannot be disallowed by pointing out that I am thinking."

Although Berkeley was the great idealist of the West he has had few followers. Yet he is still widely read—especially in university classes, possibly because of the simplicity of his presentation—and his name is still invoked both by admirers and detractors.[12]

Yogācāra

The best example of a monistic idealism in the East is that of the Yogācāra or Vijñānavāda, a Buddhist school of philosophy founded in India in the second century A.D. by Aṣvaghosa, developed in the fourth century under Aryāsaṅga and Dignāga, and introduced into China in the next century. The term *Yogācāra* refers to the practical side of the doctrine, meaning that the absolute truth or *bodhi* is attainable only by those who practice yoga. *Vijñānavāda* refers to the theoretical side, meaning the view based on the principles of critical analysis. Radhakrishnan compared the Yogācārins' attack on the Sautrāntikins (Buddhist philosophers who held that there is an actual self-existent spatial and temporal universe in which mind has only an equal place with other finite things) with Berkeley's attack on Locke's material substratum: "The task of the Yogācāra was like that of Berkeley, to expose the baseless and self-contradictory character of the unknown absolute matter of the Sautrāntika, and persuade us to drop all ideas of such an external existence. We have no warrant for supposing the cause of all things to be material substance. Matter is an idea and nothing more. Things are clusters of sensations."[13] Much of the Yogācāra literature has been preserved in Tibetan and Chinese translations from the Sanskrit.

According to the Yogācārins all data of human experience can be considered from three points of view. The view of ordinary unsophisticated people is that things are exactly as they are experienced. The sense organs are humans' windows to reality. The shimmering water seen by the thirsty traveler on the desert is water. This is *the imagined point of view*. The Yogācārins say this view must be forsaken, as it gives the human being a world of mirages, of imagined and contrived "realities." The second point of view is known as *the interdependent point of view*. The desert traveler learns that what was mistaken as water is an appearance fashioned by the interdependence of atmospheric conditions. The traveler learns to discriminate between data that is purely imaginary, and therefore nonexistent, such as the objects of daydreaming, and data like the water images on the desert that do not exist as they appear. The former may be said to be illusory in reality; the latter is illusory in appearance, i.e., the traveler did see something in the desert, but erred in thinking it was water. *The absolute or perfected point of view* transcends the interdependent point of view that things exist relative to other existing things, just as the interdependent point of view transcends the naively realistic point of view that things are as they are experienced and are experienced as they are. According to the absolute view empirical characteristics are recognized as analogues or metaphors of reality. The absolute view is in fact not a view. It is free from all signs, names, and appearances. One who takes the first view sees the mirage as water; one who takes the second view sees the water as mirage; one who takes the third view drinks the water!

The first two points of view constitute the mind system. This is the empirical level of knowing. It is always afflicted with subject-object duality. It is known as *visaya vijñāna* (sense-consciousness, object-consciousness, or discriminating-mind). Yogācāra would be a subjective idealism were this the entirety of its metaphysics. The words of the *Laṅkāvatāra Sūtra* state in the language of Berkeley that *esse est percipi*: "The sense-minds and their centralised discriminating-mind are related to the external world which is a manifestation of itself and is given over to perceiving, discriminating and grasping its *māyā*-like appearances."[14] But this is not all of the Yogācāra theory of reality. There is also a Transcendental Subject known as the *Ālaya Vijñāna*. The absolute "view" is that of *Ālaya Vijñāna*. The *Ālaya Vijñāna* is what the yogis discover in their meditation, that is, that waking consciousness is but a fragment of a whole that is much wider than the ordinary human ever dreams. The discovery of the Universal Mind is a possibility for every human being; but as long as one clings to the illusion of individuality, to particularizing, and to dichotomizing, the discovery will never be made.

In the absence of a yogic experience the nature of *Ālaya Vijñāna* can only be suggested by inadequate verbalization. Since one of the functions of *Ālaya Vijñāna* is to serve as the repository of all mental life, the term is translated as "Storehouse Consciousness." Some translators prefer "Sub-conscious Consciousness" or "Universal Mind." *Ālaya Vijñāna* is the matrix from which all that is comes into being. It is sometimes called the *tathāgata-garba*, the womb where the future is conceived, nourished, and matured. It is the source of the phenomenal world as well as of the Buddha, of the illusory as well as of the real, of evil as well as of good. *Ālaya Vijñāna* is not a substance—not even the *Ātman*—but a series of seeds, each giving rise to its successor, or, better, a stream of absolute consciousness. It is the ultimate reality from which all that is real derive their reality. In the words of Berkeley it is "that Eternal Invisible Mind which produces and sustains all things."[15] According to the *Laṅkavatāra*, "Universal Mind transcends all individuation and limits. Universal Mind is thoroughly pure in its essential nature, subsisting unchanged, and free from faults of impermanence, undisturbed by egoism, unruffled by distinctions, desires and aversions. Universal Mind is like a great ocean, its surface ruffled by waves and surges but its depths remaining forever unmoved."[16] It is "the storage and clearing house of all the accumulated products of mentation and action since beginningless time."[17]

Between Universal Mind (*Ālaya Vijñāna*) and the discriminating-mind (*visaya vijñāna*) is intuitive-mind (*manas vijñāna*):

> Between Universal Mind and the individual discriminating-mind is the intuitive-mind which is dependent upon Universal Mind for its cause and support and enters into relations with both. . . . Intuitive-mind is one with Universal Mind by reason of its participation in Transcendental Intelligence, and is one with the mind-system by its comprehension of differentiated knowledge. . . . The discriminating-mind is a dancer and a magician with the objective world as his stage. Intuitive-mind is the wise jester who travels with the magician and reflects upon his emptiness and transiency. Universal Mind keeps the record and knows what must be and what may be.[18]

Yogācārins call theirs the philosophy of *citta-mātra* (mind-only). Mind is the only reality. Everything other than mind is but ideas of mind. According to the *Surangama Sūtra* the Buddha once addressed his disciples as follows: "All the

Brothers in this Great Assembly, and you too, Ananda, should reverse your outward perception of hearing and listen inwardly for the perfectly unified and intrinsic sound of your own Mind-Essence, for as soon as you have attained perfect accommodation, you will have attained to Supreme Enlightenment."[19] In the *Laṅkavatāra* the Buddha is reported to have said that "the external world is nothing but a manifestation of mind."[20] An object in the physical world is a shadowy appearance conjured by thought. The reasoning of the Yogācārins, insofar as it can be constructed, moves like this: External objects cannot be established because they cannot be different from the consciousness of objects. Waking experiences no more require an external world for their verification than do dream experiences. So it is not possible to establish the reality of external objects, nor is it necessary.

The assertion of the nonexistence of objects, although a metaphysical position, was not stated for intellectual purposes. Buddhism is always soteriological. Metaphysical ideas are introduced only when instrumental to the attainment of the ideal condition known as Nirvāṇa. So when one reads in Buddhist literature that the world is like "a painter's canvas on which the ignorant imagine they see the elevations and depressions of mountains and valleys. . . . like a wheel of fire made by a revolving firebrand . . . like a mirror reflecting colors and images . . . like the echo of the wind . . . like a mirage of moving water seen in a desert"[21] one must keep in mind that the motivation is to guide humans into paths leading to the cessation of suffering, not merely to metaphysical wisdom.

Pluralistic Idealism

Leibniz

Gottfried Wilhelm Leibniz (1646–1716) is the best example of a Western pluralistic idealist. He was well aware of the work of Baruch Spinoza (1632–1677) who, assuming that to be is to be one and that oneness means totality, developed a theory of ultimate reality as the One Substance. Leibniz agreed that to be is to be one, but oneness for him meant indivisibility. Therefore, in the Leibnizian system ultimate reality is a harmony of independent simple substances. He once observed that the essential difference between his metaphysics and that of Spinoza was that there is but one substance for Spinoza and an infinite number for him.

Leibniz sought integration without loss of variety both in his thought and in his life. He possessed more talents and interests than he was able to indulge. He moved from project to project completing few. He promoted a design for establishing centers of learning in all the capitals of Europe where philosophers and scientists could gather to assist each other, outlined plans for an encyclopedia of human knowledge, developed programs for cooperative research in medicine and physical sciences, outlined a conceptual alphabet as the first step in the development of a universal language, and prepared a doctrine of essential Christian beliefs in an effort to terminate divisions in Christendom.

Leibniz, like all scientists and philosophers of seventeenth-century Europe, accepted the notion of substance as a fundamental fact about the natural world. All things in the natural world have properties or qualities such as color, sound, texture, temperature, flavor, taste, odor, and so forth, and everything has that which supports the qualities, that holds them together as a a thing distinct from other things of its class and from things of other classes, and that accounts for the persistence of the thing through change of qualities. It is the substance of Fido that persists throughout the lifetime of Fido from puppyhood to senility. Substance as substance cannot be observed, but substance must be for there to be an object that can be experienced. The experienced object is a substance also, a complex thing composed of simple things. So there are both complex substances and simple substances. The distinguishing characteristic of a simple substance, according to Leibniz, is indivisibility. Leibniz called simple substances "monads." He probably borrowed the term from Euclid's *Elements*, where *monas* means the unit. Leibniz began his little book *The Monadology* as follows: "The *monad*, of which we shall speak here, is nothing but a simple substance, which enters into compounds; *simple*, that is to say, without parts. And there must be simple substances, because there are compounds; for the compound is nothing but a collection or *aggregatum* of simples. Now where there are no parts, there neither extension, nor shape, nor divisibility is possible. And these monads are the true atoms of nature, and, in a word, the elements of all things."[22]

The monad cannot have parts; if it did, it would not be simple. The monad cannot have extension; if it did, it could always be halved into two shorter lengths. The monad cannot have figure; if it did, it could always be measured by simpler units. So the monad is indivisible.

Leibniz continued in his opening remarks about monads:

> Moreover, there is no fear of dissolution, and there is no conceivable way in which a simple substance could perish in the course of nature. For the same reason there is no way in which a simple substance could begin in the course of nature, since it cannot be formed by means of compounding. Thus it may be said that monads can only begin and end all at once, that is to say they can only begin by creation and end by annihilation, whereas what is compound begins and ends by parts. There is also no means of explaining how a monad can be altered or changed within itself by any other created thing, since it is impossible to displace anything in it or to conceive of the possibility of any internal motion being started, directed, increased, or diminished within it, as can occur in compounds, where change among the parts takes place. Monads have no windows, by which anything could come in or go out.[23]

To discover what a monad is like Leibniz suggested that we look within ourselves. What is the immediate experience of our selves? We discover that we are centers of spiritual activity. We are force or action. For us, to be is to be active. Likewise the monad is a spiritual atom—a source and center of activity. Monads appear to each other as material, even mechanical, bodies, but the material and the bodily is not the real essence of things. Matter is the representative manner in which one monad is symbolized in another monad's awareness. Again, we know by self-examination that we are free purposing agents, yet we see each other in terms of caused objects. I am what I have made myself to be, but you are the product of heredity and environment!

Leibniz, as idealist, had to account for matter. He did so in a very interesting way. There are two kinds of matter, he said—*materia secunda* and *materia prima*. Secondary matter is phenomenal. It does not belong to monads but to the aggregate of monads that we call *things,* and to them only as an appearance of materiality. The universe is in reality an infinity of nonspatial simple substances that present the illusion of large material bodies moving in space. Primary matter is an aspect of monads, but since monads have no extension, so primary matter is the nonextended potentiality of monads to appear as extended when grouped with other monads to form things in the natural world. Primary matter is force or energy that under certain conditions appears to be material. This seventeenth-century anticipation of Einstein's equation of matter and energy is striking. Ruth Lydia Saw, an authority on Leibniz, has observed, "Matter conceived as essentially energy-bearing, as giving rise to the well-founded appearance of extension in space and time, and of each centre of activity having what appears to be spatial relations with other centres of energy, fits admirably the state of present-day physics."[24]

One wonders why Leibniz did not say that the monads have no *doors*, since it is through doors rather than windows that things usually enter or depart. What he had in mind is that there is no causal relationship among monads. Each monad is a solipsistic universe. No monad—with the possible exception of God—is aware of other monads. No monad acts on another monad. Then how could Leibniz account for variety and change in the world? Saw suggests

> If we are looking for an analogy for the kind of change which Monads undergo, we must look at our own experiences. At any moment we can detect variety in our experiences and change from one moment to the next. At this moment, for example, I am thinking about Leibniz and, at the same time, hearing the wind in the trees, conscious that I am pleasantly warm, and that it will soon be time to stop for lunch. These other aspects are detected only when we look for them, but, nevertheless, they are aspects of one and the same state. We do not for one moment imagine our consciousness of the rustling of the leaves to be side by side with our feeling of warmth, and Leibniz is appealing to us to agree that this is a thinkable kind of multiplicity which could belong to an object not extended in space. In this way, we can

see how it is that there can be variety in a world composed of simple substances.[25]

The monads appear to be finite in that they come into being and pass away. This cannot be done by composition and decomposition since monads have no parts. They can only begin or end all at once. Leibniz, a devout Protestant, appealed to God as "the Architect of the machine of the universe."[26] God's activity in fashioning monads is designated by the term *fulguration*, which means to send out flashes like lightning. Leibniz wished to avoid the word *creation*, which would suggest the forming of things that can act independently of their maker, and the word *emanation*, which would suggest the forming of things that act dependently on their maker. God the Fulgurator selects from an infinity of possible monads those whose life histories are compatible with the life history of other fulgurated monads. Each fulgurated monad functions in pre-established harmony with every other fulgurated monad. No monad is aware of any other monad—in this sense they are windowless—nor does any monad have an effect on another. That which appears to the scientist as a cause-effect relationship among corporeal objects is but the working out of the pre-established harmony of the noncorporeal monads.

God's role in Leibniz's metaphysics is not clear. God is both the architect of the universe and the "Monarch of the divine city of Minds."[27] That is, God is both the fulgurator of all monads and the chief monad. This duality may be reflected in Leibniz's reference to the simple substances as "created monads" (therefore fulgurated by God) and also as "incorporeal automata" (therefore motivated by God as an external agency).[28] The created monads are divided into three classes: (1) rational minds, which he called "rational monads" and "spirits"; (2) animal centers of consciousness, which he called "irrational monads" or "souls"; and (3) monads that have very obscure perceptions and give no evidence of their inner spiritual nature, which he called "bare monads," "sleeping monads," and "swooning monads." All the created monads are entelechies, since they contain within themselves a latent perfection.

While the monads are windowless in the sense that they possess no means for looking out at each other, they do have relationships to each other. Leibniz's favorite metaphor is of a mirror: "every monad is a mirror that is alive or endowed with inner activity, is representative of the universe from its own point of view, and is as much regulated as the universe itself."[29] The metaphor is not adequate. What Leibniz meant was that the whole universe is portrayed in each monad in a noncausal way. What one sees in a monad is not a mirror image or an appearance of a real world but a way to understand the entire universe through the idiosyncrasies of each monad—and each monad is unique.

Jainism

The nearest approximation to a pluralistic idealism in Eastern philosophy is Jainism, a living way of life practiced today by a few million people who reside chiefly in India. Jainism was founded in the sixth century B.C. by Vardhamāna, who is usually known as Mahāvīra (Great Hero). The primary aim of Jainism is the perfection of the soul through a rigorous asceticism based on the doctrine of *ahiṁsā*, or noninjury of any living being.

Jainism began as a rejection of the Hindu conceptions of *Ātman-Brahman* and of any god of creation or worship, although liberated individuals are called *gods*. Its metaphysical positions are always tempered by *syādvāda*, "The Doctrine of Maybe." This is the conviction that reality is extremely indeterminate. Therefore any statement about ultimate reality must be qualified.

Since the universe can be looked at from a number of viewpoints, a variety of conclusions can be true. The Jains illustrate their epistemology by the oft-repeated story of the blind men who decided that an elephant is like a wall, a pillar, a winnowing fan, a rope, or a snake, depending upon which part of the elephant each blind man happened to touch. All statements about the nature of reality are subject to a sevenfold formula: (1) maybe is, (2) maybe is not, (3) maybe is and is not, (4) maybe is inexpressible, (5) maybe is and is inexpressible, (6) maybe is not and is inexpressible, and (7) maybe is, is not, and is inexpressible. The conclusion to be drawn is that all judgments have only a partial and limited application to reality.

The Jain philosophers within the limits of the caveat of *syādvāda* state that being (*sat*) is in two forms: (1) *cetana dravya* (conscious substance) and (2) *acetana dravya* (unconscious substance). The two are more commonly known as *jīva* and *ajīva*. The Hindu connotation of "self" and "nonself" should be avoided, although terms such as *souled* and *non-souled*, *spirit* and *nonspirit*, and *vital principle* and *non-vital principle* are sometimes used by the commentators. *Jīva* means abstractly the metaphysical categories of life and consciousness, and concretely the life-monads that are uncreated, imperishable, living, and conscious. *Ajīva* as a metaphysical category means nonliving and nonconscious, the contradictions of *jīva*. That which *ajīva* denotes is divided into two classes: *rūpa* (with form) and *arūpa* (without form). That which is with form is known as *pudgala* (matter). Matter is composed of an infinity of uncreated and indestructible atoms. Matter possesses four qualities: odor, color, taste, and tangibility. Sound is a mode of matter. That which is without form is *ākaśa*, *dharma*, *adharma*, and *kāla*. *Ākaśa* (space) is the container of everything, of both the universe (*loka*) and the non-universe (*aloka*). *Dharma* is the medium that makes movement possible. *Adharma* is that which makes rest possible. In the writings of Jainism *dharma* is compared to water, and *adharma* is compared to earth. *Kāla* (time) is the medium that makes change possible.

Ajīva is that which can be touched, tasted, heard, seen, and smelled; *jīva* is that which can touch, taste, hear, see, and smell. *Ajīva* is the object; *jīva* is the subject. Each atom is also a monad, that is, each *ajīva* is also a *jīva*. This view is known in the West as either *hylozoism* (all matter is alive) or *panpsychism* (all things are living). The Jain soteriology is based on the proposition that there is a one-way cause-effect relationship between the *ajīva* and the *jīva* that must be arrested. Matter is constantly affecting the proper function of spirit. Liberation (*mokṣa*) is release from the deleterious influence of matter. The Jains refer to matter as a weight that prevents *jīvas* from ascending to the top of the universe where they might remain in endless bliss.

All *jīvas* are eternal, living, conscious, and have the potential for liberation from *ajīva*, but they differ in their number of senses. Some *jīvas* have only the sense of touch. There are five classes of the one-sense *jīvas*: those associated with the earth, with water, with fire, with air, and with vegetable life. A Jain, for example, could say either "I touch the piece of chalk" or "The piece of chalk touches me." Jains are strict vegetarians. Some refrain from eating potatoes, contending that each eye of a potato is a life. *Jīvas* that have two senses—touch and taste—include worms, leeches, and other simple fauna. The three-sensed *jīvas*, like ants and moths, have the senses of touch, taste, and smell. *Jīvas* with four senses have in addition the sense of sight. They include flies, locusts, mosquitoes, and scorpions. Man and the lower animals belong to the class of five-sensed *jīvas*. The classification of *jīvas* according to the number of senses they possess seems to imply a hierarchy of development. The five-sensed *jīvas* have, through their incarnations, been more successful in throwing off matter, and are therefore closer to the *mokṣa* state than are *jīvas* with fewer than five senses.

Jainism is obviously a dualistic metaphysic, yet the claims of the Jains that there are an infinity of *jīvas* and that salvation consists in the separation of the *jīva* from matter make it possible to consider Jainism an Eastern counterpart to Leibniz's pluralistic idealism.

Mysore Hiriyanna offers the following apology for what he terms the "half-hearted character of Jaina inquiry": "The truth is that the primary aim of Jainism is the perfection of the soul, rather than the interpretation of the universe." Hiriyanna concludes, "as a result we fail to find in it an ultimate solution of the metaphysical problem."[30]

Pluralistic Materialism

Greek Atomism

Pluralistic materialism began in the Greek world as a protest against the metaphysics of the Eleatic philosophers, chiefly Parmenides, who argued as follows: reality is a plenum, that is, a Being that is full; as a plenum it is the Great One; as the Great One it is homogeneous, that is, there are no gaps, or void, or nonbeing in Being; if there is no void, physical motion or change is impossible; despite visual appearances, therefore there is no motion.

Leucippus and Democritus (fifth century B.C.) agreed that the physical world is composed of units that are full, homogeneous, and free from internal motion, but they contended that Parmenides had grossly overestimated the size and underestimated the number of the plena. Leucippus, according to Aristotle, held that

> "what is" in the strict sense of the term is an absolute plenum. This plenum, however, is not "one"; on the contrary, it is a "many," infinite in number and invisible owing to the minuteness of their bulk. The "many" move in the void (for there is a void): and by coming together they produce "coming-to-be," while by separating they produce "passing-away." Moreover, they act and suffer action wherever they chance to be in contact (for there they are not "one"), and they generate by being put together and becoming intertwined.[31]

Aristotle, the chief source of our information about these ancient pluralistic materialists, reported, "Leucippus and his associate Democritus say that the full and the empty are the elements, calling the one *being* and the other *non-being*—the full and solid being *being*, the empty *non-being* (whence they say *being* no more is than *non-being*, because the solid no more is than the empty.)"[32]

Leucippus and Democritus appear to have been commonsense philosophers, anxious to save the appearances of things, that is, plurality, movement, change, generation, decay, destruction. All of these had been shown by the Eleatics to be irrational, and therefore nonexistent. The problem to which Leucippus and Democritus addressed themselves was whether a theory of reality can be developed that does not violate what one experiences. Their answer was that the real world is composed of units that are invisible and indivisible. The latter may have been the most significant characteristic of the units, since they selected as a name for the units the Greek word *ātomon*, meaning that which cannot be sliced, Atoms are invisible because of their smallness; they are indivisible because of their unity. Each is a plenum. They are uncreated, indestructible, unchangeable, and innumerable.

Aristotle wrote regarding Democritus,

> He thinks the substances are so small as to escape our senses, but have all sorts of shapes and figures, and differences of size. From these substances, as from elements, are generated and compounded visible and sensible masses. The substances are at variance and move in the void because of their dissimilarity and the other aforesaid differences, and as they move they impinge on each other and are so completely interlocked that they touch one another or get near one another; but a single substance is never in reality produced from them by this interlocking; for it would be very naïf to suppose that two or more things could ever become one. The fact that substances stay with one another for some time the Atomists ascribe to the bodies fitting into one an-

> other and catching hold of one another; for some of them are scalene, others hook-shaped, others concave, others convex, and others have numberless other differences. He thinks they cling to one another and remain together until some stronger force arriving from the environment shakes them asunder and separates them.[33]

The atomists claimed that shape determines the taste of things. For example, sweet was associated with round atoms, sour with jagged and many-angled atoms, salty with atoms having two equal sides, bitter with very crooked and small atoms. Atoms differ externally in position and arrangement as they come together to form compound bodies.

Since the atoms have no parts, they do not move internally, but it is the nature of atoms to be always in motion with respect to each other. They "struggle," "collide," "become entangled," "intertwine," "scatter," "vibrate," and "move by mutual collisions and blows." All this activity takes place in the void. But here the atomists had problems. Parmenides had contended that the void is nothing, and that nothing cannot be. To say that nonbeing exists is to say that a nothing is a something. The atomists argued that nonbeing is the absence of being. The absence of being is not nothing; it is a no-thing, and "No-thing exists just as much as a thing."[34] "No-thing," "nonbeing," or "void" is the place between atoms, the nonatomic area in which atoms could move. The Greek word for void—*kenós*—means "the empty." The temptation to identify the notion of void and space must be resisted. Roy Kenneth Hack says about the atomists' conception of the void, "It must not be confused with empty space; the Greeks had not yet invented the notion of a continuous substratum underlying all phenomena. The void, which was also non-being, was merely an interruption of Being, which permitted beings to move and so to cause phenomena; but it was a necessary interruption."[35] There was no notion of a stuff that might or might not be occupied by atoms. Atoms were not thought to be void-occupying, as they would be space-occupying were void understood as space. The void is only where atoms are not.

John Burnet said of Leucippus, "He hardly, it is true, had words to express his discovery in; for the verb 'to be' had hitherto been used by philosophers only of body. But he did his best to make his meaning clear by saying 'what is not' (in the old corporealist sense) 'is' (in another sense) just as much as 'what is!' The void is as real as body."[36] The conception of the reality of the noncorporeal had to wait until the appearance of Socrates.

Epicurus in the third century B.C. made what he felt were necessary changes in the atomic theory. His most striking innovation was the notion that the atoms have weight. Since all atoms have equal weight, they fall at equal speed through the void. The atoms move continuously, "some of them falling straight down, others swerving, and others recoiling from their collisions."[37] Some of the atoms recoiling from collisions produce a solid; others produce a liquid. The world thus comes into being mechanically, and operates in a strictly mechanical fashion. Even the soul is atomic. Epicurus wrote that

> the soul is a body of fine particles distributed throughout the whole structure, and most resembling wind with a certain admixture of heat, and in some respects like to one of these and in some to the other. There is also the part which is many degrees more advanced even than these in fineness of composition, and for this reason is more capable of feeling in harmony with the rest of the structure as well. Now all this is made manifest by the activities of the soul and the feelings and the readiness of its movements and its processes of thought and by what we lose at the moment of death.[38]

Lucretius in the first century B.C. praised Epicurus's atomic theory for having put to rest the fears promoted by religion:

> When human life to view lay foully prostrate upon earth crushed down under the weight of religion, who showed her head from the quarters of heaven with hideous aspects lowering upon mortals, a man of Greece ventured first to lift up his mortal eyes to her face and first to withstand her to her face. Him neither story of gods nor thunderbolts nor heaven with threatening roar could quell: they only chafted the more the eager courage of his soul, filling him with desire to be the first to burst the fast bars of nature's portals . . . Therefore religion is put under foot and trampled upon in turn; us his victory brings level with heaven.[39]

It was the nontheistic cosmogony of atomism that appealed to Lucretius. Creation is constantly going on as the atoms, like particles of dust in sunlight, engage in "never-ending conflict skirmish and give battle combating in troops and never halting, driven about in frequent meetings and partings; so that you may guess from this, what it is for first-beginnings of things to be ever tossing about in the great void."[40] He placed even more emphasis on the swerve of atoms: "If they were not used to swerve, they would all fall down, like drops of rain, through the deep void, and no clashing would have begotten nor blow produced among the first-beginnings; thus nature never would have produced aught."[41]

No advances were made in materialism during the Middle Ages when Christianity was dominant. Descartes was the one who reintroduced materialism in the West in what is sometimes referred to as his "bifurcation of nature." Matter and spirit, he said, interact. Just how the interaction takes place, he did not convincingly explain.

Thomas Hobbes (1588–1679) was one of the most thoroughgoing materialists of the Western world, explaining all reality in terms of extended bodies and motion. Julien Offrey de Lemettrie's *L'homme machine* (Man the Machine), Paul Henri Thiry Holbach's *Le système de la Nature* (System of Nature), and Karl Büchner's *Energy and Matter* are representative materialistic works of the eighteenth and nineteenth centuries. Thought was in some of these works declared to have the same relation to the brain as bile to the liver or urine to the kidneys. "Man is what he eats," declared the materialists.

Cārvāka

The Eastern form of materialism that most nearly parallels Western materialisms is found, surprisingly, in the development of philosophy in India. The stereotype of Indian life and thought as antimaterialistic is partly due to the fact that the first Westerners to study Indian philosophy were themselves in the idealistic tradition—Arthur Schopenhauer, William Jones, H. T. Colebrooke, H. H. Wilson, A. E. Gough, F. Max Müller, Paul Deussen, Richard Garbe, and Ralph Waldo Emerson. Moreover the Indian intellectuals who first presented Indian philosophy to the West were idealists—S. Radhakrishnan, S. K. Belvalkar, R. D. Ranade, M. Hiriyanna, S. C. Vidyabusana, and K. C. Bhattacharyya. Far too many, both in the West and the East, think Indian philosophy is the philosophy of Śaṅkara. However, a spirit of revolt, which often took the form of agnosticism, nihilism, and pessimism, has been a part of the history of Indian thought. Fa Hian, a Chinese Buddhist who visited India between 405–411 reported there were ninety-six schools of heretics in Magadha. Hindu heretics are sometimes designated as *nāstikas* (no-sayers), indicating they do not recognize the Vedas as authoritative and thereby implying they hold there is no higher reality than the sense-perceived world.

Ājīvika was one of the early heretical sects. The sect flourished from the eighth century B.C. to the fourteenth century A.D. All that is known about these philosophers today comes to us from their opponents. They denied a predictable cause for anything. Everything is the result of fate or destiny (*niyati*). They had an atomic theory—probably the oldest atomic theory in the world. Everything is a composite of five elementary atoms: earth, air, fire, water, and a mysterious atom that bestows life. Initiation into the sect involved great cruelty, such as holding hot metal in the hands, breaking a bone, severing a muscle, or cutting off a finger to use flowing blood for rites believed to increase psychic powers. Begging was the only approved method for securing food, and one was obliged to eat whatever was placed in the begging bowl. Suicide was the only approved way to die.[42]

The first treatise of materialism in India was a work of the sixth century B.C. known as the *Bṛhaspati Sūtra*. Radhakrishnan states that this volume "is not available."[43] A more explicit statement would be that it was destroyed by the Vedic fundamentalists. The materialistic philosophies were known either as Lokāyata or Cārvāka. The term *Lokāyata* comes from *loka* (this world, or things of this world), so *Lokāyata* means "belonging to the world of the senses" or "the view of the people of this world." The term *Cārvāka* comes from *cāru* (sweet) and *vāk* (speech). Perhaps "sweet talk" was a reference to the hedonic character of the ethics of the materialists. Only one authentic text of the Cārvāka survives—

a seventh-century A.D. treatise known as the *Tattvapaplavasiṁha*. The other sources of information come from the enemies of Cārvāka, the *Sarvasiddhāntasārasaṁgraha* (ninth century A.D.) and the *Sarvadarśanasaṁgraha* (fourteenth century A.D.)

Ajita (fifth century B.C.) was one of the early materialistic philosophers about whom we know a little. He was given the nickname Keśakambalin (hair blanket) because he wore a robe made of human hair. He taught that everything in the universe, including man, is a combination of four elements: earth, air, fire, and water. Differences in things are due solely to the different proportions of the elements. At death the entire human being is dissolved back into the primary elements. There is no reincarnation. *Pain* and *pleasure*, *good* and *evil* are words that have no meaning. Knowledge can come only through the senses, and any reasoning beyond the senses is invalid.

The favorite form of dialectic of the Cārvāka philosophers was ridicule. They ridiculed the Vedic sacrifices: "If a beast slain in the Jyotiṣṭoma rite will itself go to heaven, why then does not the sacrificer forthwith offer his own father?"[44] They ridiculed the Vedic scriptures: "The three authors of the Vedas were buffoons, knaves, and demons."[45] They ridiculed the Vedic priests; the sacrifices were described as "but means of livelihood for those who have no manliness nor sense."[46] And they ridiculed religion in general:

> There is no world other than this; there is no heaven and no hell; the realm of Śiva and like regions are invented by stupid impostors of other schools of thought. The enjoyment of heaven lies in eating delicious food, keeping company of young women, using fine clothes, perfumes, garlands, sandal paste, etc. The pain of hell lies in troubles that arise from enemies, weapons, diseases; while liberation is death which is the cessation of life-breath. The wise therefore ought not to take pains on account of that [i.e., liberation]; it is only the fool who wears himself out by penances, fasts, etc. Chastity and other such ordinances are laid down by clever weaklings.[47]

Cārvāka was consistently materialistic in its theory of reality. Earth, water, fire, and air were the uncreated and indestructable original and ultimate principles. In the words of the *Sarvadarśanasaṁgraha*: "In this school the four elements . . . are the original principles; from these alone, when transformed into the body, intelligence is produced, just as the inebriating power is developed from the mixing of certain ingredients; and when these are destroyed, intelligence at once perishes also. . . . Therefore the soul is only the body distinguished by the attribute of intelligence since there is no evidence for any self distinct from the body."[48] Consciousness itself is a bodily emergent: "The consciousness that is found in the modifications of non-intelligent elements . . . is produced in the manner of the red colour out of the combination of betel, areca-nut and lime."[49]

There is some evidence that the Cārvāka philosophers at times disagreed violently about the nature of the self. One group, known as the Dhūrtta, held there is no self whatsoever. Another group, known as the Suśikṣita, held that there is a self that can be distinguished from the body, but it perishes with the destruction of the body.

The most sophisticated philosophical contribution of Cārvāka was the doctrine of *svabhāva* (self-sameness). This meant for the Cārvāka philosophers that matter is all there is. The whole cosmic process is the result of the activity of matter. Reality is not contingent on anything external to itself. Moreover the inherent characteristic of each thing is its *svabhāva*, and it is this alone that determines the destiny (*niyati*) of each thing. The whole causal principle is invalidated. All that a thing is an unfolding of its *svabhāva*. An acorn becomes an oak tree rather than a willow because of its *svabhāva*. The *svabhāva* of violin playing is sound, not music. The *svabhāva* of a clay pot is clay, not a thing for holding water. *Svabhāva* is a pluralistic notion. It can be thought of as the contradictory of the totality implied in the concept of Brahman. It is a notion of ownness or intrinsicality, a nominalistic position that denies universal concepts any reality. There is no *svabhāva* of acorns—only a *svabhāva* of each acorn. *Svabhāva* would seem to make all knowledge impossible. There could be no science of genera and species, only a botany of this particular flower, a geology of the particular rock one holds in one's hand, and a physiology and chemistry of each human body.

Metaphysical Dualism

Dualism was man's earliest view of reality. Descartes said it is "the most ancient and common" philosophy."[50] Arthur O. Lovejoy speaks of a "double dualism." One is epistemological dualism—the theory of representative perception that distinguishes objective reality from reality as perceived, such as the railroad rails that are parallel but convergent to the eye. The other is metaphysical dualism, which divides reality into a world of matter and a world of mind. Metaphysical dualism, according to Lovejoy, is the view that part of reality satisfies the following specifications—and part does not:

1. It is spatial as well as temporal.
2. Some or all parts of it continue to exist during the interperceptual intervals of any and all percipients, and no part belongs to it solely by virtue of the occurrence of a perception.
3. The extended things, or groups of characters, existing in it go through that sort of uniformly correlated change usually called causal interaction, the laws of these interactions being in some degree determinable.
4. These causal processes continue their regular sequences when not attended to by any percipient.

5. This order is a common factor in or behind the experience of all percipients.[51]

Descartes

Descartes is the clearest example of a Western metaphysical dualist. After having established his own existence as a thinking being, he noted he had "a certain passive faculty of perception." He wrote in his *Meditations*, "I was conscious that the ideas were presented to me without my consent being required, so that I could not perceive any object, however desirous I might be, unless it were present to the organ of sense; and it was wholly out of my power not to perceive it when it was thus present."[52] In *The Principles of Philosophy* he carried the notion of the otherness of objects further, noting that "every perception we have comes to us from some object different from our mind; for it is not in our power to cause ourselves to experience one perception rather than another, the perception being entirely dependent on the object which affects our senses."[53]

According to Descartes God possesses the power to produce all objects distinctly conceived. If God is the author of the conception of a world external to the mind, and if God is not a deceiver—and Descartes held God is not—then the objects of sense that one senses are indeed as independent and external as the human being senses them to be.

Descartes bifurcated reality into the material and the spiritual. But his thoughts about the spirit-matter dichotomy continually returned to the body-mind dichotomy: "It is certain that I [that is, my mind, by which I am what I am] is entirely and truly distinct from my body, and may exist without it."[54] Nature teaches me, he said, that "I am not only lodged in my body as a pilot in a vessel, but that I am besides so intimately conjoined, and as it were intermixed with it, that my mind and body compose a certain unity."[55] He was not always clear as to the manner of the "certain unity"; again in the *Principles* he wrote that "although the human soul is united to the whole body, it has, nevertheless, its principal seat in the brain, where alone it not only understands and imagines, but also perceives."[56] The interaction between mind and body, he speculated, is in the pineal gland. He does not spell out the interaction between the spiritual and the material in detail, but we can surmise that God is involved in the relationship.

Descartes, like Socrates, began as a natural scientist and became a psychologist, as he stated in *A Discourse on Method:* "But after I had been occupied several years in thus studying the book of the world, and in essaying to gather some experience, I at length resolved to make myself an object of study."[57]

Metaphysical dualism sometimes appears to be the theory of philosophers who can't make up their mind! Descartes fits this image perfectly. His personal conflict between scholastic authoritarianism and rationalism is precisely indicated in the last lines of the *Principles*: "Nevertheless, lest I should presume too far, I affirm nothing, but submit all these my opinions to the authority of the church and the judgment of the more sage; and I desire no one to believe anything I may have said, unless he is constrained to admit it by the force and evidence of reason."[58]

Sāṁkhya

The outstanding dualistic philosophy in the East is the Sāṁkhya. It is also the oldest of the Hindu *darśanas* (schools or systems—literally a *darśana* is a point of view.) The term *sāṁkhya* comes from a root meaning "to count" or "to number." The designation may have been given to the system in derision because its followers engaged in systematic enumeration of the categories of reality. In time the meaning shifted to signify discriminating knowledge.

Although some historians of Indian philosophy think the first Sāṁkhya philosophers were pre-Buddhistic, the earliest extant text, *The Sāṁkhya Kārikā* of Iśvarakṛṣṇa, is a work of the third century A.D.

The Sāṁkhya is the one genuinely creative orthodox metaphysical system in India. The other *āstika* philosophies are mainly devoted to logic, or to physical science, or to an exposition of the Vedic literature. The *Upaniṣads*, the fountainhead of Indian philosophy, are not philosophy per se. They are largely speculative statements of position rather than systematic arguments. According to an ancient Indian legend the early Vedic seers both knew the truth and knew it to be true, the later sages knew the truth but had lost the vision of its truth, and the philosophers were those who were searching for both the lost truth and the lost vision.

The Sāṁkhya philosophers, for reasons we cannot understand, in their efforts to recapture the lost wisdom stressed the metaphysical position that received a minor emphasis in the *Upaniṣads*—at least in the *Upaniṣads* which have survived. A. Barriedale Keith warns that

> it is impossible to find in the *Upaniṣads* any real basis for the Sāṁkhya system. The *Upaniṣads* are essentially devoted to the discovery of an absolute, and, diverse as are the forms which the absolute may take, they do not abandon the search, nor do they allow that no such absolute exists. There are, however, elements here and there which mark the growth of ideas which later were thrown into systematic form in the Sāṁkhya, but it is impossible to see in these fragmentary hints any indication that the Sāṁkhya philosophy was then in process of formation.[59]

The "hints" to which Keith refers are those rare passages in the *Upaniṣads* that vary from the usual emphasis on *Ātman-Brahman*. One such passage is in the *Bṛhad-Āraṇyaka Upaniṣad* where the "One without a second" experienced fear: "He was afraid. Therefore one who is alone is afraid. This one then thought to himself: 'Since there is nothing else than myself, of what am I afraid,' . . . 'Oneself is like a half-fragment,' as Vājñavalkya used to say."[60] Again in the *Chāndogya Upaniṣad* the seer attempts to explain how both those who say in the beginning there was only Being and those who say in the beginning there was only Nonbeing can be correct.[61] The Sāṁkhya philosophers picked up these nonmonistic passages and developed a dualistic metaphysic. The result is that as other systems of philosophy were developed in India their creators had to answer the problems bequeathed by the Sāṁkhya without actually declaring the Sāṁkhya to be wrong or anti-Vedic. Sāṁkhya had entered via the ground floor, and could not be tossed out. Śaṅkara declared the Sāṁkhya to be his main opponent within the Upaniṣadic tradition, yet he never accused Sāṁkhya of being *nāstika*.

Sāṁkhya was the catalyst for philosophizing in India. T. V. Thadani contended, "Indeed, to understand the Sāṁkhya is to understand the basis of all these systems, for they too deal with the same topics, but from different points of view, and are but an amplification, commentary or criticism of its ideas and conclusions."[62]

The existential goal of all Indian philosophy is stated in the opening lines of *The Sāṁkhya Kārikā*: "From torment by three-fold misery arises the inquiry into the means of terminating it."[63] The triad of misery is that brought about by ourselves, that caused by external aspects of the world including other people, and that produced by fate or by supernatural agencies. Of the three methods for getting rid of human misery—the empirical, the religious, and the philosophical—only the latter, which is the way of discriminative knowledge, is reliable. Bondage, according to Sāṁkhya philosophers, is basically wrong identification. The one in bondage errs in thinking wherein is his real nature. The spirit thinks it is the body. This means that Sāṁkhya is a *jñāna mārga*, a way of liberation by use of the intellect, rather than by devotion to a god (*bhakti mārga*), or by moral effort (*karma mārga*), or by psychological disciplines (*yoga mārga*).

The discrimination essential to liberation (*mokṣa*) according to Sāṁkhya is that between two primordial ontological principles known as *prakṛti* and *puruṣa*. *Prakṛti* (first maker)—the principle of potency, the source of the world of becoming, the changing object, and the cause of all physical and psychical effects—is often referred to as Matter. *Puruṣa* (first man)—the principle of consciousness and the inactive subject—is often referred to as Spirit. Both are eternal, having neither beginning nor end. Hence, Sāṁkhya metaphysics is dual. Yet pluralism is involved, since although *prakṛti* is single, *puruṣa* is plural. There is only one Matter but many spirits. So Sāṁkhya is an asymmetric dualism. Neither *prakṛti* nor *puruṣa* is directly perceived. Their existence is inferred.

The argument for *prakṛti* is that the physical world is an effect rather than a cause of itself; a physical effect presupposes a material cause in which the effect is immanent. The argument for *puruṣa* is that a material cause in which the effect is immanent requires a nonmaterial agent to trigger the latent effect from potentiality to actuality.

Prakṛti is the unevolved matter containing immanently all things in itself. *Prakṛti* is constituted by three *guṇas*, that is, strands, constituents, or compositive factors. These three are in a relationship that is "mutually subjugative, and supporting, and productive, and co-operative."[64] The three *guṇas* might be described as relational entities that manifest themselves as qualities. *Sattva*—the pure—is associated with pleasure and illumination; *rajas*—the active—is associated with pain and action; *tamas*—the stolid—is associated with resistance and delusion. Traditional analogues of the *sattva-rajas-tamas* are the wick-oil-fire necessary for the lighting of a lamp and a swimmer, movement of arms, and resistance of water for swimming. The state of equilibrium ceases when *sattva* becomes aware of the presence of *puruṣa*, and the evolution of the physical world begins.

It is not relevant here to trace the complicated evolutional development of the physical world from *prakṛti*. It is enough to indicate that there are two modes of evolution: a primary evolution of principles (*tattvas*) and a secondary evolution of things. The evolution, in keeping with the traditional Eastern view of time, is cyclical: a period of evolution is followed by a period of dissolution, followed by another period of evolution, ad infinitum.

Puruṣas in this system of philosophy are not lives, nor minds, but subjects. A *puruṣa* is consciousness, but that does not mean it is a conscious mind. For example, "the spirit is 'witness,' and has 'isolation,' 'neutrality,' and is the 'seer,' and 'inactive.'"[65] It is "neutral" yet it "appears as if it were active."[66] The argument for the reality of *puruṣa* is based on the evidence of purposes in the physical world. According to the argument, things that exhibit design always have a transcendent reference to an extraneous end. Hence, *prakṛti* must evolve for the sake of some principle, and that principle is *puruṣa*. Another form of the argument is based on the human drive for self-perfection. Each of us feels this drive, and the drive is toward some real end, so the end must exist.

The Sāṁkhya Kārikā is a fascinating early document in the history of Indian philosophy in that, unlike the pontifications of the *Upaniṣads*, it lists the arguments for its position. It argues for *prakṛti* as follows: "Because of the finite nature of specific objects, because of homogeneity, because of the evolution being due to the efficiency of the cause, because of separation between cause and its product, and because of the merging of the whole world (of effects),—there is the Unmanifest as the cause."[67] The arguments for *puruṣa* are: "Because all composite objects are for another's use, because there must be absence of the three attributes and other properties, because there must be control, because there must be someone to experience, and because there is a tendency towards 'isolation' or final beatitude, therefore, the spirit must be there."[68] These suggestions of arguments were fertile fields for later philosophers. Some of the flaws in their metaphysics are obvious. For example, *prakṛti* is supposed to be the principle of objectivity, yet in its *sattva* strand it is aware of *puruṣa*. Likewise, *puruṣa* is the principle of subjectivity, yet it is said to be unaware of *prakṛti*. The Advaitins say the chief error made by the Sāṁkhya philosophers was in trying to dichotomize that which is a unity.

Transcendental Metaphysics

Kant

The fourth type of theory of reality is those that hold that ultimate reality cannot be known to be spiritual or material because it cannot be known at all. The outstanding representative of this mode of metaphysical thinking in the West was Immanuel Kant (1724–1804). The modern period of philosophy began in the West when Western people, turning away from appeals to Scholastic authorities, revived the faith of the ancient Greeks in the power of the human intellect to understand the nature of reality. But which method of attaining knowledge should be used? And how certain is the knowledge that humans can attain? Philosophers like Bacon, Locke, Berkeley, and Hume favored empiricism; philosophers like Descartes, Leibniz, and Spinoza favored rationalism. Kant did not want to take sides because he saw both rationalism and empiricism are needed: "Thoughts without content are empty, intuitions without concepts are blind."[69] He said that rationalism alone can at best arrive at knowledge that is logically true, and empiricism alone can at best arrive at knowledge that is about a real world. The rationalists assume they know the real world because reality is rational. The empiricists assume there is no objectively real world to be known but only a world constructed out of sensations. In place of these dogmatic assumptions and attitudes Kant asserted what he called the *critical* method and attitudes. Kant sought to find that which is transcendental to human experience, that is, that which must be in order that knowledge be true as the rationalists claimed and that which is about a real world as the empiricists claimed.

To accomplish this Kant inaugurated what he described as a Copernican revolution in philosophy.

> Hitherto it has been assumed that all our knowledge must conform to objects. But all attempts to extend our knowledge of objects by establishing something in regard to them *a priori*, by means of concepts, have, on this assumption, ended in failure. We must therefore make trial whether we may not have more success in the tasks of metaphysics, if we suppose that objects must conform to our knowledge. This would agree better with what is desired, namely, that it should be possible to have knowledge of objects *a priori*, determining something in regard to them prior to their being given. We should

> then be proceeding precisely on the lines of Copernicus' primary hypothesis. Failing of satisfactory progress in explaining the movements of the heavenly bodies on the supposition that they all revolved round the spectator, he tried whether he might not have better success if he made the spectator to revolve and the stars to remain at rest. A similar experiment can be tried in metaphysics, as regards the intuition of objects. If intuition must conform to the constitution of the objects, I do not see how we could know anything of the latter *a priori*: but if the object (as object of the sense) must conform to the constitution of our faculty of intuition, I have no difficulty in conceiving such a possibility. Since I cannot rest in these intuitions if they are to become known, but must relate them as representations to something as their object, and determine their latter through them, either I must assume that the concepts, by means of which I obtain this determination, conform to the object, or else I assume that the objects, or what is the same thing, that the experience in which alone, as given objects, they can be known, conform to the concepts. In the former case, I am again in the same perplexity as to how I can know anything *a priori* in regard to the objects. In the latter case the outlook is more helpful. For experience is itself a species of knowledge which involves understanding; and understanding has rules which I must presuppose as being in me prior to objects being given to me, and therefore as being *a priori*.[70]

Kant's shift from "What is the nature of knowledge, the world being what it is?" to "What is the nature of the world, knowledge being what it is?" may be described as a shift from the typical Western way of doing philosophy to the typical Eastern way. The emphasis was moved from the epistemological object to the act and agent of knowing.

He pointed out that all human experiences are spatial and temporal. This is the way human sensibility is constructed. This does not mean that the things experienced are themselves spatial and temporal, but only insofar as an object of potential experience conforms to the conditions of human knowing can it be known. Things may have many other characteristics, but these cannot be known by man. If there be a world over, beyond, behind, or transcendental to the world known, that world cannot be known. *World* was a term that had two meanings for Kant. One meant the world that man can know by means of his rational and empirical methods. For the empiricist it is the world one senses, or, as Hume would say, the world one constructs from one's impressions. For the rationalist it is that described by the categories of reason. The worlds of empiricism and rationalism are worlds from a particular point of view. They are how things appear to be or are thought to be. Kant called it *the phenomenal world*. The second use of the word *world* for Kant designated a world from no point of view. This world is not a world as sensed nor a world as thought, but a world that transcends sensation and thought. It is the world of things-in-themselves. It is a world of reality rather than a world of appearance. Kant called it *the noumenal world*.

If the noumenal world transcends all knowing, how did Kant know that it exists? Had he merely postulated an imaginary world? Kant tried in a variety of ways to show why there must be a noumenal world. One way was by pointing out that space and time as forms of empirical experience are not experienced in themselves but are the conditions of having empirical experiences, and that the rational categories of quantity (unity, plurality, and totality), of quality (reality, negation, and limitation), of relation (substance and accident, cause and effect, and agent and patient), and of modality (possibility, existence, and necessity) are not thoughts in themselves but are the conditions of thought. These conditions of sense experience and rational thought transcend experience and thought, yet they are real. A commentator on Kant writes in his defense that Kant's account "certainly implies the existence of an unknown and unknowable X which 'affects' our senses with something which is 'transformed' into objective and scientific reality by being 'subjected' to certain forms—on the one hand to the forms of perception, and on the other to the form of the understanding."[71]

A second way Kant established the world of things-in-themselves is based on self-knowledge. I do not know myself as I am, but only as I appear to myself. The *I* of self-knowing—the transcendental unity of apperception—is always a subject, never an object. Yet it is, even though I cannot have an intellectual intuition of the self that is. So there is self-in-itself that transcends the self that is what appears to me as myself. Kant argued by analogy that since a noumenal subject is required in internal knowing, a noumenal object is required in external knowing.

A third argument for things-in-themselves is that they are the necessary limiting conditions of knowing. The supersensible cannot be known, but it has reality as a terminus beyond which we cannot go. Things-in-themselves check the pretensions of our knowledge. This was a somewhat Platonic argument, which must not have been fully satisfactory to Kant.

Perhaps his best defense of the existence of a noumenal world was in pointing out that human beings are more than philosophical animals. They are also moral beings. Kant said that every human being recognizes a moral law that is unconditional. He called it the "categorical imperative." He spelled it out in many forms, but most clearly as "I am never to act otherwise than so that I could also will that my maxim should become a universal law."[72] This imperative, said Kant, is part of human nature and has metaphysical implications. It implies the realities of freedom, immortality, and God. These three cannot be established by knowledge, but they are established by the claims of universal morality.

Advaita Vedāntism

Advaita Vedāntism, the form of Vedānta associated with Śaṅkara, is an excellent example of Eastern transcendental metaphysics. According to Richard

Garbe, "Nearly all educated Hindus in modern India, except in so far as they have embraced European ideas, are adherents of the Vedānta; and three-fourths of these accept Śaṅkara's interpretations of the *Brahma Sūtras*, while the rest are divided among the varying explanations of the system offered by one or other of the remaining commentators."[73] S. Radhakrishnan agrees: "In one or the other of its forms the Vedānta determines the world view of the Hindu thinkers of the present time."[74] G. R. Malkani makes an interesting—and debatable—additional assessment, claiming that Rāmānuja's Viśiṣṭādvaita Vedāntism "is largely acceptable to the Christian West" and that Śaṅkara's Advaita Vedāntism "is more truly representative of the Hindu East."[75]

Vedāntism is scholastic in the sense that it takes its fundamental teachings from the *Upaniṣads*, the *Bhagavad Gītā*, and the *Brahma Sūtras* (or *Vedānta Sūtras*) of Bādarāyaṇa, the so-called "triple basis of the Vedānta." Bādarāyaṇa's *Sūtras* are 555 brief aphorisms and mnemonic devices serving to remind scholars of the metaphysical aspects of the *Upaniṣads*. The central topic for consideration is indicated in the names of the four chapters: "The Theory of Brahman," "Consideration of Objections to the Theory of Brahman," "Ways to Attain Knowledge of Brahman," and "Consideration of the Fruits of Knowing Brahman." The three outstanding commentaries on the *Brahma Sūtras* are the nondualistic interpretation of Śaṅkara (ninth century), the modified nondualistic interpretation of Rāmānuja (twelfth century), and the dualistic interpretation of Madhva (thirteenth century).

The name of Śaṅkara's *darśana*—Advaita (non-twoness)—is a contradiction of the Sāṁkhya. Śaṅkara began his commentary with a declaration of his intent to stress unity rather than duality: "With a view to freeing one's self from that wrong notion which is the cause of evil and attaining thereby the knowledge of the absolute unity of the Self the study of the Vedānta-texts is begun."[76] He believed he was stemming the tide against the *Upaniṣads*, a tide that began with the Cārvākas as revolters and with the Sāṁkhyas as reformers.

"The complete comprehension of Brahman is the highest end of man, since it destroys the root of all evil such as ignorance, the seed of the entire *saṁsāra* (cycle of births and deaths)," wrote Śaṅkara.[77] Brahman, however, in a sense is known even before the knowing, for Brahman is the knower. Brahman is the Self. In other words, the existence of Brahman is obvious; the essence of Brahman is not obvious, or, as Śaṅkara said, "there is a conflict of opinions as to its special nature."[78]

Śaṅkara began his attempt to present the nature of Brahman by describing Brahman as the cause of creation, preservation, and destruction of the world—the triad mythologically symbolized as Brahmā, Viṣṇu, and Śiva: "That omniscient omnipotent cause from whence proceed the origin, subsistence, and dissolution of this world—which world is differentiated by names and forms, contains many agents and enjoyers, is the abode of the fruits of actions, these fruits having their definite places, times, and causes, and the nature of whose arrangement cannot even be conceived by the mind,—that cause, we say, is

Brahman."[79] The physical world has name and form, that is, it can be specified both linguistically and metaphysically, but Brahman, the cause of the physical world, has neither name nor form. The physical world, then, does not come from a nonintelligent substance like the *prakṛti* of the Sāṁkhya, nor from atoms as had been proposed by the Vaiśeṣika philosophers, nor from nonbeing as claimed by the Mādhyamika philosophers, nor from its own nature, that is, as cause of its self, nor from any sort of transmigratory substance.[80] "Brahman . . . being devoid of form . . . cannot become an object of perception."[81] Brahman cannot be known inductively. Śaṅkara added that "inference also and the other means of proof do not apply to it."[82] Brahman cannot be known deductively. Śaṅkara continued by noting that Brahman "like religious duty . . . is to be known solely on the ground of holy tradition."[83] But this does not mean that *śruti* cannot be assisted by reason. It is "reasoning which disregards the holy texts and rests on individual opinion only [that] has no proper foundation."[84] "Brahman is eternal, all-knowing, absolutely self-sufficient, ever pure, intelligent and free, pure knowledge, absolute bliss."[85] In other words, Brahman is absolute being (*sat*), absolute consciousness (*chit*), and absolute value (*ānanda*). But these must not be understood as qualities of a substance. Brahman as *saccidānanda* is being-itself or fullness of being, consciousness-itself or self-luminous consciousness, and value-itself or infinite bliss. Brahman is the ground of being, consciousness, and value. Śaṅkara did not apply *sat, chit* and *ānanda* to Brahman as positive characteristics or properties; rather *saccidānanda* denotes the integral foundation of all things that do or do not have being, that are or are not conscious, and that do or do not have value. In other words, although Brahman is not *anṛta* or *asat* (nonexistence or nonreality), not *jada* or *acit* (inertness or inconscience), and not *duḥkha* (sorrow, suffering, misery), Brahman is the foundation of all negativities as well as all positivities.

Śaṅkara found it difficult to explain what Brahman is, for the obvious reason that Brahman is no *what*. Brahman is not a thing, a being, an entity—not even a god. *Brahman* is the name given to denote a condition of potentiality that manifests itself in beings. It is the matrix not only of beings, but also of knowledge and value. From this dynamic, timeless, undifferentiated, unlimited continuum—this *sat-chit-ānanda*-ness—has come our universe, our gods, and our selves. Brahman becomes a *what* only in the process of becoming. A distinction must not be made where there is no distinction, that is, between Brahman and Brahman-izing. A question like "Why does Brahman take on phenomenal forms?" misses the point; in order for Brahman to be Brahman, Brahman must Brahman-ize. Manifesting and pluralizing is part of the necessity of Totality. The Absolute must individualize to be the Absolute.

One of the contributions Śaṅkara made to the Upaniṣadic conception of Brahman was his contention that "Brahman is apprehended under two forms; in the first place as qualified by limiting conditions owing to the multiformity of the evolutions of name and form (i.e., the multiformity of the created world); in the second place as being the opposite of this, i.e., free from all limiting conditions whatever."[86] The former is the Brahman with qualities, hence it is known as *Saguṇa Brahman.* It is an object of knowledge and worship. It is Brahman from a point of view. This is Brahman considered as an object of *aparā vidyā*, that is, the lower or phenomenal knowledge, the knowledge in which the subject-object distinction is preserved. The latter is the Brahman without qualities, hence it is known as *Nirguṇa Brahman.* It is the Brahman from no point of view. This is Brahman in the framework of *parā vidyā*, that is, the higher or noumenal knowledge, the "knowledge" in which the subject-object distinction is irrelevant.

Śaṅkara found support for the two kinds of knowing in *Muṇḍaka Upaniṣad* 1.1.4, but the use to which he put the distinction was his own. The two forms of Brahman in the metaphysics of Śaṅkara correspond to the two forms of the self: the nonmigrating Self (*Ātman*) and the migrating self (*jīva*). But there are not in fact two selves or two Brahmans, only two forms of human apprehension. This enabled him to account for passages in the *Upaniṣads* that were inconsistent with his own conclusions, and also made it possible for him to utilize the theistic passages in the *Bhagavad Gītā.*

Another contribution of Śaṅkara was his use of the conception of *māyā.* The world is the pure sport (*līlā*) of Saguṇa. The entire "created world" is *māyā*; it is a world of "as if"—as if it were real, as if it were knowable, and as if it were valuable. There is no creator, and there is no "created world." The world as a creation is a phenomenon. Creation and creator are appearances only. The Sāṁkhya is *dvaita* in its separation of material cause (*prakṛti*) and moving cause (*puruṣa*). But Śaṅkara's metaphysic is *advaita*, since for him Brahman is both "material cause" and "moving cause." Brahman is the real cause; the world is an apparent effect. What Śaṅkara seems to have meant is that we fall into the *māyā* state whenever we fail to realize the oneness of reality. Any experience constituted by or following from the distinction between subject and object, or between self and nonself, is a *māyā* experience. *Māyā* is that ontic-noetic state in which limitations (*upādhis*) are imposed or superimposed upon reality.

In the doctrine of *māyā* Śaṅkara was not treating the world as though it did not exist, nor was he eliminating the illusion that the world does exist; rather he was calling attention to the conditions under which human minds perceive and conceive the world. The characteristics we say the world has are the characteristics reality must have in order for it to be experienced by human sense organs and to be thought by human minds. The world as humans experience it is a world of phenomena and perspectives that stands midway between the *sat* mode of existence, that is, the absolute, eternal, infinite condition of the Brahman, and the *asat* mode of existence, the impossible condition of "the son of a barren woman." According to Advaita Vedānta there are two forms of *māyā*: (1) the *māyā* that takes one object for another, such as mistaking a rope for a snake, and (2) the *māyā* that attributes to an object a characteristic that does not belong to it, such as looking at a white stone through a piece of amber glass and seeing the stone as amber. The first form of *māyā* is the error we make when we think the physical world is real; the second form of *māyā* is the error we make when we think the individual self is real. The physical world is a phenomenal or *māyā* substance; the self has a phenomenal or *māyā* quality, namely, its individuality.

The impact of Advaita Vedāntism on the lives of Hindus is very difficult to assess, but perhaps V. S. Naipaul has captured it when he observes, "The outer world matters only in so far as it affects the inner. It is the Indian way of experiencing."[87] The result is an astonishing indifference to external condition.

Mādhyamika

A transcendental metaphysics developed within Buddhism that is known in India as Mādhyamika and Śūnya-vada and in China as San-Lun Tsung. Mādhyamika (Middle Way) refers to the effort of these philosophers to find an intermediate between affirming and denying, to avoid the Law of Noncontradiction. They wished to use the relativity of all thought to find a position between scepticism and absolutism. They were also concerned about the antitheses between the eternal and the temporal, being and nonbeing, permanence and change, rest and movement, *nirvāṇa* and *saṁsāra*. Śūnya-vada (Emptiness doctrine) refers to the view that ultimate reality transcends knowing. San-Lun Tsung (Three Treatise School) indicates that the doctrine is based on three texts: *Chung Kuan Lun* (Middle Treatise), *Shih- ērh Mēn Lun* (Twelve Gate Treatise), and *Pai Lun* (Hundred Treatise). The school was founded in India in the second century A.D. by Nāgārjuna and flourished there until about 1000. It helped shape the Advaita Vedāntic view of reality. The ideas of Mādhyamika probably came to China in the second century and had become the San-Lun Tsung by the sixth century. In 625 the school came to Japan as Sanron. It survives in Ch'an Buddhism in China and in Zen Buddhism in Japan. T. R. V. Murti describes it as "the central philosophy of Buddhism."[88] Alan W. Watts writes, "When, therefore, I use the word *Buddhism* without further qualification it should be understood that I am referring to the Mādhyamika school of Nāgārjuna."[89]

The history of Buddhism contains four major metaphysical systems: (1) Vaibhāṣika, which holds that both the material and the spiritual worlds are real, and that external objects are directly perceived; (2) Sautrāntika, which holds that both the mental and the spiritual worlds are real, and that external objects are not perceived but are known by inference; (3) Yogācāra, which holds that the material world is void of reality and that only the spiritual world is real; and (4) Mādhyamika, which holds that all is void (*śūnya*). The history of Buddhistic thought might be better represented by dividing it into three chronological periods: (1) an early realistic phase (Vaibhāṣika and Sautrāntika), (2) a middle transcendental phase (Mādhyamika), and (3) a late idealistic phase that attempted to soften the negativism of Mādhyamika (Yogācāra).

Nāgārjuna analyzed the Holy Truths (*āryastaya*) of Buddhism into two types: the empirical and the transcendental. "The teaching by the Buddhas of the *dharma* has recourse to two truths: the world-ensconced truth and the truth which is the highest sense. Those who do not know the distribution of the two kinds of truth do not know the profound 'point' in the teaching of the Buddha. The highest sense [of the truth] is not taught apart from practical behavior, and without having understood the highest sense one cannot understand *nirvāṇa*."[90] The distinction is not, as Plato said, between opinion and knowledge, but between mundane truth and ultimate truth. The former is needed for practical living and the latter for final release, but in the world of *saṁsāra* in which we live both are needed. One cannot attain *nirvāṇa* save within *saṁsāra*. The objects of both truths are the same; the approach is different. Mundane or worldly truth is needed to manage the affairs of life; ultimate truth is needed to avoid attachment to the affairs of life.

Chi-tsang (549–623) of San-Lung Tsung said that the twofold truth should be considered as operating at three levels. Worldly truth at the first level is naive realism. What appears to be real is considered to be real. Ultimate truth at the first level rejects naive realism, knowing that the *dharmas* (elements of existence) are empty. Worldly truth at the second level, accepting both the worldly truth of the first level and the ultimate truth of the first level, arrives at a metaphysical dualism. Ultimate truth at the second level, refusing to accept the worldly truth of the first level and the ultimate truth of the first level, arrives at a metaphysical nondualism. Worldly truth at the third level accepts both the duality of the worldly truth of the second level and the nonduality of the ultimate truth of the second level. Ultimate truth of the third level rejects both the duality of the worldly truth of the second level and the nonduality of the worldly truth of the second level. This is the Middle Way.

Chi-tsang's twofold truth at three levels was illustrated in the words of Ch'ing-yüan (c. 740), which I paraphrase as follows:

> Level 1 Before I had studied Zen for thirty years, I saw mountains as mountains, and waters as waters.
>
> Level 2 When I arrived at a more intimate knowledge, I came to the point where I saw that mountains are not mountains, and waters are not waters.
>
> Level 3 But now that I have got its very substance I am at rest. For it is just that I see mountains once again as mountains, and waters once again as waters.

The Middle Way is a path between affirming and denying. If reality is neither being nor nonbeing, it is empty (*śūnya*). The Mādhyamika philosophers, taking account of the fact that the zero in Sanskrit can be represented either by *śūnya* (the empty) or by *purna* (the full), spoke of the *dharmas* as both empty and full of nothing. The enlightened being (*bodhisattva*) is one who combines his great wisdom (*prajñā*) of knowing that all selves are empty and his great compassion (*karuṇā*) of resolving to save all selves. Reality is the relative that is not being, not nonbeing, not both being and nonbeing, and not neither being nor nonbeing. Hence, for Nāgārjuna the Absolute is the relative.

Śaṅkara's system differs from Nāgārjuna's in that he negates the Four-corner Negation; he denies that it is true that reality is the relative that is not being, not nonbeing, not both being and nonbeing, and not neither being nor nonbeing. Hence, for Śaṅkara the Absolute is the nonrelative.

The dialectic of the Mādhyamika is still debated by historians of Buddhist philosophy. At least five conclusions have been drawn. One conclusion is that the Mādhyamika teaches a nihilism. Everything is unreal. "The doctrine of Śūnya-vāda has been understood in India, by non-Buddhistic philosophers in general, to mean that the universe is totally devoid of reality, that everything is *śūnya* or void," claimed Satischandra Chatterjee and Dhirendramohan Datta.[91] Surendranath Dasgupta also called it "nihilism," and explained "what is really meant is that things can only be indicated as mere appearances one after another, for they have no essence or true nature. . . . As the phenomena have no essence they are neither produced nor destroyed; they really neither come nor go. They are merely the appearance of *māyā* or illusion. The void (*śūnya*) does not mean pure negation, for that is relative to some kind of position. It simply means that none of the appearances have [*sic*] any intrinsic nature of their own (*niḥsvabhāvatvam*)."[92] Likewise Mysore Hiriyanna stated that all Hindu thinkers "agree in holding that the void is the only truth according to the Mādhyamika. They describe the school as nihilistic and have no difficulty in refuting that apparently absurd position."[93] He added that the Jains also hold the Mādhyamika to be nihilistic.[94] Joseph De Bona goes so far as to claim all Buddhism is nihilistic: "Nihilism, the doctrine that things are by nature ego-less and devoid of *ātman* or self-substance, was common to all Buddhism."[95]

A second conclusion is that while the phenomenal world is unreal, the noumenal world is real, although devoid of phenomenal characteristics. Chatterjee and Datta spoil Hiriyanna's universal claim about Indian philosophers in stating their position: "But when we study this philosophy more closely, we come to realize that the Mādhyamika view is not really nihilism, as ordinarily supposed, and that it does not deny all reality, but only the apparent phenomenal world perceived by us. Behind this phenomenal world there is a reality which is not describable by any character, mental or non-mental, that we perceive. Being devoid of phenomenal characters, it is called *śūnya*."[96]

A third conclusion is that Mādhyamika presents the doctrine of *śūnyatā* to remind us that the world of sense experience is always a relativism. Stcherbatsky usually translated *śūnyatā* as "relativity." Junjiro Takakusu shared this view: "The idea of relativity seems to be strongly presented in the Indian Mādhyamika School."[97] John Blofeld summarized the teaching of the Mādhyamika school in four teachings, revealing his own interpretation as relativism:

> 1. It is better to describe the world as void than to say it exists.
> 2. There is neither void nor existence.
> 3. There is nothing which can be described as non-void or non-existence.
> 4. On the other hand, the converse is true that there is nothing which can be described as not being non-void or not being non-existence.[98]

Clarence Burton Day said that according to Mādhyamika "everything is relative to an Absolute (Void) which cannot be defined."[99] T. R. V. Murti, however, pointed out that these interpretations may err in laying hold of but one meaning of *śūnya*. He stated in the glossary of his *The Central Philosophy of Buddhism*: "*śūnya*, *śūnyatā*, the terms are used in two allied meanings: (i) the phenomena are *śūnya*, as they are relative and lack substantiality or independent reality; they are conditioned (*pratītya-samutpanna*), and hence are unreal; (ii) the Absolute is *śūnya* or *śūnyatā* itself, as it is devoid of empirical forms; no thought-category or predicate ('is', 'not-is', 'is and not-is', 'neither is nor not-is') can legitimately be applied to it; it is Transcendent to thought (*śūnya*)."[100]

A fourth conclusion is that the Mādhyamika dialectic is a judgment on the limitations of human reason. It clears the mind for intuiting reality. This is the view of Murti: "The Mādhyamika denies metaphysics not because there is no real for him; but because it is inaccessible to Reason. He is convinced of a higher faculty, Intuition (*prajñā*) with which the Real (*tattva*) is identical."[101] "Negation is thus the despair of thought; but it is at once the opening up of a new avenue—the path of intuition. Negation is the threshold of intellectual intuition. *Śūnyatā* is not only the negation of *dṛṣṭi* (view, judgment), but is *Prajñā*. . . . *Śūnyatā* is negation of negations; it is thus a re-affirmation of the infinite and inexpressibly positive character of the Real."[102] Radhakrishnan's position on Mādhyamika was similar to Murti's, although he seemed to stress the limitations of language rather than the limitations of reason. Radhakrishnan wrote,

> About the ultimate reality we cannot say anything. . . . To the Mādhyamikas reason and language apply only to the finite world. To transfer the finite categories to the infinite would be like attempting to measure the heat of the sun by the ordinary thermometer. From our point of view the absolute is nothing. We call it *śūnyam*, since no category used in relation to the conditions of the world is adequate to it. To call it being is wrong, because only concrete things are. To call it non-being is equally wrong. It is best to avoid all descriptions of it.[103]

This interpretation is consistent with Alan W. Watts's fine insight: "Buddhism

. . . is not a culture but a critique of culture."[104]

A fifth conclusion is that the Mādhyamika philosophers were trying to point out that words, reason, and even intuition denote no self-existent reality. No thing exists absolutely, independently, nor even by reason of being constructed by thought. Both sensible and ideal objects are empty. The dialectic is a means for realizing this emptiness. Frederick J. Streng says the dialectic has two functions: (1) "an effective force for realizing the emptiness of things" and (2) "the means of quelling the pain found in existential 'becoming' which results from longing after an eternal undisturbed entity."[105] Streng thinks that the dialectic is used chiefly for soteriological purposes—"a means of ultimate transformation." It is both the expression of reality and the technique for achieving a transformation. "Emptiness" connotes both the emptiness of any "Absolute" one may imagine, and also the emptiness of quests for this "Absolute." Emptiness is a technique to remind human beings that salvation is immediately at hand, but not identical with the present situation. The spiritual life is achieved within the practical life. Wisdom is the joy of freedom in everyday existence. Longing after an eternal, unchanging, self-existent Ultimate is a diversion. The dialect is a means for dissipating the desire for such an Absolute. "Dwelling in emptiness" means living in an openness to experience free from bondage to the flux of existence and from bondage to the self. Problems like those of the hierarchy of values based on an absolute ground, evil as rooted in an objective reality, and human freedom and divine predestination are discovered to be "answers" to unreal "problems." Human beings are saved from themselves and from the claims of existence by appreciating the lack of self-existence of these "things"—their "own-being" (*svabhāva*) is "other-being" (*parabhāva*). The other side of *śūnyatā* is "the interrelatedness of everything in existence."[106] Agehananda Bharati presents this view unqualifiedly: "Buddhism has no ontology, no metaphysics; Hinduism has a powerful ontology—this is the one unbridgeable difference between all of its forms and Buddhism of all schools."[107] He warns that "ontological terms should be ostracized in the translation of Buddhist texts."[108]

Which conclusion did Nāgārjuna intend? He should be allowed the last words:

> Emptiness is proclaimed by the victorious one as the refutation of all viewpoints; but those who hold "emptiness" as a viewpoint—[the true believers] have called those "incurable." . . . The production of a self-existent thing by a conditioning cause is not possible, [for,] being produced through dependence on a cause, a self-existent thing would be "something which is produced." . . . How, indeed, will a self-existent thing become "something which is produced"? . . . Certainly the self-existence of an other-existent thing is called "other-existence." Further, how can a thing [exist] without either self-existence or other-existence? If either self-existence or other-existence exist, then an existing thing, indeed would be proved. If there is no proof of an

existent thing, then a non-existent thing cannot be proved. Since people call the other-existence of an existent thing a "non-existent thing." Those who perceive self-existence and other-existence, and an existent thing and a non-existent thing, do not perceive the true nature of the Buddha's teaching.[109]

Taoism

The last example of an Eastern transcendental metaphysic comes from Taoism, a remarkable Chinese philosophy that escaped the Confucian stress on morality and ceremony. Confucianism centers on man; Taoism centers on nature. The Chinese way of life at its best strikes a balance between the two, although the folklore of the Chinese contains many stories of conflict. According to one a craftsman in three years of work created a leaf that could not be distinguished from a real leaf. A Taoist observed that if nature took three years to make one leaf, leaf-bearing plants would be bare.

Taoism stems from a small book entitled the *Tao Teh Ching*, often called "the 5000-word classic," said to have been writen by Lao Tzu in the sixth century B.C. The word *ching* means book. *Tao* is an ontological term, and *teh* is an axiological term. In the words of D. T. Suzuki: "*Tao* literally means 'a path,' or 'a way,' or 'a course,' but it is more than a map for orientation schematically drawn up for the traveler to follow. The Tao is our actually walking on this 'way' or coursing on or through it. No, it is more than that. It is the walking itself, or the coursing itself, which is Tao. The Tao is not where we follow the way as indicated in the map. We are the Tao, the walker and the Tao are the same."[110] *Tao* is a process term—nature naturing. *Teh* refers to the value considerations resulting from *Tao*. *Teh* is the way life ought to be lived, reality being what it is. An English equivalent of the title might be *The Book of the Way Things Go and the Consequences for Human Behavior.*

The first chapter of the *Tao Teh Ching* contains the fundamentals needed to understand Taoism as a transcendental metaphysic. Wing-tsit Chan translates it as follows:

> The Tao that can be told of is not the eternal Tao;
> The name that can be named is not the eternal name.
> The Nameless is the origin of Heaven and Earth;
> The Named is the mother of all things.
>
> Therefore let there always be non-being, so we may see their subtlety,
> And let there always be being, so we may see their outcome.
> The two are the same,
> But after they are produced, they have different names.
> They both may be called deep and profound.
> Deeper and more profound,
> The door of all subtleties![111]

I offer the following as a transcreation:

> The Totality that can be expressed verbally is not the timeless and unchanging Totality.
> The Totality that can be thought in concepts is not the timeless and unchanging Totality.
> The origin of the unitary physical universe is that aspect of Totality called "Nonbeing."
> The origin of the pluralistic physical universe is that aspect of Totality called "Being."
> "Nonbeing" calls attention to Totality as known intuitively.
> "Being" calls attention to Totality as known in a subject-object relationship.
> But "Nonbeing" and "Being" are only two names for Totality.
> An understanding of this is the way to the understanding of all mysteries.

Tao is the indefinite, inexpressible, transcendent-immanent ground of the universe. All reality issues from *Tao* by emanation rather than creation.

Three metaphysical levels are referred to in the *Tao Teh Ching*. One is *Tao* as "myriad things."[112] This refers to the detailed, separated, individual things that maintain themselves, reproduce themselves, destroy other selves, and finally perish. The second is *Tao* as Being. This is referred to as "the mother of all things."[113] It is "Named" in the sense that it can be known as an object. It is the Being aspect of *Tao*. It is *Tao* in its immanent characteristics. The third is *Tao* as Nonbeing. This is *Tao* referred to as "The Great," "The Great Form," "The One," "The Changeless," and "The Eternal." It is "Nameless" in the sense that it cannot be known as an object. It is the Nonbeing aspect of *Tao*. However, terms like *aspects* and *characteristics* are deceptive. *Tao* is not Being (*yu*), nor Nonbeing (*wu*), but Being-Nonbeing, or *yu-wu*. Chapter 40—"Reversion is the action of Tao. . . . All things in the world come from being. And being comes from non-being."[114]—might suggest that Nonbeing is prior chronologically and/or ontologically to Being, but as Chan points out "to produce means not to originate but to bring about." In chapter 2 we are informed "Being and Non-being produce each other." The relationship between *wu* and *yu* is not *wu*→*yu*, but *wu*⇄*yu*, or [*wu* (*yu*) and *yu* (*wu*)]. However, it is difficult to escape the conclusion that Nonbeing is ultimate. For example, Fung Yu-lan writes,

> This does not necessarily mean that there was a time when there was only non-being and nothing, and that then there came a time when being came into being from non-being. It only means that if we analyse the existence of the heavens and the earth and all creatures, then we see that there must first be being before there can be beings such as the heavens and the earth and all creatures. Therefore, speaking logically, being is something which stands first of all. The meaning of "first" here is not first in point of time, and the mean-

> ing of "being" is not being in point of actuality. From the point of view of actual existences, there cannot be being but only beings.[115]

Tao as Nonbeing is not a negative concept.

According to Wing-tsit Chan,

> Other Chinese schools of thought conceived of non-being simply as the absence of something, but in Taoism it is not only positive; it is basic. This was epoch-making in the history of Chinese philosophy. According to Homer W. Dubs, it is also new in Occidental thought. He says, "Here is a solution to the problem of creation which is new to Western philosophy: the universe can arise out of nothing because nonexistence itself is not characterless or negative." In his opinion, "here is a metaphysical system which starts, not with matter or with ideas, but with law (*Tao*), nonexistence, and existence as the three fundamental categories of reality."[116]

The *Tao* is said to be Nameless (*wu-ming*). Eloquent speakers stutter.[117] The wise do not speak—

> He who knows does not speak.
> He who speaks does not know.[118]

2

The Self in the Natural World—Causality

Cause and time are concepts that all understand until they begin to examine them. A common sense notion of cause is that it is a regular sequential relationship between two things or events. A fire under a pot of water causes the water to boil. Modern scientists would add that the causal relationship means that reliable predictions are possible. Yet we daily experience regular sequential relationships that meet these criteria but are not causal relationships. No one claims day causes night.[1] The cause-effect relationship is obviously more than a relationship that is regular, sequential, and predictable.

The Cause-Effect Relationship

Primitive human beings established a practical causal relationship with their environment long before causality was a philosophical problem. "How can we avoid the cold?" and "What will stop hunger pangs?" were causal quests. "Who sends the wind?" and "Why is the sun so hot?" were causal questions that led to the first mythologies. The search for answers to cause-effect questions may be regarded as one of the foundations of the entire intellectual enterprise. We assume objects, events, forces, and processes are related in a manner such that we can understand, predict, and, in some cases, control our natural world.

Some philosophers suggest that the way to understand causality is to look first within ourselves. Samuel Alexander wrote,

> If you wish to discover the nature of causality, look first to your mind. You are conscious of your own power in willing in so far as you experience the continuous transition of an idea of some end into the consciousness of taking the final steps to its attainment. . . . It is itself the experience of exerting power. With this analysis in our mind we may ask ourselves whether causality in the physical world is not in turn the continuous transition of one physical event into another. To do so is not to impute minds to physical things, as

if the only things which could be active must, on the strength of the experience referred to, be minds. It is merely to verify under obscurer conditions what is manifest in the working of our mind.[2]

Causality is defined in the *Dictionary of Philosophy* edited by Dagobert D. Runes as "the relationship between a cause and its effect." This is a circular definition. A parallel could be to define marriage as a relation between a husband and a wife, that is, marriage as a relation between a married man and his spouse. Causality is not the relationship between a cause and its effect, but the relationship between objects, events, states, qualities, forces, processes, and ideas such that the occurrence of one is necessary, or sufficient, or both necessary and sufficient for the occurrence of the other. Any satisfactory definition of causality must include reference to these three varieties of cause. (1) A necessary causal relationship is one in which an identified thing, such as an object, event, state, quality, force, process, or idea, is required for the production of another thing, but there is no certainty that it will accomplish the production. (2) A sufficient causal relationship is one in which an identified thing will produce another thing, but there may be other ways to accomplish the production. (3) A necessary and sufficient causal relationship is one in which an identified thing will with certainty accomplish the production of another thing, and there is no other way to accomplish the production. Imagine a woman who consults a chemist about three spots on her living room rug. The chemist explains, "Spot no. 1 will require the use of ammonia, but I'm not sure it will come out. Ammonia is necessary. Spot no. 2 can be removed with soap and water. That will be sufficient. But, if you wish, you would use any commercial cleaner. Now spot no. 3 is something else. 'Spot Remover Delux' is the trade name of a clearner you can get at the supermarket. It will remove spot no. 3—and, in my opinion, nothing else will remove it." In formal logic necessary causality is expressed as "only if X then Y," sufficient causality as "if X then Y," and necessary and sufficient causality as "if and only if X then Y."

Identification of the cause is seldom a simple matter. For example, Mrs. Brown discovers her cake is a failure, and seeks the cause. She finally realizes that she read one ingredient as two tablespoons rather than two teaspoons. So that was the cause. Or was it because she was not wearing her glasses when she made the cake, or because she had had a quarrel with her husaband, or because she was thinking of her mother's ill health, or because she was listening to the radio, or because the radio announcer was reporting a new arms conflict, or because she had a headache, or because the kitchen was too warm? Every one of these may have been a partial cause. The "real cause" may have been none of these, or all of these, or all of these plus many more.

The totality of partial causes may include all phenomena of the universe. "All events, including this event, is the cause of this event" may be the necessary statement of the full causality of each event. But does this leave any meaning for cause? Must cause therefore mean that event which under the present conditions the author wishes to select as the major contributing factor to the production of another event? It was thinking like this that prompted Bertrand Russell to describe causality as "a relic of a bygone age, surviving, like the monarchy, only because it is erroneously supposed to do no harm."[3]

Causality is often regarded as a reigning assumption in the sciences, although articles on science without causality appear in philosophical journals. However, as A. C. Ewing has written, "It is indeed sometimes said that science nowadays is able to dispense with cause, but what the people who say this have in view is some metaphysical conception of cause with which they do not agree."[4]

Some philosophers of science make a distinction between a stronger and a weaker meaning of causality. The distinction hinges on the identity or non-identity of causality and determinism. Causality is the belief that every event has a cause. Determinism is the belief that the entire future of the universe is fixed by the past and the present, and therefore is predictable. The stronger meaning of causality identifies causality and determinism. The weaker meaning of causality denies the identity, holding that all events are caused but the future is not completely predictable. Why is this the case?

Aristotle said chance is the unforeseen crossing of two lines of causation. But unforeseen by whom? William James said we live in "a pluralistic, restless universe."[5]

Scientists and philosophers of science are usually displeased with a conception of cause that states there is a causal power or force between events identified as cause and effect. Also there is objection to causality when it implies that exact and firm predictions are possible. Natural scientists prefer to state their conclusions and predictions as empirical probabilities or statistical averages rather than mathematical certainties.

No credible scientist would ever announce that he or she had discovered an uncaused event. Such a notion is unthinkable within the sciences, although it is sometimes found in religions. Hence theologians may argue not only that there are causes within the universe but also that the universe itself is caused, and that the "First Cause" is God. If asked, "Who made God?" they reply God is the uncaused cause, the *causa sui* (cause of itself). Scientists may respond that this is a very special use of the concept, or that the creation of the universe is not an event, or that they will revise the causal principle to take into account this violation of the principle, or, recalling Laplace's reply to Napoleon's query as to the place of God in his *System of the World*, they may say, "We do not need this hypothesis." In this connection it is curious to note that Laplace did introduce a "Supreme Intelligence" who is the knower of all causes but not the creator of the world or the self-creator.

Aristotle on Causality

Four men who have shaped the Western thinking about causality are Aristotle, David Hume, J. S. Mill, and Werner Heisenberg. Aristotle set the pattern for the Western view of the cause-effect relationship. Aristotle's thinking about cause was always in the context of production, action, change, and movement. He began by examining four kinds of change. (1) *Artificial* change is that form in which an agent external to an object brings about a change in the object, as when a cabinetmaker turns a pile of lumber into a desk. (2) *Natural* change is when the source of change is within the object, as when as acorn grows into an oak tree. (3) *Lucky* change is when an agent unwittingly brings about a change that he would have brought about had he known all the facts, as when a man accidentally finds in the marketplace a person whom he has been seeking for days. (4) *Haphazard* change is when indeliberate change in lower animals or inanimate objects produce a result that might have been planned, as when a stone happens to fall in such a way as to make a comfortable seat for a person.

Aristotle also thought of change in four other ways: (1) as generation, creation, or coming-into-being and destruction, annihilation, or ceasing-to-be; (2) as change of place, movement, locomotion; (3) as change from rest to motion, and from motion to rest; and (4) as change of quality, as when the surface of a loaf of bread changes from white to brown in the baking process.

In analyzing the kinds of change, Aristotle looked for what he called the *aitía*. This Greek word is often translated "causes," although expressions like "the necessary conditions for coming-into-being," or "the factors needed for change," or "the whys and wherefores of anything" might be better. The plural rather than the singular may have been deceptive, since Aristotle treated cause as a configuration of necessary conditions of natural processes and artificial productions rather than as four independent ingredients of change. The question he put to himself was "What *conditions* are necessary to account for change?" not "What *things* are necessary to account for change?" He answered that there is a material condition (material cause), a pattern or plan condition (formal cause), an activity condition (efficient or moving cause), and a goal condition (final cause). Thus in making a house the material cause is the wood, stone, brick, glass; the formal cause is the blueprint; the efficient cause is the work of masons, carpenters, plumbers; and the final cause is the purpose of making a dwelling in which a family will live. In natural production, for example, the growth of an oak tree, there must be the acorn, the "form" of oak tree in the acorn, the growth produced by soil, rain, and sun, and the goal or *telos* of a perfect oak tree. Aristotle thought of the four causes as *aspects* of such processes as house-building and oak-tree-growing, that is, as *things* only in the context of creating, altering, moving, and destroying. But it was easy to interpret his analysis of the fourfold nature of causality into four entities that must precede anything. Aristotle's conditions were interpreted in a thinglike manner and were put to use by Christian philosophers in the Middle Ages to establish the existence of God (efficient cause), who acted on matter (material cause—which seemed also to have been created by God) to create a world according to a design planned by God (formal cause) for a purpose (final cause).

The problems these Scholastics raised by their speculations I shall not examine here other than to note that cause and effect are like husband and wife—a husband is a man in a marriage relationship and a wife is a woman in a marriage relationship such that if the wife dies the husband ceases to be a husband; he becomes a widower. If the husband dies the wife ceases to be a wife; she becomes a widow. Just as one cannot refer to *husband* or *wife* save in marriage relationship, so one cannot refer to "cause"—even a "First Cause"—save in a causal relationship. Hence, the First Cause of the world has no ontic status before creation, just as a husband has no ontic status before a marriage. It was David Hume who reminded Western philosophers of the relational nature of causality.

Hume on Causality

"Nothing is more curiously inquired after by the mind of man than the causes of every phenomenon; nor are we content with knowing the immediate causes, but push on our inquiries till we arrive at the original and ultimate principle. We would not willingly stop before we are acquainted with that energy in the cause by which it operates on its effect; that tie, which connects them together; and that efficacious quality on which the tie depends."[6] So wrote David Hume in the section of his *Treatise of Human Nature* titled "Conclusion of this Book." At the opening of his consideration of the problem of causality he wrote,

> There is no question which, on account of its importance, as well as difficulty, has caused more disputes among ancient and modern philosophers, than this concerning the efficacy of causes, or that quality which makes them be followed by their effects. But before they entered upon these disputes, methinks it would not have been improper to have examined what idea we have of that efficacy, which is the subject of the controversy. This is what I find principally wanting in their reasonings, and what I shall here endeavour to supply.[7]

Hume, after pointing out that the idea of the efficacy of causes—that quality that forces an effect to follow from a cause—is the central problem of the idea of causality, called attention to the terms that he said are "nearly all synonymous": "I begin with observing that the terms of *efficacy, agency, power, force, energy, necessity, connection,* and *productive quality* are all nearly synonymous; and therefore it is an absurdity to employ any of them in defining the rest."[8] What Hume had in mind can be illustrated by water. Those who think of a cause as efficacy contend that the properties of water are color, weight, odor, taste, and temperature, as well as the power to make things grow, to dissolve salt, to drown an air-breathing animal, and to support wooden objects.

At this point in the *Treatise* Hume identified the methodology of his study. Rather than proceeding in the rationalistic manner of making a definition of cause and examining the idea to see what is entailed, in an empirical manner he sought the impression, that is, the sensation, passion, or emotion,[9] from which the idea of force or efficacy is derived: "By this observation we reject at once all the vulgar definitions which philosophers have given of power and efficacy, and instead of searching for the ideas in these definitions, must look for it in the impressions from which it is originally derived."[10] An example of what Hume was rejecting is the first lines of Spinoza's *Ethics*: "I understand that to be Cause of Itself (*causa sui*) whose essence involves existence and whose nature cannot be conceived unless existing."[11]

Causality is a relationship, and a cause is an object in a causal relationship, said Hume. But there are other relationships. Hume enumerated seven philosophical relations: resemblance, identity, relations of time and place, proportion in quantity or number, degrees in any quality, contrariety, and causation.[12] These relations may be divided into two classes. The first four are relations of ideas and can be derived from ideas alone; for example, from the idea of a triangle can be deduced the idea of two right angles. This relation is invariable. It is the foundation of rationalism, yielding logical certainties. The other three relations—identity, time and place, and causation—are relations of matters of fact. They cannot be derived from ideas alone; "This triangle is white" cannot be deduced from the idea of a triangle. This relation is variable. It is the foundation of empiricism, yielding only probabilities.

The three philosophical relations that cannot be derived from ideas alone are also discovered in the natural world, so, although Hume did not identify them as such, they might be called *the natural-philosophical relations*. Hume wrote that

> the relations of contiguity and distance betwixt two objects may be changed merely by an alteration of their place, without any change on the objects themselves or on their ideas; and the place depends on a hundred different accidents, which cannot be foreseen by the mind. . . . Two objects, though perfectly resembling each other, and even appearing in the same place at different times, may be numerically different: and as the power, by which one object produces another, is never discoverable merely from their idea, it is evident cause and effect are relations, of which we receive information from experience, and not from any abstract reasoning or reflection.[13]

The causal relation is unique in that it is the only one of the three natural relations "that can be traced beyond our senses, and informs us of existences and objects which we do not see or feel."[14] Hume, as an empiricist holding that all realities can be sensed, was puzzled about the "existences" and "objects" called *causes* and *effects* since they are not seen, heard, felt, tasted, or smelled. If causes and effects are objects, then the impression that produces the idea of cause and effect can be identified. What is that impression?

In his attempt to identify the impression that produces the idea of cause Hume noted three relations that are essential to the cause-effect relationship. He might have called them subrelations. The first is contiguity: "I find in the first place, that whatever objects are considered as causes or effects, are contiguous; and that nothing can operate in a time or place which is ever so little removed from those of its existence."[15] The second is the temporal priority of the cause: "The second relation I shall observe as essential to causes and effects, is not so universally acknowledged, but is liable to some controversy. It is that of priority of time in the cause before the effect."[16] After a lengthy discussion of why the cause must precede the effect, Hume added that "the affair is of no great importance."[17] He then listed the third relation, which "is of much greater importance, than any of the other two above mentioned."[18] This is a "necessary connection."[19] What impression produces this idea? It is not found among the known qualities of objects nor among the known relations. Hume would not admit that he had found an idea that is not preceded by an impression. Since he could not locate the impression in the objects external to the knower, he said, "We must therefore proceed like those, who being in search of anything that lies concealed from them, and not finding it in the place they expected, beat about all the neighbouring fields, without any certain view or design, in hopes their good fortune will at last guide them to what they search for."[20]

Hume had discussed this problem earlier in the *Treatise*, but at this point in the argument he appears to have forgotten what he had previously written. In book 1, part 1, section 4 he said that the faculty of the imagination is guided by "some universal principles," or "some associating quality," or some "uniting principle among ideas" that is a "gentle force" associating ideas. The "gentle force" is the work of "Nature . . . pointing out to everyone those simple ideas, which are most proper to be united into a complex one. The qualities, from which this association arises, and by which the mind is, after this manner, conveyed from one idea to another, are three, viz., resemblance, contiguity in time or place, and cause and effect."[21] Now, instead of regarding causality as a "gentle force" of nature, he asked where in the relation of causality is located the subrelation of necessary connection. Finding that he could not locate necessary connection in either of the other two qualities or subrelations of causality, Hume reported, "I find that upon the appearance of one of the objects the mind is determined by custom to consider its usual attendant, and to consider it in a stronger light upon account of its relation to the first object. It is this impression, then, or determination, which affords me the idea of necessity."[22] The "necessary connection," "power," "efficacy," "force," "energy," "productive quality," and/or "agency" is located in the knower rather than in the known, in the epistemological subject rather than in the epistemological object. "Experience is a principle which instructs me in the several conjunctions of objects for the past. Habit is another principle which determines me to expect the same for the future."[23] Necessary connection—the heart and core of causality—is the "principle which makes up reason from cause and effect."[24]

So what is a cause for Hume? If one wishes to define a cause qua philosophical relation, it is "an object precedent and contiguous to another, and where all the objects resembling the former are placed in the like relations of precedency and contiguity to those objects that resemble the latter."[25] If one wishes to define a cause qua natural relation, it is "an object precedent and contiguous to another, and so united with it that the idea of the one determines the mind to form the idea of the other, and the impression of the one to form a more lively idea of the other."[26]

At the close of book 1 when Hume looked back at what he had accomplished and what he had failed to accomplish, he compared himself to a sailor hoping to compass the globe in a leaky weather-beaten vessel. His philosophy, he said, placed him in "forlorn solitude" and left him "utterly abandoned and disconsolate."[27] "I have exposed myself to the enmity of all metaphysicians, logicians, mathematicians, and even theologians."[28] "All the world conspires to oppose and contradict me."[29] The reason for the opposition, said Hume, was that he showed that the energy in the cause by which it operates on the effect is not in the cause but in the mind and experience of the observer. He noted:

> and how must we be disappointed when we learn that this connection, tie, or energy lies merely in ourselves, and is nothing but that determination of the mind which is acquired by custom, and causes us to make a transition from an object to its usual attendant, and from the impression of one to the lively idea of the other? Such a discovery not only cuts off all hope of ever attaining satisfaction, but even prevents our very wishes; since it appears, that when we say we desire to know the ultimate and operating principle as something which resides in the external object, we either contradict ourselves, or talk without a meaning.[30]

But Hume's fears were needless. The book did not create the sensation he had expected. As he wrote in his autobiography, "Never literary attempt was more unfortunate than my *Treatise of Human Nature*. It fell dead-born from the press, without reaching such distinction as even to excite a murmur among the zealots." During his lifetime Hume was recognized as author of *History of England*, but today he is better known for his analyses of cause and the self and for his role as "spiritual father of Kant."

Mill on Causality

John Stuart Mill (1806–1873) began his *System of Logic, Ratiocinative and Inductive, Being a Connected View of the Principles of Evidence, and the Methods of Scientific Investigation*, book 3, chapter 5, section 1 with these words: "The phenomena of nature exist in two distinct relations to one another; that of simultaneity, and that of succession. Every phenomenon is related, in an uniform manner, to some phenomena that coexist with it, and to some that have preceded and will follow it."[31] The uniformities he had in mind were "the Laws of Number" and "the Laws of Space." He examined these, and then sought for another law of succession with the same rigorous certainty and universality that he found in numerical and spatial laws. He noted:

> Now among all those uniformities in the succession of phenomena, which common observation is sufficient to bring to light, there are very few which have any, even apparent, pretension to this rigorous indefeasibility: and of those few, one only has been found capable of completely sustaining it. In that one, however, we recognise a law which is universal also in another sense; it is coextensive with the entire field of successive phenomena, all instances whatever of succession being examples of it. This law is the Law of Causation. The truth, that every fact which has a beginning has a cause, is coextensive with human experience.[32]

The universality of "the Law of Causation" is "a most important and really fundamental truth,"[33] because the notion of cause is "the root of the whole theory of Induction."[34]

Mill warned that he had no intention of getting involved in the notion of a First Cause: "I premise, then, that when in the course of this inquiry I speak of the cause of any phenomenon, I do not mean a cause which is not itself a phenomenon; I make no research into the ultimate, or ontological cause of anything."[35] He then noted that the metaphysicians of his time had obviously not learned much from the work of Hume.

> The notion of causation is deemed, by the schools of metaphysics most in vogue at the present moment, to imply a mysterious and most powerful tie, such as cannot, or at least does not, exist between any physical fact and that other physical fact on which it is invariably consequent, and which is popularly termed its cause: and thence is deduced the supposed necessity of ascending higher, into the essences and inherent constitution of things, to find the true cause, the cause which is not only followed by, but actually *produces*, the effect. No such necessity exists for the purposes of the present inquiry, nor will any such doctrine be found in the following pages.[36]

The only cause that induction requires, argued Mill, is the cause that can be gained from experience. No one experiences a First Cause.

Mill then defined causation as "that invariability of succession . . . found by observation to obtain between every fact in nature and some other fact which has preceded it."[37] Causation is universal: "And the universality of the law of causation consists in this, that every consequent is connected in this manner with some particular antecedent, or set of antecedents."[38] He hastened to add that he meant "invariably connected." There are no chance events in the phenomena of nature. The antecedents are usually multiple, one of which will be called the cause; the others will be called conditions. Often the condition that came last into existence is dignified by the name *cause.*[39] He added that "in practice that particular condition is usually styled the cause, whose share in the matter is superficially the most conspicuous, or whose requisiteness to the production of the effect we happen to be insisting on at the moment."[40] However, the cause, "philosphically speaking, is the sum total of the conditions positive and negative taken together; the whole of the contingencies of every description, which being realized, the consequent invariably follows."[41]

At this point Mill offered an interesting addition to his analysis of causation. The definition of cause as "the antecedent which it invariably follows" does not mean "the intecedent which it invariably *has* followed in our past experience."[42] The term *cause* necessitates that "we should believe not only that the antecedent always *has* been followed by the consequent, but that, as long as the present constitution of things endures, it always *will* be so."[43] He illustrated why night cannot be cause or condition of day:

> If the sun ceased to rise, which, for aught we know, may be perfectly compatible with the general laws of matter, night would be, or might be, eternal. On the other hand, if the sun is above the horizon, his light not extinct, and no opaque body between us and him, we believe firmly that unless a change takes place in the properties of matter, this combination of antecedents will be followed by the consequent, day; that if the combination of antecedents could be indefinitely prolonged, it would be always day; and that if the same combination had always existed, it would always have been day, quite independently of night as a previous condition. Therefore is it that we do not call night the cause, nor even a condition, of day.[44]

This prompted Mill to rethink his definition of cause. The notion of cause, he said, involves the idea of necessity, and necessity means unconditionalness. "Invariable sequence, therefore, is not synonymous with causation, unless the sequence, besides being invariable, is unconditional."[45] And so Mill again refined his definition of cause: "We may define, therefore, the cause of a phenomenon, to be the antecedent, or the concurrence of antecedents, on which it is invariably and *unconditionally* consequent."[46]

Mill asked himself whether the cause-effect relationship is always an antecedent-consequent relationship. He referred to a dogma of the scholastics—*cessante causa cessat et effectus* (a continuing cause is necessary for the continuence of the effect)—and answered that it depends on the nature of the relationship. Some things, once produced, do not require the continued presence of the agents that produced them; thus a sword run through the body kills a person, but the sword need not stay in the body for the person to remain dead. But other conditions, once produced, do require the continued presence of the agents that produced them; for example, the pressure that forced the mercury up a tube must remain to sustain it in the tube.

Mill also presented five experimental methods that he described as "the only possible modes of experimental inquiry, of direct induction *a posteriori*, as distinguished from deduction."[47]

> (1) *The Method of Agreement*: "If two or more instances of the phenomenon under investigation have only one circumstance in common, the circumstance in which alone all the instances agree, is the cause (or effect) of the given phenomenon."[48]
> (2) *The Method of Difference*: "If an instance in which the phenomenon under investigation occurs, and an instance in which it does not occur, have every circumstance in common save one, that one occurring only in the former; the circumstance in which alone the two instances differ, is the effect, or the cause, or a necessary part of the cause, of the phenomenon."[49]
> (3) *The Joint Method of Agreement and Difference*: "If two or more instances in which the phenomenon occurs have only one circumstance in common, while two or more instances in which it does not occur have nothing in common save the absence of that circumstance; the circumstance in which alone the two sets of instances differ, is the effect, or the cause, or a necessary part of the cause, of the phenomenon."[50]
> (4) *The Method of Residues*: "Subduct from any phenomenon such part as is known by previous inductions to be the effect of certain antecedents, and the residue of the phenomenon is the effect of the remaining antecedents."[51]
> (5) *The Method of Concomitant Variations*: "Whatever phenomenon varies in any manner whenever another phenomenon varies in some particular manner, is either a cause or an effect of that phenomenon, or is connected with it through some fact of causation."[52]

A Scholastic View of Causality

It would be a serious misunderstanding of Western philosophy to think that all Western philosophers were sympathetic to those who, like Hume and Mill, tried to develop an empirical theory of causality. Hume was not exaggerating when he said metaphysicians, logicians, mathematicians, and theologians were opposed to his view. Theologians were still thinking in terms of what Aquinas called "causal agents." Christians, said Aquinas, "must hold that the will of

God is the cause of things"[53] and "in that man is rational, it is necessary that he have free choice."[54] God as "the first in the order of agents" must be the cause of all events, and humans cannot be rational beings unless they have the possibility of making genuine choices. How is it possible to have both divine predestination and human freedom?

Aquinas said that "the will of God is the cause of things, and that He acts by the will, and not, as some have supposed, by a necessity of His nature."[55] For example, God speaks truthfully not because he is Truth but because he chooses to speak truthfully. Aquinas offered three reasons for this. First, since both intellectual agents (those who act from choice and natural agents—those who act by reason of their nature) act for an end, "the natural agent must have the end and the necessary means predetermined for it by some higher intellect; as, the end and definite movement is predetermined for the arrow by the archer. Hence the intellectual and voluntary agent must precede the agent that acts by nature. Hence, since God is first in the order of agents, He must act by intellect and will."[56] Second, "[s]ince . . . the divine being is undetermined, and contains in Himself the full perfection of being, it cannot be that He acts by a necessity of His nature, unless He were to cause something undetermined and indefinite in being."[57] Third,

> it is shown by the relation of effects to their cause. For effects proceed from the agent that causes them in so far as they pre-exist in the agent; since every agent produces its like. Now effects pre-exist in their cause after the mode of the cause. Therefore, since the divine being is His own intellect, effects pre-exist in Him after the mode of intellect, and therefore proceed from Him after the same mode. Consequently, they proceed from Him after the mode of will, for His inclination to put in act what His intellect has conceived pertains to the will. Therefore the will of God is the cause of things.[58]

If God is the cause of all things, does that mean that God is the cause of all that humans do? Aquinas answered affirmatively.

> Now if a thing cannot attain to something by the power of its nature, it must be directed thereto by another; thus, an arrow is directed by the archer towards a mark. Hence, properly speaking, a rational creature, capable of eternal life, is led towards it, directed, as it were, by God. The exemplar of that direction pre-exists in God; just as in Him is the exemplar of the order of all things towards an end. . . . Now the exemplar in the mind of the doer of something to be done is a kind of pre-existence in him of the thing to be done. Hence the exemplar of the aforesaid direction of a rational creature towards the end of life eternal is called predestination. For to destine is to direct or send. Thus it is clear that predestination, as regards its objects, is a part of providence.[59]

But if predestination is part of God's providence, and if some humans are redeemed and some are damned, does God's providence include the damnation of some? This strange doctrine, known as "double predestination," was supported by Aquinas in an interesting way, namely, by an appeal to the chain of being.

> The reason for the predestination of some, and reprobation of others, must be sought in the goodness of God. Thus God is said to have made all things through His goodness, so that the divine goodness might be represented in things. Now it is necessary that God's goodness, which in itself is one and simple, should be manifested in many ways in His creation; because creatures in themselves cannot attain to the simplicity of God. Thus it is that for the completion of the universe there are required diverse grades of being, of which some hold a high and some a low place in the universe. That this multiformity of grades may be preserved in things, God allows some evils, lest many good things should be hindered. . . . God has willed to manifest His goodness in men: in respect to those whom He predestines, by means of His mercy, in sparing them; and in respect of others, whom he reprobates, by means of His justice, in punishing them. . . . Yet why He chooses some for glory, and reprobates others, has no reason, except the divine will. Whence Augustine says: "Why He draws one, and another He draws not, seek not to judge, if thou dost not wish to err."[60]

It is also interesting to note that earlier Aquinas said that God acts by reason of his free will rather than by his nature, and later he maintained God provides diverse grades of being because the "completion of the universe" requires it. One might wonder how Aquinas could avoid the conclusion that God in his goodness desires the redemption of all mankind. The answer is that the chain of being necessitates that there be both lost and saved.

After establishing that God is the cause of all things, Aquinas would seem to be required to admit that humankind is the cause of nothing. But he could not allow this, for then God's counsels, exhortations, commands, and prohibitions would be meaningless. Man's free choice is inherent in God's commandments. Aquinas distinguished three kinds of actions: (1) without judgment, (2) with nonfree judgment, and (3) with free judgment. The first refers to the acts of inanimate objects; a stone falls without thought. The second describes the acts of lower animals; they act from judgment, but not from free judgments; a sheep runs from a wolf by reason of natural instinct. The third refers to the acts of human beings. Aquinas said that

> man acts from judgment, because by his apprehensive power he judges that something should be avoided or sought. But because this judgment, in the case of some particular act, is not from a natural instinct, but from some act of comparison in the reason, therefore he acts from free judgment and retains the power of being inclined to various things. For reason in contingent matters may follow opposite courses, as we see in dialectical syllogisms and rhetorical arguments. Now particular operations are contingent, and therefore in such matters the judgment of reason may follow opposite courses,

and is not determinate to one. And in that man is rational, it is necessary that he have free choice.[61]

Arguments for predestination, predeterminism, foreknowledge, omniscience, prescience, and providence have appeared in Christianity since the writings of Paul.[62] An interesting modern solution is that predestination is true, but not metaphysically true. For example, according to William Pauck, "In the last resort, it is a soteriological and not metaphysical doctrine, for it is not designed to assert the truth that everything is predetermined by God (although it must be admitted that the doctrine of divine providence has always stood in a close relation to the teaching on predestination); it is designed in order to give doctrinal expression to the religious conviction that man is altogether dependent upon God for his salvation."[63] Another interesting defense of divine omniscience is that God does not know everything now, but rather knows everything that it is possible to know.[64]

Heisenberg on Causality

The English astronomer A. S. Eddington in his Gifford Lectures on *The Nature of the Physical World*, delivered in early 1927, said, "In the old conflict between freewill and predestination it has seemed hitherto that physics comes down heavily on the side of predestination."[65] He admitted that he found it incredible that everything is completely predetermined, and yet, he added, "I have not been able to form a satisfactory conception of any kind of law or causal sequence which shall be other than deterministic."[66] But "a new situation has arisen. It is a consequence of the advent of the quantum theory that *physics is no longer pledged to a scheme of deterministic law*. Determinism has dropped out altogether in the latest formulations of theoretical physics and it is at least open to doubt whether it will ever be brought back."[67]

Eddington later wrote that the above remarks were made in this form in his Gifford Lectures. He did not state the grounds for the remarks. He noted in rewriting the text that the attitude of "indifference" to determinism had been replaced by "an attitude more definitely hostile."[68] He referred to a discovery in quantum physics made public in the summer of 1927 by Werner Heisenberg. He called it a general principle, ranking with the principle of relativity, and christened it "the principle of indeterminacy." He stated the principle as follows: "a particle may have position or it may have velocity but it cannot in any exact sense have both."[69] Greater accuracy can be attained in specifying position at the cost of less accuracy in the specifying velocity, and vice versa. Eddington confessed,

There has been no time for more than a hurried examination of the far-

> reaching consequences of this principle; and I should have been reluctant to include "stop-press" ideas were it not that they appear to clinch the conception towards which the earlier developments were leading. The future is a combination of the causal influences of the past together with unpredictable elements—unpredictable not merely because it is impracticable to obtain the data of prediction, but because no data connected causally with our experience exist. It will be necessary to defend so remarkable a change of opinion at some length. Meanwhile we may note that science thereby withdraws its moral opposition to freewill.[70]

Eddington's hasty survey of Heisenberg's discovery resulted in an astonishing line of reasoning that must have proceeded as follows:

1. Heisenberg has discovered indeterminancy in the atom.
2. Determinism is predictability by appeal to the relationship of cause and effect.
3. Causes force or compel effects.
4. Freedom is the opposite of force or compulsion.
5. Heisenberg has found freedom in the activity of the atom.
6. Physics is no longer pledged to a scheme of deterministic law, and so it withdraws "its moral opposition to freewill."
7. Physics has shifted from support of predestination to support of freedom.
8. "It will perhaps be said that the conclusion to be drawn from these arguments from modern science, is that religion first became possible for a reasonable scientific man about the year 1927. . . . If our expectation should prove well founded that 1927 has seen the final overthrow of strict causality by Heisenberg, Bohr, Born and others, the year will certainly rank as one of the greatest epochs in the development of scientific philosophy."[71]

Eddington in his "hurried examination" equated causality with compulsion and chance with freedom. Heisenberg had found an element of unpredictability or chance in his study of atomic behavior, and Eddington wished to be one of the first to announce in "stop-press" fashion that physics had shifted from support of predestination to support of freedom. It seems hard to believe that a scientist of his caliber could have so sophomorically confused natural law (the law of description) and moral law (the law of prescription). It was much as if one held the law of the stop sign and the law of falling bodies were both constraining laws, that is, "You must stop" and "Unsupported bodies must fall."

Twelve years later in *The Philosophy of Physical Science* Eddington admitted his error in a face-saving manner: "In the discussion of freewill provoked by the modern physical theories, it has, I think generally been assumed that, since the ordinary laws of inorganic matter leave its behaviour undetermined within a certain narrow range, there can be no scientific objection to allowing a volition of consciousness to decide the exact behavior within the limits of the aforesaid range. I call this hypothesis A."[72] Eddington admitted that he supported this view in *The Nature of the Physical World*, and added that his "earlier discussions were marred by a failure to recognize that hypothesis A is nonsense."[73]

The principle that Eddington called "the principle of indeterminancy" was announced by Heisenberg in *Zeitschrift für Physik* in 1927. Heisenberg preferred to call it the "Copenhagen interpretation of quantum theory,"[74] since the experiments that the principle interprets were performed in that city.

In classical Newtonian mechanics, and even in Einstein's theory of relativity, the state of a single system at a specified time and place can be given precisely in numbers that represent position and momentum; for example, the astronomer in such a system can predict the time and place of a future event such as an eclipse of the moon. As quantum physics developed it was assumed that what is true in the macrocosm is also true in the microcosm. But the Newtonian view of the world was based on the assumption that motion and position are defined from the view of points of rest. What does one do in the world of the atom where there is no fixed point? In classical physics a particle has position but no momentum; in modern physics a particle has momentum but no position. Einstein had developed his theories of relativity in this context.

Niels Bohr, realizing that a term like *particle* is misleading when discussing radiation emitted by the atom, began speaking of "matter waves," rather than of particles. He knew that the images of the wave and the particle are mutually exclusive—a thing cannot be a wave and a particle at the same time—and yet he found that by shifting from one view to the other he was able to illustrate experiments in atomic research. He called this "the principle of complementarity." What was complementary, however, was not the wave and the particle per se but the particle view and the wave view of the atom. Bohr attempted to solve the apparent contradiction by referring to electromagnetic waves as "probability waves" rather than "real waves." Probability waves are not three-dimensional waves like radio waves, but are waves in a many-dimensional configurational space. They are mathematical quantities. The "waves" he had in mind were more like waves of the future than waves of the ocean.

Meanwhile Heisenberg had discovered another deviation from Newtonian physics. In his laboratory in Copenhagen, experimenting with the motion of electrons through a cloud chamber, he discovered that from a study of the position and velocity of an electron he could not predict accurately an event comparable to the predicting of an eclipse of the moon in astronomy. He said, "One could speak of the position and of the velocity of an electron as in Newtonian mechanics and one could observe and measure these quantites. But one could not fix both quantities simultaneously with an arbitrarily high accuracy."[75] "Position" and "velocity" have no operational meaning in quantum physics. They do not enable physicists to determine when an electron will be where.

This inability to predict began to be called "the relations of uncertainty" or "the principle of indeterminancy." Causal determinism is not operative at the heart of reality.

Heisenberg reminisced in 1955 about discussions with Bohr that lasted many hours into the night and ended in near despair. At the end of the discussions he would go for a walk in the neighboring park repeating again and again the question: Can nature possibly be as absurd as it seems in those atomic experiments?

Einstein assumed that an error had been made somewhere, and that when the error was corrected, the strictly interpreted principle of causal determinism would win out. He asserted testily, "God does not play dice."

Others, like Eddington in 1927, rejoiced that gaps had been found in the predictions of Newtonian mechanics and attempted to use the gaps as loopholes for free will. Some recalled that C. S. Peirce believed in the reality of chance in the world. He dignified the belief by the term *tychism* (the Greek word for luck). William James had distinguished "soft determinism"—the view that, while it is true that everything happens because of conditions that make it impossible for anything else to happen, there is still enough loose play in the universe to allow for freedom of the will and moral responsibility—and "hard determinism"—the view that all events, including moral behavior, are the result of causes such that the occurrence of the events can be predicted.

Before deciding that the principle of indeterminacy has any relevance to the problem of human freedom one should ask what relation chance or indeterminacy has to freedom. Is one free—physically, economically, psychologically, morally—because one is not caused? The answer is negative because the opposite of freedom is not causality but compulsion.

Perhaps the best approach to the consideration of human freedom and causality is to ask under what conditions one feels free. Would one feel free in an indeterminate world in which predictions were not possible? Again the answer must be negative because the feeling of making free choices is dependent upon the predictability of what will happen from the choices one makes. In a world in which food sometimes nourishes, sometimes poisons, sometimes causes total blindness, and sometimes turns to stone in the mouth, would one ever feel free to eat? How could one feel free to act in a world in which gravity was an unpredictable force? One would never feel free to toss anything in the air, not knowing whether it would fall to the earth, rise indefinitely, remain in midair, or sail off at an angle.

Western thinkers have perhaps spent more time and energy on the problem of free will than the matter deserves. Although free will is often listed as a central problem in introductory philosophy textbooks, the consideration has curious and humorous aspects. According to an old story, a New England preacher was told one Sunday morning that God had determined since eternity that he was to preach in a certain church that morning. He replied, "Then I am not going to preach." I recall once being given a minilecture by a fellow philosopher in a hotel lobby on why the belief in free will was absurd. Upon concluding, he said, "Now I'm going into the dining room early. There is always a better choice of menus at this hour." Perhaps all one can say about freedom and determinism is that the former is inconceivable without the latter.

Heisenberg's contribution to the Western view of causality is not scientific support to the arguments for freedom of the self. But he has made some very significant contributions. One is in the area of language. Heisenberg held to the traditional language of Newtonian mechanics:

> The Copenhagen interpretation of quantum theory starts from a paradox. Any experiment in physics, whether it refers to the phenomena of daily life or to atomic events, is to be described in the terms of classical physics. The concepts of classical physics form the language by which we describe the arrangement of our experiments and state the results. We cannot and should not replace these concepts by any others. Still the application of these concepts is limited by the relations of uncertainty. We must keep in mind this limited range of applicability of the classical concepts while using them, but we cannot and should not try to improve them.[76]

But he found that concepts like *position, velocity, thing,* and *fact* have no operational meaning when applied to small particles. He observed, "The ordinary language was based upon the old concepts of space and time and this language offered the only unambiguous means of communication about the setting up and the results of the measurements. Yet the experiments showed that the old concepts could not be applied everywhere."[77] And he claimed that in atomic experiments "we have to do with things and facts, with phenomena that are just as real as any phenomena in daily life. But the atoms or the elementary particles themselves are not as real; they form a world of potentialities or possibilities rather than one of things and facts."[78]

F. S. C. Northrop thinks that Heisenberg's "contention that quantum mechanics has brought the concept of potentiality back into physical science" is a "novel and important thesis."[79] Potentiality is rooted in the fact that position and velocity of wave particles take the form of statistical prediction. The atomic physicist cannot predict when a wave particle will be in a specific position partly because the language of position and velocity is not appropriate, and partly because the prediction refers to statistical averages. The tension between the necessity of describing atomic experiments in the terms of classical physics and the knowledge that the terms are not accurate is "the root of the statistical character of quantum theory," according to Heisenberg.[80]

Philipp Frank summarizes the role of the causal law in atomic physics as follows: "There are no laws by which we can predict from any observable initial conditions the precise future locations of point-events. In other words, there are no state variables the initial values of which we can keep within such a narrow margin that we can achieve a precise predictability of single point-events in the future."[81] Whereas Newtonian mechanics describes a certain event, the probability function describes a whole ensemble of possible events.

According to Heisenberg

> it is important to remember that in natural science we are not interested in the universe as a whole, including ourselves, but we direct our attention to some part of the universe and make that the object of our studies. In atomic physics this part is usually a very small object, an atomic particle or a group of such particles, sometimes much larger—the size does not matter; but it is important that a large part of the universe, including ourselves, does *not* belong to the object.
>
> Now, the theoretical interpretation of an experiment starts with the two steps that have been discussed. In the first step we have to describe the arrangement of the experiment, eventually combined with a first observation, in terms of classical physics and translate this description into a probability function. This probability function follows the laws of quantum theory, and its change in the course of time, which is continuous, can be calculated from the initial conditions; this is the second step. The probability function combines objective and subjective elements. It contains statements about possibilities or better tendencies ("potentia" in Aristotelian philosophy), and these statements are completely objective, they do not depend on any observer; and it contains statements about our knowledge of the system, which of course are subjective in so far as they may be different for different observers. In ideal cases the subjective element in the probability function may be practically negligible as compared with the objective one. The physicists then speak of a "pure case."[82]

The above quotation also calls attention to another contribution of the indeterminacy principle to the principle of causality. The quantum-theoretical interpretation of atomic events is based on measuring devices constructed by the observer "and we have to remember that what we observe is not nature in itself but nature exposed to our method of questioning."[83] So "one must not forget that in the drama of existence we are ourselves both players and spectators."[84] The indeterminacy element is rooted in the subjectivity of the observer. The act of observing alters the object being observed. Although this makes objectivity impossible, one must remember that the physical world withour the observer is not the total physical world.

The Chinese View of Causality

Metaphysics was not a major concern of the classical Chinese philosophers. One of the rare discussions of causality appears in *Hsiao Ch'ü* (Minor Illustrations), a volume on the methods of dialectics written during the Warring States period (403–221 B.C.). This work of the Mohist school of philosophy was a handbook to aid the Mohists in their opposition to the followers of Confucius. Mo Tzu (470–381 B.C.), the founder of the school, was the first opponent of Confucius and the first important philosopher after Confucius. He wrote essays against the Confucian love of music and ceremony and against what he regarded as Confucius's atheism. Y. P. Mei, who translated the *Mo Tzu* into English in 1929, refers to Mo Tzu as "the neglected rival of Confucius."

In the *Hsiao Ch'ü* the author discusses causality in the framework of dialectics, claiming there are six uses of dialectics, namely, to distinguish (1) right from wrong, (2) good government from bad government, (3) similarity from difference, (4) names from the actualities for which they stand, (5) what is beneficial from what is harmful, and (6) what is certain from what is uncertain. One of the ways to distinguish the certain from the uncertain is to find the statements that correctly set forth cause or causes.

A cause (*ku*), according to the *Hsiao Ch'ü* is "that with the obtaining of which something becomes."[85] There are two kinds of causes: minor cause and major cause. An example of a minor cause is the point as cause of a line. There cannot be a line withour a point, but a point in itself does not constitute a line. This is designated in Western philosophy as the necessary cause. An example of a major cause is the act of seeing and sight. There can be sight if and only if there is an act of seeing. This is designated in Western philosophy as the necessary and sufficient cause. There is no mention of the sufficient cause. The assumption is that the world is causal and that the mind of man is competent to discover the causes. Other Chinese philosophers used the concept of causality but made little effort to understand its meaning.

The Buddhist Theory of Causality

Kamalaśīla, an eighth-century Indian Mādhyamika Buddhist, once observed, "Among all the jewels of Buddhist philosophy its theory of Causation is the chief jewel."[86] T. R. V. Murti considered causation "the central problem in Indian philosophy."[87] According to Buddhism the world of our ordinary experience, which the Buddhists call "the world of the conditioned," is completely causal. The world of the unconditioned, the world described as the Buddha-nature and *nirvāṇa,* presumably is not causal, since it is said to be unthinkable and incomprehensible. In the conditioned world every cause arises dependent upon a combination of causes that it necessarily succeeds and is linked to a combination of effects that necessarily succeed it. The Buddhists appear to have accepted uncritically the view that an effect-producing power is inherent in the things that are causes. The whole world of the conditioned is in functional dependence upon a coordinated totality of conditions.

There is no First Cause in Buddhism. This is inherent in the Buddhist conception of a cyclical theory of time. Therefore, there is no quest for the originating cause in the chain of causes; all causes are contingent. Each cause is a link (*nidāna*) in a chain of conditions necessary for the process of anything's being. Every event is the result of events, and every event is part of the coordinated cause of events. Every *dharma* (element of existence) is conditioned (*saṁskṛta*), that is, made by the combination and concurrence of conditions. Literally *saṁskṛta* means "where this is, there that is."

The search for causes in Buddhism is never a search for specific causal factors; causes appear in a causal matrix. Causation is always in a set of cofactors. An event is a cause only in a contextual arrangement of events. A formula often used in Buddhism is "Nothing single comes from single." The world of the conditioned is therefore an interconnected whole of events. The effect is nothing over and above the presence of the totality of causes. Therefore, one cannot speak of a beginning or ending of a cause. A cause is not an element in a gestalt—it is the gestalt. Its reality depends upon the total environment, and also upon the conditions under which it is being considered. Buddhists might make themselves clearer to Western-trained minds were they to speak of the manifold conditions necessary for an event rather than the cause of an event. Takakusu wrote, "It is clear that the Causation Theory of Buddhism is not like the theory of causality of classical physical science which is a fixed theory. In Buddhism every Stage is a cause when viewed from its effect; when viewed from the antecedent cause, it is an effect. It may be also said that there is a cause in the effect, and an effect in the cause. There is nothing fixed in this theory."[88]

Buddhists insist that causes do not *explain* existence; causes *are* existence. The cause is the thing or event itself. To exist is to be a cause. An ancient text ascribed to the Buddha himself states, "All (real) forces are instantaneous. (But) how can a thing which has (absolutely) no duration, (nevertheless have the time) to produce something? (This is because what we call) 'existence' is nothing but efficiency, and it is this very efficiency which is called a creative cause."[89] F. Th. Stcherbatsky commented, "In other words, existence is dynamic, not static, and it is composed of a sequence of point-instances which are interdependent, i.e., which are causes."[90]

The causal law within Buddhism is known as *pratītya-samutpāda* (the law of dependent origination). The term means literally "because of that occurring, this occurs." The law is applied in a cyclical arrangement visualized as a twelve-spoked wheel—the Existence Wheel (*Bhava-chakra*)—and is variously designated: "The Cycle of Causation and Becoming," "The Twelve-Divisioned Cycle," "The Cycle of Co-ordinated Co-production," "The Cycle of Combined Dependent Origination," "The Wheel of Dependent Production," "The Chain of Causation," "The Cycle of Causation and Becoming." When the law is used in soteriological contexts, it is called "The Wheel of Life," "The Circle of Birth and Death," or "The Wheel of Bondage." The Wheel represents the process of the conditioned life as one of continual phenomenal change (*saṁsāra*) pluralistically caused. It is usually said to be composed of twelve *nidānas* (spokes of the wheel, or links in the chain). Images of a wheel or a chain misrepresent, since the relationship of the *nidānas* is best described as a flow, and wheels and chains do not flow. The twelve *nidānas* are divided into two of the former life, eight of the present life, and two of the future life.

The two *nidānas* of the past, are (1) *avidyā* (ignorance, blind mind, and delusion) and (2) *saṁskāra* (blind will, disposition, tendency or motive to live). They remain after death and represent the cause of the next life.

The eight *nidānas* of the present are divided into five effects of the past that appear in the present and three causes in the present. The five are (1) *vijñāna* (subconscious mind, the first moment of a new form), (2) the five *skandhas* (body, feelings, understanding, will, and pure consciousness, which are in the embryo before the formation of the sense organs), (3) *sad-āyatana* (that is, the prenatal development of the organs of sense) (4) *sparca* (contact, as when the organs and consciousness begin to cooperate, with the sense of touch dominating), and (5) *vedanā* (perception, the sensations now definite.) These five form the individual. The individual then enters the sphere of self-creation. The three causes of the present are (1) *tṛṣṇa* (thirst, desire, or craving for existence and experience, marked particularly by the awaking of the sexual instinct), (2) *upādāna* (cleaving, attaching oneself to an object or activity), and (3) *bhava* (existence, the formation of being through the realization of the objective of one's life). These three *nidānas* of the present represent the stage of conscious self-creation. They remind the Buddhist that one is what one desires, craves, and becomes.

The two *nidānas* of the future are the effects of *tṛṣṇa, upādana,* and *bhava* and are also the cause of *avidyā* and *saṁskāra*. They are (1) *jāti* (rebirth) and (2) *jarā-maraṇa* (death, decay). When viewed as flow in the perspective of the wheel, they are the future in the sense of the time when the causes of the present open out and close—and they contain also the causes for life still further in the future.

The whole "Wheel of Conditioned Becoming" I express in the following manner:

Because of ignorance, blind will occurs,
and because of blind will, subconscious mind occurs,
and because of subconscious mind, name and form occur,
and because of name and form, the prenatal development of sense occurs,
and because of prenatal development of sense, contact occurs,
and because of contact, perception occurs,
and because of perception, desire occurs,
and because of desire, cleaving occurs,
and because of cleaving, existence occurs,
and because of existence, rebirth occurs,
and because of rebirth, death occurs,
and because death occurs, ignorance occurs, and so on.

But Buddhism would be misrepresented unless the wheel were stated both in the order of occurence and in the order of cessation.

> Because of the cessation of ignorance, blind will ceases,
> and because of the cessation of blind will, subconscious mind ceases,
> and because of the cessation of subconscious mind, name and form cease,
> and because of the cessation of name and form, the prenatal development of sense ceases,
> and because of the cessation of prenatal development of sense, contact ceases,
> and because of the cessation of contact, perception ceases,
> and because of the cessation of perception, desire ceases,
> and because of the cessation of desire, cleaving ceases,
> and because of the cessation of cleaving, existence ceases,
> and because of the cessation of existence, rebirth ceases,
> and because of the cessation of rebirth, death ceases.

The wheel image, in other words, is designed not only to explain the origin of *duḥkha* (the transience that leads to anguish), but also to point the way to the ending of *duḥkha*. It reminds Buddhists that on the one hand they ought not to have been born, but on the other hand being born gives them the opportunity to attain *nirvāṇa*.

The wheel image also helps the Buddhist understand how all events are conditioned. The flow (*saṁsāra*) is such that each *nidāna* must be thought of in two aspects: *nidāna*-qua-cause and *nidāna*-qua-effect. Each *nidāna* is both the effect of all other *nidānas* including itself-qua-cause and the cause of all other *nidānas* including itself-qua-effect. For example, *nidāna* 6 (the numbering has no significance other than to distinguish one *nidāna* from the other eleven) is qua-effect coproduced by the other *nidānas* and by 6-qua-cause, and *nidāna* 6-qua-cause coproduces with all other *nidānas*-qua-cause of all other *nidānas*-qua-effect. But even this formula errs in assuming that a *nidāna* can be singled out from its *saṁskṛta* context.

An understanding of the conditioned nature of all reality is the ultimate insight to be attained in the world of the conditioned. According to Buddhist tradition a prospective Buddha attains this insight just before realization of full Buddhahood.

The Indian View of Causality

To understand properly this very important part of Indian philosophy the student must begin with the study of an early civilization in the subcontinent of Asia. The Indo-Aryans who lived in the valley of the Indus River in the second millennium B.C. had conflicting loyalties to two gods, Indra and Varuṇa. The former symbolized strength; the latter, order. Indra was a warrior whose fighting was motivated at least in part by the love of conflict. Indra, the god of storm and monsoon, threw his thunderbolts to release the waters of heaven and send them coursing down the river beds. He was a god of vigor and enthusiasm, a slayer of dragons, a drunkard, and a braggart. His devotees sang, "Indra is King over all that moves and moves not. . . over all living men he rules as Sovran."[91] Varuṇa was the god of cosmic order. He was the universal monarch whose all-seeing eyes—the sun and the moon—watched over the world. While Indra sent rivers overflowing their banks, Varuṇa kept rivers within their banks: "the rivers flow by the power of Varuṇa."[92] Efforts to combine the two gods into one, as in a prayer addressed to Indra-Varuṇa in *Ṛg Veda* 7. 83, appear to have been unsuccessful. The conflict between Indra and Varuṇa, the conflict between power and justice, was the same conflict that bothered Plato in *The Republic*. But Varuṇa eventually conquered the minds and hearts of the Indian people, as indicated by such diverse evidence as the elevation of priests and scholars to first place in the caste system, the doctrine of *ahiṁsā* (non-violence), the victory of Mahatma Gandhi's pacificism over Subhas Chandra Bose's militarism in the Congress party, and the moral posturing of Indian representatives in the assembly of the United Nations. A refrain in *Ṛg Veda* 8. 41—"Let all the others die away"—proved to be prophetic.

Varuṇa was probably first regarded as the god of the order of the cosmos, then as the god of the order of the sacrificial rites to deities, and finally as the god of social and moral order. Varuṇa carried a rope with which he bound oaths. He was a notary public in whose presence one made promises. He was the third party at all agreements. He was also a priest before whom one confessed sins and asked forgiveness; "May we be free from sin against that Varuṇa, who has compassion upon him who commits offence."[93] He was the divine protector and savior: "Keep us all our days in the right path, and prolong our lives."[94] Every hymn to Varuṇa in the *Ṛg Veda* contains a petition for the remission of sins, for example, "If, Varuṇa, we have ever committed an offence against a benefactor, a friend, a companion, a brother, a near neighbor, or Varuṇa, a dumb man, remove it from us."[95]

The early Indians, whose thoughts have been preserved in the hymns of the *Ṛg Veda,* referred to the order of the cosmos with an abstract term *Ṛta,* which is strikingly similar to the Greek term *Lógos*. *Ṛta* was a universal and eternal law underlying the orderliness of the universe. Day and night, winter and summer, seedtime and harvest, the rotation of the heavenly bodies, and the regularity of the monsoons were manifestations of *Ṛta*. "The dawn follows the path of *Ṛta* the right path; as if she knew them before. She never oversteps the regions. The sun follows the path of *Ṛta*."[96] *Ṛta* was described as "Varuṇa's eternal statute,"[97] but it is uncertain whether the concept of *Ṛta* or the concept of Varuṇa was developed first. *Ṛta* was the early Hindu conception of natural law. It embodied the notion of inner justice; night with its coolness was a compensation for day with its heat, the monsoon was a recompense for the drought that preceded, and harvesting was the reward for the labor of planting and cultivating. *Ṛta* was the nature of things. The *Ṛta* of water was to seek a lower level. The world was not a chaos of chance events, but events were predictable. The ancient Indians had discovered the causal principle.

The Sanskrit term for causality is *kāryakāraṇa-bhāva*. The root *kāra* means making, producing, fashioning. *Kārya* is that which is made. *Kāraṇa* is that which makes. *Bhāva* means a state of being. So *kāryakāraṇa-bhāva* designates a relationship of that which is made to that which makes it. The cause-effect relationship in the West is the effect-cause relationship in India. The difference may be due to the customary chronological orientation in the West and the ontological orientation in India. Causality or causation is "effectuality" or "resultness" in India. The word *kāraṇa* rarely appears in the *Upaniṣads*. One appearance is at the opening of the *Śvetāśvatara Upaniṣad*, the theistic *Upaniṣad*, and that refers to First Cause: "Those who discourse on Brahman say: What is the cause? [*kāraṇam*] (Is it) Brahman? . . . Time, inherent nature, necessity, chance, the elements, the womb or the person (should they) be considered the cause?"[98]

The builders of philosophical systems in India raised two questions about *kāryakāraṇa-bhāva*: (1) Are the *kārya* (effect) and the *kāraṇa* (cause) *sat* (real) or *asat* (unreal)? (2) Is the *kāraṇa* a mode of the *kārya;* or, in Western terminology, is the effect an emergent or an emanation? Is the effect to be described as a new substance or as new properties? The philosophers developed four theories (*vādas*) of the nature of causality: (1) *asatkāraṇavāda,* the unreal cause theory; (2) *satkāraṇavāda,* the real cause theory; (3) *asatkāryavāda,* the unreal effect theory; and (4) *satkāryavāda,* the real effect theory.[99]

Asatkāraṇavāda requires little explanation here, as it is the Buddhist theory of causality and has already been examined. The theory is not the preposterous claim that one can get something from nothing, but rather that one can get something from no *thing*. Buddhism as a process philosophy asserts that the cause is not a substance. There is no self-sufficient and self-sustaining reality that can be identified as a cause. Buddhism eschews static metaphysics. Everything is in flux (*sāmtāna*), or, as the Buddha is reported to have said, "Everything is on fire." A "thing" is a series of events. The circle of fire is the illusion created by a swiftly revolving torch. In a metaphysics of momentariness (*kṣanikavāda*) *cause* is the name given to all the *nidānas* acting in a *kārana* manner. Thus there is no *kārana* having *sat* nature.

The view of causality in Advaita Vedānta when considered from the aspect of Brahman is called *satkāraṇavāda* (the real cause theory), and when considered from the aspect of the temporal and spatial manifestations of Brahman it is called *vivartavāda* (the appearance theory). According to Advaita Vedānta there is but one Reality—the Absolute Totality, which is Nirguṇa Brahman. Human beings in their ignorance (*avidyā*) attribute to Brahman characteristics that are not truly the attributes of Brahman. These are known as superimpositions (*adhyāsas*). One of the most striking of these is cause. Therefore, it is common for humans to state that the physical world, individual selves, and divine beings are the effects of Brahman the First Cause. These, however, are but the *māyā* of Brahman, that is, the illusory appearances or manifestations of Totality. Hence to call Brahman the cause of the world is not correct, because there cannot be a cause save in a cause-effect relationship (or effect-cause relationship), and for the same reason the world cannot be called an effect. Causality itself is a superimposition of the human mind upon Brahman; but since the *kārana* is said to be Brahman, it cannot be denied reality. Hence, the theory is called *satkāraṇavāda*. In a sense the cause of the physical world is not Brahman but human beings who superimpose false attributes upon Brahman.

Asatkāryavāda is the theory of causality of the Nyāya-Vaiśeṣika philosophers. According to this theory the cause and the effect are two substances. The cause must cease in order for the effect to come into being. The effect is the counter-entity of the cause. The effect is a new reality; it does not subsist in the cause. According to these philosophers a cause has three necessary characteristics: (1) *pūrvaṛtti* (antecedence)—the cause must always precede the effect; (2) *niyatapūrvavṛtti* (invariability)—the cause and effect must be so related that qualitative and quantitative differences in the cause will be paralleled with the same differences in the effect; and (3) *ananyathāsiddha* (necessity)—the relation between cause and effect must be such that the latter unconditionally follows the former. Nothing is transferred from cause to effect. There is a power inherent in the atoms such that a new substance with new characteristics emerges. For example, the atoms of clay, stick, wheel, and water when brought into certain relations destroy a cause and produce a new being (*ārambha*)—a pot. Hence, this theory is sometimes called *ārambhavāda* (the theory of new creation).

The ontic separation of the cause and the effect was obviously a problem for the Nyāya-Vaiśeṣika philosophers. They introduced the category of *abhāva* (negation or nonexistence to overcome this problem). They distinguished four kinds of nonexistence: (1) the nonexistence of a thing as another thing, such as a clay pot is not a wooden spoon; (2) the nonexistence of a thing after its destruction; (3) nonexistence as impossibility, such as the child of a barren woman; and (4) the nonexistence of a thing before its production, so that the nonexistent clay pot has a reality as cause in the atoms of clay, stick, wheel, and water. In the making process the nonexistent clay pot ceases to be and the existing clay pot comes into being. But the philosophers may have created more problems for themselves. They forgot that it is one thing to obvert the statement of quality, like "this is not red" to "this is nonred," and quite a different matter to obvert an existential statement, such as "this does not exist" to "this does nonexist." They were forced to admit they had two kinds of existence: (1) existent existence of the effect and (2) the nonexistent existence of the cause! If in the causal process the cause is eliminated and the effect appears, one might wonder how it can be called a process. Causality under such a theory becomes legerdemain.

Satkāryavāda or *pariṇāmanvāda* (the modification or change theory) is the view of the Sāṁkhya philosophers. According to this theory cause is a potentiality that is modified in the process, and emerges as the effect. The entire world is an evolutionary development from *prakṛti* (matter, nature, or object). *Prakṛti*, the generative material source of all, is dynamic, self-efficient, and self-contained, but it is not self-sufficient, since it acts only when catalyzed by the presence of *puruṣa* (spirit or subject). The evolutes of *prakṛti* are real transformations. Yet nothing completely novel comes into being, since the evolutes as effect pre-exist in *prakṛti*. Evolution is a self-becoming from the determinate matrix of all that is and all that is to become. Within the evolved world things are continually emerging from material causes, and are continually merging back into their material causes. The clay that became a pot because of the pot-potentiality of the clay will in time return to clay with its pot-potentiality. Causality is the unfolding of the unmanifested within the cause. The Sāṁkhya philosophers' criticism of *asatkāryavāda* is that when the cause and the effect are two independent entities causality ceases to be a relation and becomes a magic show in which all things are possible. The effect must be of the same essence as the cause, and what is nonexistent in the cause cannot be produced. In the Ganganatha Jha translation of *Sāṁkhya Kārikā* the words *cause* and *effect* appear in quotation marks to remind the reader that they are names having no specific denotation. "Effect" is "cause" transformed from potentiality to actuality.

The concept of *Ṛta* (universal order) and the principle of *kāryakāraṇa-bhāva* (the condition of effect and cause) resulted in two very important features in the life of the Indians. These are *dharma* (the responsibilities inherent in one's station in life) and *karma* (the law of the deed). The former will be examined in the next chapter, but consideration of *karma* belongs in a discussion of causality. *Karma* is defined in Benjamin Walker's *Hindu World* as "the principle of universal causality resulting from action."[100] *Karma* can be regarded as the extension of *Ṛta* from the natural world to the moral world. It is the doctrine that necessary and sufficient causes account for events in the total life of each individual human being. The doctrine of *karma* and transmigration were generally accepted in India by the sixth century B.C. Max Weber, writing in the early part of the twentieth century, stated, "All Hindus accept two basic principles: the *saṁsāra* belief in the transmigration of souls and the related *karman* doctrine of compensation. These alone are the truly 'dogmatic' doctrines of all Hinduism, and in their very interrelatedness they represent the unique Hindu theodicy of the existing social, that is to say, caste system."[101] Nicol Macnicol said, "It is true on the whole of every Indian type of religion . . . that its most obvious and commanding feature is this *karma* aspect of life and destiny."[102] Louis Renou said the essentials of the Indian religion "could have been covered by the theory of *karma*."[103] Balbir Singh stated, "Hardly has any other conception commanded anything like the same unanimity among Hindu thinkers—nay, among all the Indians including the Jainas and the Bauddhas—as the law of *karma*, and there is probably nothing in respect of which the thinking of the Indians can be more sharply distinguished from that of the West than by the way in which it has been interpreted to account for that sphere of human activity which brings in its trail certain significant ethico-metaphysical implications."[104]

According to the doctrine of *karma* every act of a human being is both an effect and a cause.[105] An act or a situation is the result of forces set in operation by previous acts, and at the same time it may set in operation other forces that will come to fruition in other acts and situations. Some of the results of acts will appear in the present incarnation; others will appear in future incarnations. *Karma* requires the doctrine of reincarnation to make it intelligible, since gross observation indicates that not all of the causes initiated by an act come to fruition within the lifetime of the actor, and some of the results of acts cannot be traced to causes within the lifetime of the one experiencing the results.

Western people often have difficulty understanding *karma* because they interpret the law of the deed too simply, assuming it means that the soul upon death enters anothers body. *Karma* might better be understood as corollary of the doctrine of *Ātman*. The Upaniṣadic doctrine of *Ātman* is the essential ontological oneness of humanity. *Karma* is the essential chronological oneness of all human being. *Karma* and *saṁsāra* constitute a mythological expression of oneness of all forms of life in all time. Each life is affected by and affects every other form of life in a common *karma*. Each contributes to the fund of life, and each receives from that fund. The doctrine affirms the corporate unity of life and the corporate responsibility shared by all that lives. We are not monadic individuals, but mutually interacting parts of one living world. The world in which we now live has been formed and determined by lives before us, but we are a part of that forming. The world in which others will live after us is being shaped by us, but we are a part of that receiving. Each self is both cause and effect of the self that is now incarnate. Each self is nexus of past and future, and also nexus of the one and the many. In the words of Aurobindo, *karma* and reincarnation assure us "that not only the elements of our physical body, but those of our subtler vital being, our life-energy, our desire-energy, our powers, strivings, passions enter both during our life and after our death into the life-existence of others."[106]

Another Western misunderstanding of the doctrines of *karma* and *saṁsāra* arises from the view that the doctrines are concerned with the continuation of consciousness, that is, it is often considered as an alternative to the Christian belief in immortality. But *karma* and *saṁsāra* are mainly concerned with the conservation of values. They are an assurance that the good, the beautiful, and the true have value transcending the short span of a human life from birth to death. The doctrines may have grown out of a peculiar fear expressed in a few places in the *Upaniṣads*, namely, the fear of *punarmṛtyu* (the death of death), the fear that the postmortal life will end as totally as does the mortal life.[107]

Another Western misunderstanding that associates *karma* with fate seems too wide of the mark to be considered. Yet, strangely, this misunderstanding is found in the *Mahābhārata*, the great epic of India.[108] The concept of fate (*daiva*, literally "peculiar to the gods") appears to have been brought in to reconcile the conception of *karma* as impartial causality with *prasāda,* divine grace. In other words, *daiva* was an effort to preserve *Ṛta* and *karma* in times that stressed belief in a personal god. The effort ignores a fundamental element of *karma*—that one creates one's own fate, bears one's own burdens, and reaps only what one has sown.

Karma determines both that there will be another incarnation and what the nature of that incarnation will be. Sometimes *karma* is divided into "good *karma*" and "bad *karma,*" depending upon whether the next incarnation is above or beneath the dignity of the present incarnation. The incarnation need not be a human being. Some Hindus have speculated that the *jīva* can migrate into any form of animal or plant life, but such speculations are based largely on the imagination of the speculator. Most forms of Hinduism assume that only a human being has the opportunity to exhaust *karma* and liberate the *jīva* from reincarnation. Probably too much speculation has been built on the notion that reincarnation is a penalty for sin rather than an opportunity to grow into the full possibilities of life. Some ways of acting are more productive of karmatic results than are other ways; according to the *Bhagavad Gītā* the motive of the act determines the *karma*-producing nature of the act. Acts motivated by a pure sense of duty with no regard to the consequences are acts that exhaust *karma* without producing new *karma.*

Karma is divided into *āravdha karma* and *anāravdha karma.* The former is the result of an act that has begun to bear its fruits; the latter is the result of an act that has not yet borne its fruits. *Anāravdha karma* is further divided into *prāktana karma,* the results of action in previous births that have not yet borne fruit, and *kryamāna karma,* the results of action in this incarnation that have not yet borne fruit. The ramifications of the doctrine of *karma* are not confusing if one keeps in mind that *karma* is integral to the Indian convictions of the orderliness of the cosmos.[109]

3

The Self in the Natural World—Time

A twentieth-century American physicist and astronomer, J. T. Fraser, in reporting his feelings during World War II, wrote, "Watching the clash of cultures and the attendent release of primordial emotions stripped of their usual niceties, I could not help observing that man is only superficially a reasoning animal. Basically he is a desiring, suffering, death-conscious and hence, a time-conscious creature."[1] Fraser concluded that "time must and should occupy the center of man's intellectual and emotional interest."[2] It is impossible for anyone to take only a historical interest in time, since time concerns every person intimately and immediately. The human being is the only earthly being who has an awareness of time. Charles Lamb wrote to his sister: "Nothing puzzles me more than time and space, and yet nothing puzzles me less, for I never think about them."[3] But surely most people do think about time and space, and what they think is closely intertwined with the thought of their particular historical period. For example, the main concern of the ancient Greeks was the present. The Hebrews were interested in the past, and especially in the origin of things (*beresheth,* "in the beginning"). New Testament authors stressed the notion of the right time (*kairós,* "the fullness of time.") Christianity introduced eschatological concerns: the end of history and the world process, the anticipation of death, resurrection, final judgment, the life everlasting.

Western philosophers, physicists, and mathematicians agree that time is a very difficult topic for study. Thorleif Boman thinks time is "one of the most difficult and insoluble problems at the ultimate boundary of our thinking about the world."[4] Alfred North Whitehead, one of the greatest mathematicians and philosophers of the twentieth century, said that "it is impossible to meditate on time and the mystery of the creative passage of nature without an overwhelming emotion at the limitations of human intelligence."[5] A. Cornelius Benjamin, a philosopher of science, at the close of his article on "Ideas of Time in the History of Philosophy" wrote, "As we reach the end of this historical sketch of the attempts on the part of the philosopher to understand time, can we say that the problem has been solved? Certainly not. Much of the language employed, though suggestive, is too vague; unresolved paradoxes are still present; and many 'solutions' are achieved through the generous use of analogies and metaphors. Has the problem been clarified? Probably, to a certain degree."[6] A popular quotation from Augustine expresses well the dismay often felt about time: "What, then is time? If no one ask of me, I know; if I wish to explain to him who asks, I know not."[7] Frederick Copleston, historian of philosophy, warns that "the last word on space and time has scarcely been said even in the post-Einstein era."[8]

The problem of time cannot be dodged. According to C. J. Whitrow "a satisfactory theory of the structure of the universe" depends on the ideas of space and time.[9] Philosophers also regard the ideas of space and time as crucial; Samuel Alexander wrote, "It is not, I believe too much to say that all the vital problems of philosophy depend for their solution on the solution of the problem what Space and Time are and more particularly how they are related to each other."[10] J. T. Fraser looked askance at contemporary philosophical efforts to study time. Finding that "philosophical writings divide sharply between those that insist on imitating exact science and those that would prefer to ignore it," he concluded, "To root an integrated understanding of time in contemporary philosophy would guarantee it a schizophrenic childhood."[11] Regardless of the accuracy of Fraser's assessment of contemporary philosophy, one must mediate between time as a concept and time as an experience, and a holistic viewpoint is the philosophers' traditional forte.

Two Kinds of Time

C. D. Broad's article on time in the *Encyclophedia of Religion and Ethics* begins with an interesting warning: "Temporal characteristics are among the most fundamental in the objects of our experience, and therefore cannot be defined."[12] Broad's distinction between experience and definition is an important clue to the understanding of time. The word *time* is used to denote both what the physicists symbolize by *t* and what the psychologists mean when they talk about a person's temporal experience. The former is the objectively measurable duration of an event or the sequence of events. If the former is time as thought, the latter is time as lived. The two times have been given the following labels:

Time as Thought	*Time as Lived*
Objective time	Subjective time
Real time	Apparent time
Conceptual time	Perceptual time
Natural time	Human time

Outer time	Inner time
External time	Internal time
Plysical time	Psychological time
Cosmic time	Clinical time
Clock time	Felt time
Mechanical clock time	Biological clock time

This distinction is similar to the division between the sciences and the humanities to which C. P. Snow called attention in his *Two Cultures*. The division is adumbrated in sentences like "I know it was only an hour, but the time I spent in the dentist's chair seemed like five or six hours" and "The hour at the party slipped by before we knew it." Objective time is measured by the rotation of the earth on its axis, the revolution of the earth around the sun, the phases of the moon, the appearances of comets, heart beats, and clocks of every conceivable kind.

The difference between primitive and modern scientific conceptions of objective time may be indicated by noting that in some rural sections of India the basic time unit is the time required to boil rice, whereas in modern physics the second as the basic unit is defined as 9,192,631,770 cycles of the frequency associated with the transition between two energy levels of the isotope cesium 133.[13] Western people have not always measured objective time precisely. Galileo used his pulse-beat to discover the regularity of the swinging pendulum. In ancient Egyptian hieroglyphics a moment of time was indicated by a hippopotamus head thrust out of water, that is, the shortest period of time was that of the hippo taking a look around. Objective time is measured not only by clocks but also by the period between meals, bowel movements, menstruations, trips to the barber shop, dental examinations, automobile lubrications, changes of typewriter ribbons, replacement of furnace filters, repainting of houses, and so on. Subjective time is indicated by the television weather forecaster who says, "Temperatures will rise as the day wears on." Verbs like "drags," "crawls," "flies," "creeps," and "speeds" are used for the common experience of time moving slowly or swiftly. Shakespeare presents subjective time in *As You Like It*, act 3, scene 2:

Rosalind. Time travels in divers paces with divers persons. I'll tell you who Time ambles withal, who Time trots withal, who Time gallops withal, and who he stands still withal.

Orlando. I prithee, who doth he trot withal?

Rosalind. Marry, he trots hard with a young maid between the contract of her marriage and the day it is solemnised; if the interim be but a se'n-night, Time's pace is so hard that it seems the length of seven year.

Orlando. Who ambles Time withal?

Rosalind. With a priest that lacks Latin and a rich man that hath not the gout, for the one sleeps easily because he cannot study, and other lives merrily because he feels no pain; the one lacking the burden of lean and wasteful learning, the other knowing no burden of heavy tedious penury. These Time ambles withal.

Orlando. Who doth he gallop withal?

Rosalind. With a thief to the gallows; for though he go as softly as foot can fall, he thinks himself too soon there.

Orlando. Who stays it still withal?

Rosalind. With lawyers in the vacation; for they sleep between term and term, and then they perceive not how Time moves.

Every person appears to have a pacemaker that regulates the speed of metabolism, and thus the rhythm and precision of timekeeping. One evidence of this is the sense of "proper time" for learning. There is a proper time for learning to control one's temper, to adjust oneself to the needs and wishes of other people, to learn how to speak a language, to master algebraic skills. Another is the length of intervals to which people are sensitive. Some psychologists identify an "indifferent zone" within which individuals cannot distinguish lengths of sound. For example, many people cannot hear intervals of sound under eigth-tenths of a second in length. This seems to be culturally conditioned. Asiatic Indians who have learned to appreciate their classical music often comment that Western music seems full of holes. For example, whereas a Western vocalist moves directly from do to mi, the classical Indian vocalist sounds re in moving from do to mi. A hearer who perceives time in intervals a hundred times shorter than those perceived by either the Western person or the Indian would find the music of Bach or Mozart to be disjointed sounds. Time perception also varies in each person depending upon general health, psychological conditions, hunger, anxiety, fear, enjoyment. Henri Piéron was one of the first psychologists to discover that variations of bodily temperature alter the sense of time. He found that a person experiences an hour of clock time to be slower when he or she has a fever.[14]

There are five major varieties of subjective or psychological time: (1) present, (2) duration, (3) future, (4) past, and (5) simultaneity and succession. The present—the psychological unit of time—is usually three or four seconds in length. The unit of psychological time corresponds to the second of physical time. Duration is the psychological time to which one refers when speaking of time passing more quickly for one person than for another. Duration denotes some degree of permanence. Some psychologists estimate that duration refers to an event lasting at least ten seconds. This seems extremely arbitrary; for example, it would seem very strange to refer to a fifty-meter dash as taking place in less than a duration of time. Future time is the anticipation of events. This time varies with the age of the person. A seven-year-old's perception of the future is quite different from that of a seventy-year-old. The time base between Christmases for a seven-year-old is one-seventh of his life, but for a seventy-year-old it is one-seventieth. Sense of time also varies with the nature of the anticipated event; for example, a month seems much longer to a young couple awaiting the day of their marriage than it does to a homesick traveler or a criminal facing the day of his execution. Age affects subjective past time in a different manner. The seventy-year-old thinks of his experiences as a seven-year-old as "only yesterday," but the seven-year-old may refer to events of last year as "a long time ago." Simultaneity and succession as subjective time is the experience of events as occurring together or as occurring before and after each other. The experience obviously depends upon what is meant by "at the same time." This experience, like that of the past and the future, depends upon one's age and also upon such psycho-physical factors as endomorphy, ectomorphy, mesomorphy, fatigue, hunger, anxiety, worry, and general health.

Objective time is not the time we experience but the time we think about. It is the stream in which experienced changes take place. Perceptual time is necessarily finite; conceptual time may be infinite. Perceptual time is heterogeneous; conceptual time is homogeneous. There are two kinds of objective time: absolute and relative.

Absolute time may be further divided into absolute real time and absolute ideal time. The classical definition of absolute real time is Isaac Newton's: "Absolute, true and mathematical time, of itself, and from its own nature, flows equally without relation to anything external, and by another name is called duration. . . . For times and spaces are, as it were, the places as well of themselves as of all other things. All things are placed in time as to order of succession; and in space as to order of situation."[15] Newton referred to absolute time as "receptacle time," in that it contains an infinite number of instants. It is the container of all temporal events. An event does not define instants of time; rather, instants of time are the means of locating events. It exists quite independently of all clocks. Clocks measure or record time; they do not define the temporal matrix. Newton referred to absolute space as "God's sensorium."

Absolute ideal time is the ideal lengths of time with which all measurements are synchronized. The ideal unit of time is to time measurements as the ideal yardstick in the Bureau of Standards at Washington, D.C., is to all measurement of lengths in America. That absolute ideal until recently was judged to be the revolution of the earth around the sun; but the ideal measurement is now the second as indicated in the radioactivity of the element cesium.

Relative time is time dependent on events. Lucretius in *De Rerum Natura* affirmed relative time and denied absolute time: "Time also exists not by itself, but simply from the things which happen the sense apprehends what has been done in the past, as well as what is present and what is to follow after. And we must admit that no one feels time by itself abstracted from the motion and calm rest of things."[16] Newton, of course, felt what Lucretius said no one feels. Lucretius would have been on firmer ground had he stated that no one *denies* relative time. Newton defined relative time as follows: "Relative, apparent, and common time, in some sensible and external (whether accurate or unequable) measure of duration by the means of motion, which is commonly used instead of true time; such as an hour, a day, a month, a year."[17]

Two kinds of relative time can be differentiated. Relative time as duration is the time of an activity having a beginning and an ending. The time span is relative to its beginning and its ending. Relative time as succession is the physical location of events as before or after other events. Relative time as duration could subsist in a universe of only one event—providing the event has an ending that can be related to its beginning. Relative time as succession could subsist only in a world that has at least two events. Leibniz opposed Newton's absolute real time on the ground that time has no reality unless it possesses coexisting parts, that is, time is an order of successions. Time, he said, is the relations among events, and these relations are formed by events.

Western Theories of Time

The modern Western conception of time is shaped more by physics and mathematics than by philosophy. Yet study of the philosophical views helps us understand the conception.

In the ancient Greek world time was thought of as the right time (*kairós*). Hesiod's *Works and Days* was a farmer's almanac giving the best times for planting and reaping. From it we learn that the Greeks thought time moved in cycles. In addition to the yearly cycle of sowing, cultivating, and harvesting there was a cycle of the years: the golden age, the silver age, the bronze age, the heroic age, and the iron age. At the close of the iron age Zeus would destroy the race of men, and the ages would be repeated in another great cycle.

The cyclical theory of time is often thought to be nonprogressive. It has been described as the squirrel cage theory, a movement round and round in place. But a spiral (or cycle) can be either a two-dimensional winding, coiling, or circling around a center and gradually receding from it, as is the case of the spiral curve of a watch spring, or three-dimensional, helixal, as is the thread of a screw or a circular staircase. The helix view is cleary indicated in the Jain theory of time as ascending cycles (*avasarpiṇī*) and descending cycles (*utsarpiṇī*). The Christian philosopher Origen rejected cyclical time, although he recognized it as a position held by some. His own interpretation was that of repetitive and nonprogressive time:

> And now I do not understand by what proofs they can maintain their position, who assert that worlds sometimes come into existence which are not dissimilar to each other, but in all respects equal. For if there is said to be a world similar in all respects (to the present) then it will come to pass that Adam and Eve will do the same things they did before; there will be a second time the same deluge, and the same Moses will again lead a nation numbering nearly six hundred thousand out of Egypt; Judas will also a second time

> betray the Lord; Paul will a second time keep the garments of those who stone Stephen; and everything which has been done in this life will be said to be repeated,—a state of things which I think cannot be established by any reasoning.[18]

Augustine, finding the cyclical theory of time a wandering around in a circle, fixed the Western view of time as moving in a straight line. The image is often of an arrow shooting out into the unknown. According to the Greeks, time (*chrónos*) is the boundary within which we live our lives. One student of mythology has argued that the image of Chronos as an old man with scythe and hourglass is the result of an ancient confusion with Kronos, the Titan who mutilated his father Uranos.[19] Time in the Western world has been evaluated oxymoronically—it is that which destroys, and yet it is that which provides opportunity for improvement.

Plato's discussion of time appears in his cosmogonical myth, the *Timaeus*. The Creator sought to make his creation an exact copy of the perfect original.

> When the father and creator saw the creature which he had made moving and living, the created image of the eternal gods, he rejoiced, and in his joy determined to make the copy still more like the original; and as this was eternal, he sought to make the universe eternal, so far as might be. Now the nature of the ideal being was everlasting, but to bestow this attribute in its fullness upon a creature was impossible. Wherefore he resloved to have a moving image of eternity, and when he set in order the heaven, he made this image eternal but moving according to number, whilc eternity itself rests in unity; and this image we call time.[20]

Eternity is the everlasting now. Time is the everlasting movement from past to future. Eternity always is; time always becomes. Unfortunately, Plato spoiled his consideration of time by adding that time and the heaven were created at the same time: "Time, then, and the heaven came into being at the same instant."[21]

"Does time exist?" asked Aristotle. One part of time—the future—is not yet, and one part of time—the past—has been and is not. So existing time is made up of two nonexisting parts. "One would naturally suppose that what is made up of things which do not exist could have no share in reality."[22] To one who imagines time is made of atomic units known as moments or "nows" Aristotle pointed out that the "now" is a boundary of the past and the future, and as a boundary it has no dimensions of its own.

According to Aristotle time is not movement, nor is it independent of movement. Yet time is related to movement because time is perceived only when we have perceived "before" and "after" in movement. Time is that which is bounded by two "nows," one before and one after. "Hence time is not movement, but only movement in so far as it admits of enumeration. . . . Time then is a kind of number. . . . Time obviously is what is counted, not that with which we count."[23] Time implies "now," and "now" implies time. But the "now" does more than separate past and future—it also connects past and future into a continuous time. Therefore Aristotle defined time as "number of movement in respect of the before and after," and added that time is "continuous since it is an attribute of what is continuous."[24]

Aristotle asked if time is mind-dependent: "Whether if soul did not exist time would exist or not, is a question that may fairly be asked. . . . But if nothing but soul, or in soul reason, is qualified to count, there would not be time unless there were soul."[25] He offered no answer other than to note that if movement can exist without soul—as it can—and if time is an attribute of movement—as it is—then perhaps time can exist apart from the mind that counts the movements.

As for the cyclical nature of time, Aristotle argued that since time is measured by motion, and motion is measured by time, and since it is the regular circular motion of the heavenly bodies that is above all else the measure of time, therefore "even time itself is thought to be a circle."[26]

Augustine's discussion of time in *The Confessions,* book 11, chapters 10 through 31, is a charmingly frank and detailed record of his efforts to determine the nature of time. The account begins by his imagining a person asking, "What was God doing, before He made heaven and earth?"[27] Augustine says he will not reply as an unnamed person did by answering, "He was preparing hell for those who pry into mysteries."[28] He adds he would rather confess ignorance than ridicule one who asks probing questions. Augustine then asserts that before God made heaven and earth he made nothing. He admits the inquirer may wonder that "the God Almighty, and All-creating, and All-sustaining, the Architect of heaven and earth" would delay such an important work.[29] But, replies Augustine, if God is the creator of everything, then he is also the creator of all times—past, present, and future. So there could be no time before God created times, and since "In the beginning God created heaven and earth," there could be no time before the creation of the world. Augustine does not seem to be aware that he is saying that God created the world and time at the same time! This would imply a super-time by which to measure the simultaneity of the two creations. But, continues Augustine, there was no time before the work of Creation. Yet God was before the Creation. He as "an ever-present eternity" preceded past time and will continue to be beyond all future time. If God may be said to have years, his years are not as human years. Ours come and go; his do not. "All Thy years stand at once since they do stand; nor were they when departing excluded by coming years, because they pass not away; but all these of ours shall be when all shall cease to be. Thy years are one day, and Thy day is not daily, but to-day; because Thy to-day yields not with to-morrow, for neither doth it follow yesterday. Thy to-day is eternity. . . . Thou hast made all time; and before all times Thou art, nor in any time was there not time."[30]

At this point in his argument Augustine becomes more philosophical and less theological, confessing that although the nature of time baffles him, he is confident on one point. "Yet I say with confidence, that I know that if nothing passed away, there would not be past time; and if nothing were coming, there would not be future time; and if nothing were, there would not be present time."[31] Time is relative to events. It is not an absolute within which events may or may not take place, but a measure of events.

Augustine notes that we speak of a time that is long and a time that is short. But what is a long or short past time, a long or short future time, or a long or short present time? The past is not now, and the future is not yet. A "not now" and a "not yet" cannot be long or short. As for the present, how long or how short is it? The present *year*, the present *month*, the present *week*, the present *day*, the present *hour*, the present *minute*, and the present *second* can be measured. But what is the present *itself* that we indicate in the expression "time present"? According to Augustine, "If any portion of time be conceived which cannot now be divided into even the minutest particles of moments, this only is that which may be called present; which, however, flies so rapidly from future to past, that it cannot be extended by any delay. For if it be extended, it is divided into the past and future; but the present has no space."[32] The past has no length because it is not now, the future has no length because it is not yet, and the present has no length because present is only the division between past and future. It is the boundary that separates past and future.

"That I measure time, I know. But I measure not the future, for it is not yet; nor do I measure the present, because it is extended by no space; nor do I measure the past, because it no longer is."[33] Augustine then realizes *where* time is measured: "In thee, O my mind, I measure times. . . . the impression which things as they pass by make on Thee, and which, when they have passed by, remains, that I measure as time present, not those things which have passed by, that the impression should be made. This I measure when I measure times."[34] A "long future" time is "a long expectation of the future," and a "long past" is "a long memory of the past."[35] Augustine illustrates his discovery with an example of reciting a familiar psalm. When one stops in the middle of the recitation, the past is that which is now in memory, the future is expectation of what one will recite, and the present is the consideration through which the expectation can become memory.

Time, then, is an activity of created minds, and "there could be no time without a created being."[36] The mind of God is different. For him all things past and future—memory and expectation—are known as one knows a familiar psalm. God—"a mind, so greatly abounding in knowledge and foreknowledge"—is such that "whatever is so past, and whatever is to come of after ages, is no more concealed from Him than was it hidden from me when singing that psalm, what and how much of it had been sung from the beginning, what and how much remained unto the end."[37]

Augustine thinks of time as a passing reality that can be perceived and measured only in its passing. But again, how can one measure the passing of future time that is not yet, or of past time that is not. Augustine will not give up the notion that past time and future time do have a reality. But *where* can they be? He slips back into the theological mode and affirms there must be a future time, for God instructed the prophets about future events, and if future time is not, it certainly cannot be taught. One cannot teach a not! This leads Augustine to a fresh insight: rather than stating "There are three times, past, present, and future," one might more fittingly say "There are three times; a present of things past, a present of things present, and a present of things future."[38] This leads him to the recognition that time is not an external reality. It exists somehow in the soul. A still better formulation is to refer to "present of things past" as "memory," to "present of things present" as "sight," and to "memory of things future" as "expectation." Time, in his ratiocination, is no longer perceived as objective; it is subjective.

Before committing himself to a subjective measurement of time Augustine remembers that a learned man once observed that the motions of the sun, moon, and stars constitute time. This is not the view that motion measures time, but that "time" is a name for the movement itself. This cannot be, he thinks, because Joshua was able to persuade God to make the sun stand still so that he might have more time to complete a battle. The sun stood still, but time went on. "For, although a body be sometimes moved, sometimes stand still, we measure not its motion only, but also its standing still, by time; and we say, 'It stood still as much as it moved;' or, 'It stood still twice or thrice as long as it moved.' . . . Time, therefore, is not the motion of a body."[39]

The winsome honesty of Augustine as he tried to solve the problem of time must not tempt us to ignore the fact that Augustine slipped from the problem of the nature of time expressed in his question "What is time?" to a very different problem, namely, "How is time measured?" The measurement of time in the mind tells us little about the nature of time.

Another Western philosopher whose views on time must be mentioned is Kant. According to him time and space are necessary conditions of human sense perception. It makes no sense to say that an external thing is or is not temporal. Rather than stating that an object or event is in time, or that the object or event is placed in time, one must state that time is a structure of the mind such that unless the possible experience can take on a temporal aspect it cannot be experienced by human beings. Kant explains that

> time is not an empirical concept that has been dervied from any experience. For neither coexistence nor succession would ever come within human perception, if the representation of time were not presupposed as underlying things *a priori*. Only on the presupposition of time can we represent to ourselves a number of things as existing at one and the same time (simultaneously) or at different times (successively.) Time is a necessary representation that underlies all intuitions. We cannot, in respect of appearances in general, remove time itself, though we can quite well think time as void of

> appearances. Time is, therefore, given *a priori.* In it alone is actuality of appearances possible at all. Appearances may, one and all, vanish; but time (as the universal condition of their possibility) cannot itself be removed.[40]

One might ask therefore, "Is time real?" To this Kant replies,

> Certainly time is something real, namely, the real form of inner intuition. It has therefore subjective reality in respect of inner experience; that is, I really have the representation of time and of my determinations in it. Time is therefore to be regarded as real, not indeed as object but as the mode of representation of myself as object. . . . Thus empirical reality has to be allowed to time, as the condition of all our experiences; on our theory, it is only its absolute reality that has to be denied. It is nothing but the form of our inner intuition. If we take away from our inner intuition the peculiar condition of our sensibility, the concept of time likewise vanishes; it does not inhere in the objects, but merely in the subject which intuits them.[41]

The relations of time and space have often been examined by Western philosophers and physicists. Samuel Alexander in *Space, Time, and Deity* argued that the fundamental metaphysical category is space-time, the basic level of reality, which is composed of the relations of elements that he called "point-instants," that is, the limiting case of a motion. The ordering of space-time with reference to particular point-instances is known as a "perspective." From the perspective of a carpenter the rings of a tree are simultaneous; from the perspective of a botanist the tree rings represent different dates in the growth of the tree. Space-time, as we have already noted, contains a *nisus* or creative tendency—a deity—as does each level of reality, and, in the case of space-time, the deity is mind. Moreover, in the conjoining of space and time the time component is the catalyst for the dynamic creative process from which emerges the next level—the level of mind. Alexander put this in capsule form in a remarkable and puzzling statement: "Time is the mind of Space and Space the body of Time."[42]

Meanwhile, Albert Einstein, following an hypothesis of Eugene Minkowski, replaced the separate notions of space and time by a unified notion of space-time. The three spatial measurements and the one temporal measurement are inseparable coordinates of physical reality. This becomes especially obvious when one thinks of locating an event rather than an object. For instance, a reporter covering a midair collision of two airplanes would identify not only the three spatial locations of the event but also the temporal location—the fourth dimension. Another use of the space-time continuum is the unit of spatial measurement in astronomy—the light year, or the distance light travels in one year. The space-time unity is indicated also, according to Einstein, in that speeds approximating the speed of light shrink physical objects and slow time. One of his illustrations considers identical twin brothers, one of whom travels on a spaceship away from earth while the other remains on earth. Upon his return the traveling twin discovers that his brother has aged more than he, since the aging process of the earthbound brother will have continued relative to earth time, and that of the traveling brother will have continued relative to the speed of the spaceship. More sharply stated, Einstein claimed that passengers on a spaceship traveling at a speed one twenty-thousandth less than the speed of light will upon their return to earth discover that the one-year journey as measured by the clocks on board the spaceship was a one-hundred-year journey as measured by the clocks on the earth. Time is relative to motion in space, or in Alexander's terminology, time is a perspective.

Henri Bergson (1859–1941) found this argument for plurality of times absurd. He countered with a spatial analogy:

> I am an artist and I have to portray two subjects, John and James, the one standing next to me and the other, two or three hundred yards away. I draw the former life-size and shrink the latter to the size of a midget. A fellow artist standing next to James and also desirous of painting the two will proceed inversely; he will show John very small and James in normal size. We shall, moreover, both be right. But because we are both right, are we therefore justified in concluding that John and James have neither normal nor a midget's stature, or that they have both at once, or anything we like? Of course not. Shape and size are terms that have an exact meaning in connection with a posed model; it is what we perceive of the height and width of an individual when we are standing next to him, when we can touch him and measure his body with a ruler. Being next to John, measuring him if I like and intending to paint him in his normal height, I grant him his real size; and in portraying James as a midget, I am simply expressing the impossibility of my touching him—even, if we may be permitted to say so, the degree of this impossibility; the degree of impossibility is exactly what is called distance, and it is distance for which perspective makes allowance. In the same way, in the system in which I live and which I mentally immobilize by conceiving as a system of reference, I directly measure a time that is mine and my system's; it is this measurement which I inscribe in my mathematical representation of the universe for all that concerns my system. But in immobilizing my system, I have set the others moving, and I have set them moving variously. They have acquired different speeds. The greater their speed, the further removed they are from my immobility. It is this greater or lesser distance of their speed from my zero speed which I express in my mathematical representation of other systems when I assign them more or less slowed times, all, of course, slower than mine, just as it is the greater or lesser distance between James and me which I express by shrinking his figure more or less. The multiplicity of times which I thus obtain does not preclude the unity of real time; rather it presupposes it . . . [43]

True time or pure time, said Bergson, is "real duration" (*durée réelle*). Duration is immediately experienced as an active and ongoing flow. Scientists exteriorize this feeling of duration into a spatialized time made up of instants, and then confusedly identify this fixed world of the sciences as the real world of direct experience. Philosophers and scientists who think in mathematical and static fashions are guilty of confusing the measurement of time with the nature of time. Mathematical time cannot represent the real experience of time as duration. Time, said Bergson, belongs to the order of quality, and no analysis can resolve it into pure quantity.

The Indian View of Time

Dhan Gopal Mukerji wrote that "the Hindu does not believe in time."[44] By this strange statement he meant, among other things, that Hindus have not preserved historical records. Hindus believe earthly temporal existence should be transcended rather than enjoyed. Nirad C. Chaudhuri says in his autobiography, "At one time in my life there was nothing which came as a greater surprise to me, a student of history, than the disparagement of history by educated Indians of my class. In our schools and colleges history was supposed to be the last resort of the dullard endowed with a good rote-memory."[45]

Time (*kāla*) is described in ancient Hindu literature as a magician who works his witchcraft on man. Time both "burns all things"[46] and exercises a "generative power."[47] In the *Mahābhārata* time is treated as fate: "Whatever is done is done under the influence of *Kāla*. . . . *Kāla* is the cause of all and that for this reason we both, acting under the inspiration of *Kāla,* do our appointed work and therefore . . . we two do not deserve censure from thee in any way."[48]

The ancient Hindus distinguished the timebound and the timeless, placing the greater value on that which is beyond the changes of birth-death and creation-destruction. Values inhered in being rather than becoming, in permanence rather than change, and in eternity rather than in time. According to Hajime Nakamura,

> In the classical Indian languages, there are no words which corresponded to the concept "to become." The verb formed from the root *bhū* can be translated as both "to become" and "to exist." These two aspects of perceived reality, conceived as antithetical by the Western mind, are not even distinguished. "To become" is merely an aspect of "to exist." . . . To express the idea of change at all, Indians had to make shift with the words *anyathā bhavati* or *anyathābhāva*—"being otherwise." Becoming is expressed in terms of being, dynamic is seen as a phase of static.[49]

The Heraclitean observation "All things flow" had to be expressed derogatively as "All existences are impermanent" (*sarvam anityam*). The Brahman's *ānanda* (value) is rooted in the Brahman's *sat* (being), that is, in fixity, permanence, timelessness, imperishability.

This ancient disregard of time is sometimes found in modern India. For example, in modern Hindustani the word *kal* means both "yesterday" and "tomorrow," *parson* means both "the day after tomorrow" and "the day before yesterday," and *atarson* means both "three days ago" and "three days from now." The meaning depends on the context.[50]

The philosopher, looking for an Indian analysis of the concept of time, or the historian, seeking reliable records of historical events in India, may conclude that the Indians have little interest in the passing of the days. But this is not the case. One of the most ancient of Hindu prayers—the *Gāyatrī*—is a petition to the sun that the day may be propitious:

> That desirable glory of god Savitar may we receive.
> May he inspire our thoughts.[51]

Kālidāsa, a fifth century A.D. poet, wrote a lovely poem celebrating the importance of making good use of fleeting time:

> Look to this day!
> For it is life, the very breath of life.
> In its brief course lie all the varieties and realities of your existence:
> The bliss of growth;
> The glory of action;
> The splendor of beauty.
> For yesterday is already a dream, and tomorrow is only a vision.
> But today, well lived, makes every yesterday
> A dream of happiness, and every tomorrow a vision of hope.
> Look well, therefore, to this day!

The Indians divided the year by the appearance of the monsoon and by the northward path (*uttarāyaṇa*) and the southward path (*dakṣinayāna*) of the sun. The week was a five-day week. They borrowed the seven-day week from the Greek invaders of the fourth century B.C. They named the days after the Indian equivalent for the presiding planets according to the Greek-Roman system. Cosmic time in the Hindu tradition is measured in great cycles (*kalpas*) of 4.3 million human years, which is said to be twelve thousand divine years. Each *kalpa* is divided into four ages (*yugas*): *Kṛta, Treta, Dvāpara,* and *Kālī.* The universe, like the year, moves in two great periods: a period of activity, called a "Brahmā Day," which lasts for a thousand *kalpas,* and a period of rest, called a "Brahmā Night," which also lasts for a thousand *kalpas.*

The Chinese View of Time

The Chinese developed mechanical clocks six centuries before the appearance of the clock in the West. Yet the Chinese philosophers had little interest in the problem of time. According to Wing-tsit Chan, "Chinese philosophers, both ancient and modern, have been interested primarily in ethical, social, and political problems. Metaphysics developed only after Buddhism from India had presented a strong challenge to Confucianists. Even then, basic metaphysical problems, such as God, universals, space and time, matter and spirit, were either not discussed, except in Buddhism, or discussed only occasionally, and then always for the sake of ethics."[52]

One interesting aspect is that the practical-minded Chinese philosophers did not separate space and time. They used the two words jointly: *yü-chou* (space-time). This seems to have grown out of their interpretation of time as a duration that required movement in space. The early logicians of China were interested in the relativity of time. Their statement "The sun at noon is the sun declining" was an effort to remind themselves that noon depends upon one's point of view.[53]

Confucius and his followers disapproved of any philosophical speculations not directly related to the affairs of humans in society. Time (*shih*) entered their thinking only with respect to the proper time for the sage to act in social and political life. Likewise the Taoists thought of time only as the right time to act and the right time to refrain from action. Time was considered in the framework of duties and opportunities.

The Chinese, unlike the Indians, kept accurate historical records. Their records of early empires go back to the second millennium B.C., although only the dates after 841 B.C. are fully reliable. By the Han Dynasty (206 B.C.–A.D. 220) they had developed two ways to keep track of time in addition to recording the rise and fall of empires. One was known as the "ten stems." This was a designation for the ten days of the early ten-day week. Another was the "twelve earthly branches." This was a designation for the twelve months. The twelve also designated certain beasts, certain directions, and certain hours of the day:

Month	*Beast*	*Direction*	*Hours of the Day*
1. *tzu*	rat	N	11 P.M.–1 A.M.
2. *ch'ou*	ox	NNE	1–3 A.M.
3. *yin*	tiger	ENE	3–5 A.M.
4. *mao*	hare	E	5–7 A.M.
5. *ch'en*	dragon	ESE	7–9 A.M.
6. *ssu*	snake	SSE	9–11 A.M.
7. *wu*	horse	S	11 A.M.–1 P.M.
8. *wei*	sheep	SSW	1–3 P.M.
9. *shen*	monkey	WSW	3–5 P.M.
10. *yu*	cock	W	5–7 P.M.
11. *hsü*	dog	WNW	7–9 P.M.
12. *bai*	boar	NNW	9–11 P.M.

These two sets of signs for times—"ten stems" and "twelve earthly branches"—were combined to form a cycle of sixty terms to stand for a cycle of sixty days and for a second cycle of sixty years. The assigning of animals to each of the twelve periods contributed to the lore of lucky and unlucky times that has been an important part of Chinese culture. Rationalistic and realistic philosophers have not succeeded in diminishing the Chinese fascination for horoscopes, fortune telling, and magic.

The Buddhist View of Time

The Buddhist view of time correlates to the Japanese view of time, since it is in Japan that Buddhism developed this aspect of its nature. Unlike the Hindu, the Buddhist rejoices in the changing patterns of life, and, unlike the Indian, the Japanese emphasizes the sensible, the concrete, and the immediately apprehended. According to D. T. Suzuki,

> Behind Japanese intuitions we can say there is philosophy of time in opposition to philosophy of space. . . . The specific feature of the philosophy of time is that it turns inwardly and intuitionally apprehends the facts of consciousness, whereas the philosophy of space is always conscious of an external world and endeavours to interpret inner experiences in terms of space. This means that space-philosophy postulates something permanently existing outside the thinker himself who hungers for immortality. Even time in this system is translated into a form of space; it is comprehended as a kind of blank sheet spread from eternity to eternity, on which each instant moves, somewhat in the way individual objects fill space. Time here is conceived as a continuum composed of individual moments succeeding one after another apparently without interruption.[54]

Suzuki says space philosophy is like building a stone cathedral. Each stone is cut to right size, then the stones are put together according to a definite plan, making a grand and imposing unit that stands apart from its surroundings. Time philosophy is like building a straw-thatched tearoom in which the timber is used as it comes from the woods, often unplaned, cut just enough to fit different parts of the hut, and the whole structure harmonizes well with the woods in which it reposes. The Absolute is the phenomenal. The philosophy of Buddhism is the philosophy of intuition. It "takes time at its full value. It permits no ossification . . . of each moment. . . . Momentariness is therefore characteristic of this philosophy. Each moment is absolute, alive, and significant."[55] Suzuki adds, in reference to the *haiku* and the *sumiye*, "The Japanese mind trained in the time-philosophy of Buddhism is quick to catch each moment of nature and expresses its impression in a seventeen-syllable poem or in a few strokes of the brush."[56]

Dogen, the thirteenth-century founder of the Sōto-Zen sect of Buddhism, stressed the importance of making good use of time: "Time flies more swiftly than an arrow and life is more transient than dew. We cannot call back a single day that has passed." Therefore, added Dogen, "We ought to love and respect this life and this body, since it is through this life and this body that we have the opportunity to practice the Law and make known the power of the Buddha."[57]

Another feature of the Japanese Buddhist view of time is expressed in the phrase *sonouchi ni* (in the course of time). Whereas time in the West is that which terminates a class meeting, a basketball game, a life, or that which one tries to "beat,"[58] as in track meets, horse races, and downhill skiing, in Japan *sonouchi ni* means waiting for one's turn. This is the democratic idea that all individuals are almost equal, and hence they can take turns one after another. It is closely linked with the Japanese sense of harmony and balance. Social order rather than individual good is implicit in the performing of one's duties, in the proper cycles of national holidays, in the seasons of nature, and in the development of human lives.

4

The Self in the Social World

In this chapter three questions about the life of the human being in the social world will be considered: (1) Is sociality a natural or an acquired characteristic? (2) What is the democratic quest? (3) What are the possibilities of going beyond the national state?

The Human Being as a Social Animal

No one disputes the Aristotelian claim that the human is social, although there are hermits, recluses, and anchorites who choose to live outside society. The people in T. S. Eliot's "The Cocktail Party" are loners. Edward says,

> There was a door
> And I could not open it. I could not touch the handle.
> What is hell? Hell is oneself,
> Hell is alone, the other figures in it
> Merely projections. There is nothing to escape from
> And nothing to escape to. One is always alone.

And Celea confesses later,

> No . . . it isn't that I want to be alone,
> But that everyone's alone—or so it seems to me.
> They make noises, and think they are talking to each other;
> They make faces, and think they understand each other.
> And I'm sure that they don't.

In ancient Athens living outside the city-state was a legal substitute for state execution. Socrates preferred to drink hemlock rather than ostracize himself from the Athenian community. One who chose to live alone in Greek society was said to be *ídios*. From *ídios* is derived the word *idiot*. But is man social by nature or by nurture? Does he form social groups because he wants to or because he has to? Is the state an expression of mutual love or mutual distrust?

Plato on the Origin of the State

Plato in *The Republic* describes a long conversation between Socrates and Plato's two brothers, Glaucon and Adeimantus, about justice. When they run into difficulties trying to locate justice in the individual, Socrates suggests they might have more success in defining justice in the community: "We think of justice as a quality that may exist in whole community as well as in an individual, and the community is the bigger of the two. Possibly, then, we may find justice there in larger proportions, easier to make out."[1] Adeimantus agrees. Socrates suggests they consider the origin of the state: "My notion is . . . that a state comes into existence because no individual is self-sufficing: we all have many needs."[2] Socrates imagines human beings living in isolation—or perhaps in small families—and unable to feed, clothe, and house themselves. The individuals appeal to others to help them satisfy their needs. "So, having all these needs, we call in one another's help to satisfy our various requirements; and when we have collected a number of helpers and associates to live together in one place, we call that settlement a state."[3] A state consists of men living "in one place" in which each "man gives another what he has to give in exchange for what he can get."[4] The minimum population must include a farmer to provide food, a weaver to provide clothing, and a builder to provide housing. Upon second thought Socrates decides to add a shoemaker, and perhaps one or two more craftsmen to provide for personal wants. Upon further reflection the three agree that if the farmer is to be a good farmer he will need a plough, and if he trains himself to be a good blacksmith, he will not likely be also a good farmer. So the state will need smiths, carpenters, artisans, shopkeepers, merchants, shipowners, hunters, fishermen, and so on. The appetites of the people increase. The state that originated to provide the base necessities becomes the luxurious state with rich food, wine, perfumes, unguents, paintings, sculpture, adornments, dancers, and courtesans. Finally, there will be a need for guardians of the states. The problem of justice becomes that of each doing that which his station in the state requires for the good of the state.

The state according to Plato originates to satisfy simple human needs that the individual is unable, or able only with difficulty, to supply. Plato does not claim that humans form the state because they are by nature social. Humans need food to nourish the body, clothing to warm the body, and housing to avoid the harshness of the elements. Presumably, if individuals could supply their own needs, they would not form the state.

Aristotle on the Origin of the State

The state for Plato is an artifact—a mutual help association—created to satisfy needs that cannot be satisfied by individuals. Not so for Aristotle. For him "the state is a creation of nature."[5] But the evidence for Aristotle's claim that the state is a natural production is the same as that offered by Plato for his claim that the state is an artificial production, namely, "the individual, when isolated, is not self-sufficing."[6] Moreover, Aristotle referred to the establishment of the family as an effort to supply humans' "everyday wants,"[7] "daily needs,"[8] and "bare needs."[9] Apparently Aristotle was not satisfied with Plato's utilitarian theory of the origin of the state. He wanted to locate the origin of communities in the structure of the natural world rather than in human desires for food, clothing, and shelter; but when he discussed the establishment of *a* family, *a* village, or *a* state, he was as utilitarian as Plato.

Plato imagined a primordial condition in which human beings lived isolated from each other, but Aristotle said that "the state is by nature clearly prior to the family and to the individual."[10] The priority he had in mind is not temporal priority but ontological priority. He argued that "the whole is of necessity prior to the part; for example, if the whole body be destroyed, there will be no foot or hand, except in an equivocal sense, as we might speak of a stone hand."[11] The analogy must be carefully applied. If a human being is killed, the hand, which was a part of the whole, is a hand only in the sense that it may for a time look like a hand, but it cannot function as a hand. If the state is destroyed, individual human beings, which were parts of the whole, become "individual human beings," appearing as if they were indeed individual human beings, but they are not, because they can no longer function as individual human beings. "Man is by nature a political animal."[12] According to Aristotle "the nature of a thing is its end,"[13] the "nature" of a thing is "what each thing is when fully developed,"[14] and "to be self-sufficing is the end,"[15] so the nature/end/function of man is to become fully developed in the sense that he become self-sufficing. He does this by forming "a union of those who cannot exist without each other."[16] According to Aristotle "in common with other animals and plants, mankind have a natural desire to leave behind them an image of themselves,"[17] and therefore a male human being and a female human being establish a family in which the male is the "natural ruler"[18] and the female is the "subject."[19] Surely Aristotle knew that no plants, and perhaps only a few nonhuman animals, establish a "family," and also that satisfaction of the human natural desire to leave behind an image does not require the establishment of a family. The "union" necessary for procreation is a sexual union, not a familial union. "A social instinct is implanted in all men by nature"[20]—the instinct or natural desire to leave an image of oneself—and "the first thing to arise [from this instinct] is the family" as "the association established by nature for the supply of men's everyday wants."[21] The family is said to be the first "association"[22] and the village the first "society."[23] "But when several families are united, and the association aims at something more than the supply of daily needs, the first society to be formed is the village."[24] The third step in this presumably chronological evolution is the state, which is described not as an "association" nor as a "society," but as a "complete community": "When several villages are united in a single complete community, large enough to become nearly or quite self-sufficing, the state comes into existence."[25] Although the state originates in an effort to satisfy "the bare needs of life,"[26] the state continues to exist "for the sake of the good life."[27] "Political society" he said elsewhere, "exists for the sake of noble actions, and not of mere companionship."[28] The life of virtue is the ultimate reason for a state, and this is why the state is found among human animals rather than among brute animals who have no share in happiness or in a life of free choice.[29] Therefore,

> It is clear then that a state is not a mere society, having a common place, established for the prevention of mutual crime and for the sake of exchange. These are conditions without which a state cannot exist; but all of them together do not constitute a state, which is a community of families and aggregations of families in well-being, for the sake of a perfect and self-sufficing life. . . . Our conclusion, then, is that political society exists for the sake of noble actions, and not of mere companionship.[30]

According to Aristotle the evidence for postulating a social instinct in human beings is not only their desire to have offspring, but also their ability to speak: "man is more of a political animal than bees or any other gregarious animals," since "man is the only animal whom she [Nature] has endowed with the gift of speech."[31] It is speech that makes possible a sense of goodness and evil, and of justice and injustice—values that have meaning only in the context of families, villages, and states.

Any man or woman who cannot live in human society is not to be accounted human. Such a being is "a beast." Anyone who is self-sufficient is also not human, but "a god."[32] This strange observation is open to two interpretations. One, taking the words *beast* and *god* substantively, denies that any human being can be human outside the social condition; the other, taking the words adjectively, allows for bestial beings who cannot accommodate themselves to the opportunities and responsibilities of living in human society and for divine beings who do not need other human beings for their own self-realization and perfection. The second interpretation seems to be the correct one.

> If, however, there be some one person, or more than one, although not enough to make up the full complement of a state, whose virtue is so pre-eminent that the virtues or the political capacity of all the rest admit of no comparison with his or theirs, he or they can be no longer regarded as part of a state; for justice will not be done to the superior, if he is reckoned only as the

> equal of those who are so far inferior to him in virtue and in political capacity. Such an one may truly be deemed a God among men. Hence we see that legislation is necessarily concerned only with those who are equal in birth and in capacity; and that for men of pre-eminent virtue there is no law—they are themselves a law.[33]

Elsewhere Aristotle praised the great-souled (*megalópsychos*), magnanimous, or properly proud man, the man "concerned with honour on the grand scale."[34] He is the man "unable to make his life revolve round another."[35] He confers benefits, but is ashamed to receive them.[36] He asks nothing from others and withholds nothing from others.[37] This justifiably proud man is no doubt the one whom Aristotle mentioned in *The Politics* as the perfected man.[38] If this interpretation is correct, then the highest good is not to be found within society as stated at the opening of *The Politics*—"All communities aim at some good, the state or political community, which is the highest of all, and which embraces all the rest, aims at good in a greater degree than any other, and at the highest good"[39]—but in the character of the person who transcends social instinct.

Medieval Christianity and the State

The conflict latent in Plato's stress on social contract and Aristotle's stress on social instinct was not noticed in the West for many centuries. Christianity introduced elements of religious revolt but little of political revolt. St. Paul advised obedience to recognized authorities: children should obey their parents,[40] servants should obey their masters,[41] and Christians should pray for kings and those in authority.[42] Augustine in *The City of God* stated that each person is a citizen of two "cities." One is the earthly city, the city of souls sharing a common lost condition due to the sin of Adam; the other is the heavenly city, the community of those redeemed through the work of Jesus the Christ. The sociality of the former is that of man's common sinful nature; the sociality of the latter is that of a common faith. Augustine argued that slavery, political persecutions, and other social evils are indeed evils, but they should be patiently endured as part of the punishment for the sins of man. Augustine wrote *The City of God* at the time when northern tribes were first pushing into the Roman Empire, yet he neither rejoiced nor lamented the impending fall, since his concern was salvation of the souls of men.

The contractual interpretation of the state was stressed in the West as Europe moved from a feudal society to a monarchial society. As kings acquired power formerly held by the church, they attempted to establish that they, like the pope, ruled by divine right. Alighieri Dante (1265–1321) in *De Monarchia,* taking his clue perhaps from Augustine's two cities, asked two questions: (1) Is it necessary for the well-being of the world that there be a single temporal monarch to parallel the pope as spiritual monarch? (2) Does the temporal monarch derive his authority from God?

In answering the first question Dante appealed to Aristotle's *Politics:*

> There the acknowledged authority states that when several things are directed towards a single end it is necessary for one of them to act as director or ruler and for the others to be directed or ruled. This statement is supported not only by the glorious renown of its author but also by inductive reason. Again, if we consider an individual man we see the same principle verified: since all his faculties are directed towards happiness, his intellectual faculty is the director and ruler of all the others—otherwise he cannot attain happiness. If we consider a home, the purpose of which is to train its members to live well, we see that there has to be one member who directs and rules, either the "pater familias" or the person occupying his position, for as the Philosopher says, "every home is ruled by the eldest." . . . Similarly if we examine a city, whose purpose is to be sufficient unto itself in everything needed for the good life, we see that there must be one governing authority—and this applies not only to just but even to degenerate forms of government. If this were not so, the purpose of civil life would be frustrated and the city, as such, would cease to exist. Lastly, every kingdom (and the end of a kingdom is the same as that of a city but with a stronger bond of peace) needs to have a king to rule over and govern it; otherwise its inhabitants will not only fail to achieve their end as citizens but the kingdom itself will crumble as is affirmed by the infallible Word: "Every kingdom divided against itself shall be laid waste."[43]

In answer to the second question Dante contended that God has contracted with the pope to ensure that human beings will find the happiness of eternal life and with the king that they may enjoy peace and happiness in the earthly life:

> Unerring Providence has therefore set man to attain two goals: the first is happiness in this life, which consists in the exercise of his own powers and is typified by the earthly paradise; the second is the happiness of eternal life, which consists in the enjoyment of the divine countenance (which man cannot attain to of his own power but only by the aid of divine illumination) and is typified by the heavenly paradise. . . . This explains why two guides have been appointed for man to lead him to his twofold goal: there is the Supreme Pontiff who is to lead mankind to eternal life in accordance with revelation; and there is the Emperor who, in accordance with philosophical teaching, is to lead mankind to temporal happiness. . . . Thus it is obvious that the temporal Monarch receives his authority directly, and without intermediary, from the Source of all authority.[44]

The doctrine of the divine right of kings reached its climax in 1680 in Robert Filmer's *Patriarcha: A Defence of the Natural Power of Kings against the Unnatural Liberty of the People.* Filmer frankly admitted in the preface that the purpose of the book was "to establish the throne of our great restorer, our present King William—to make good his title in the consent of the people, which, being our only one of all lawful governments, he has more fully and clearly than any prince in Christendom; and to justify to the world the people of England whose love of their just and natural rights, with their resolution to preserve them, saved the nation when it was on the very brink of slavery and ruin." Filmer's argument is that God gave to Adam and "the rest of the patriarchs" authority, power, and dominion over their children and offspring to rule and govern them. The charge was renewed to Noah after the Flood. Adam, Noah, et al. were, according to Filmer, not only the fathers of families but also the first kings. The king is father of his country and his subjects. God has willed that the father has will over his children, and hence the king as father has will over his subjects. A child must not disobey his parents, a servant must not turn on his master, and a subject must not rebel against the king.

Filmer's patriarchalism was a slavish and literal interpretation of Christian scripture, especially the book of Genesis. He made two assumptions: (1) the source of the monarch's power is rooted in God's covenant with Adam and Noah, and (2) an original contract must never be changed.

In Locke's *The First Treatise of Government* is a scathing attack on Filmer. For example, Locke asked whether the will of the father over his children, and hence the will of the king over subjects, includes exposing, selling, and eating of offspring—atrocities that had been practiced in some parts of the world.[45]

Hobbes and the State

The contract theory of the state was given a secular interpretation by Thomas Hobbes (1588–1679). According to him the natural condition of human beings is intolerable misery:

> Nature has made men so equal in the faculties of the body and mind as that, though there be found one man sometimes manifestly stronger in body or of quicker mind than another, yet, when all is reckoned together, the difference between man and man is not so considerable as that one man can thereupon claim to himself any benefit to which another may not pretend as well as he. For as to the strength of body, the weakest has strength enough to kill the strongest, either by secret machination or by confederacy with others that are in the same danger as himself.[46]

The human being is instinctly antisocial. Each seeks gain, safety, and reputation in competition with the similar quests of others. The result is that in the natural condition there is war—either actual fighting or the disposition thereto. Everyone is enemy to every other person. The only security possible is that which each can attain through his own strength and/or invention. Thus the human life is "solitary, poor, nasty, brutish, and short."[47]

Since the natural condition of the human being includes war, every one has the right to everything, including the other's body. "And therefore, as long as this natural right of every man to everything endures, there can be no security to any man, how strong or wise soever he be, of living out the time which nature ordinarily allows men to live."[48] In the interest of everyone a commonwealth is created with a sovereign power, which Hobbes called "The Leviatian" or "The Mortal God." The commonwealth possesses the rights and powers formerly held by individuals. According to Hobbes the people make the following contract among themselves and with the sovereign: "I authorize and give up my right of governing myself to this man, or to this assembly of men, on this condition, that you give up your right to him and authorize all his actions in like manner."[49] Thus do human beings, lacking social instincts, contract with other human beings in order to achieve security and peace.

Locke and the State

John Locke's *The Second Treatise of Government*—the two appeared anonymously in 1690 with the title *Two Treatises of Civil Government*—refutes Hobbes. Locke sought to deny "that men live together by no other rules but that of beasts, where the strongest carries it, and so lay a foundation for perpetual disorder and mischief, tumult, sedition, and rebellion."[50] Locke did not ridicule Hobbes, as he, unlike Filmer, was a worthy opponent.

According to Locke the natural human state is dual—a state of "perfect freedom"[51] and a state of "perfect equality."[52] Locke realized at once that he had overstated the natural condition, since neither freedom nor equality can be "perfect," that is, complete or absolute. He added that although the state of nature is "a state of liberty, yet it is not a state of license."[53] The dual condition is limiting. The limitation is called "the law of nature." "The state of nature has a law of nature to govern it, which obliges every one; and reason, which is that law, teaches all mankind who will but consult it that, being all equal and independent, no one ought to harm another in his life, health, liberty, or possessions."[54] The law of nature is a prescriptive law built into human rationality. Each knows that he or she "may not, unless it be to do justice to an offender, take away or impair the life, or what tends to the preservation of the life, the liberty, health, limb, or goods of another."[55] This prescriptive law that one ought not to injure another is the social instinct of which Aristotle wrote. The natural state is prepolitical, but not presocial, as Hobbes thought. The human being is by nature a decent person, and not the selfish, greedy, aggressive being Hobbes thought him to be. It is interesting to note that when Locke described the "state of perfect equality" he referred not to equal abilities but to equal rights: "And if anyone in the state of nature may punish another for any evil he has done, everyone may do so; for in that state of perfect equality, where naturally there is no superiority or jurisdiction of one over another, what any may do in prosecution of that law, everyone must needs have a right to do."[56] However, the right to punish is "no absolute or arbitrary power to use a criminal, when he has got him in his hands, according to the passionate heats or boundless extravagance of his own will; but only to retribute to him, so far as calm reason and conscience dictate, what is proportionate to his transgression."[57]

"Every man has a right to punish the offender and be executioner of the law of nature," declared Locke.[58] Every person in the state of nature has the right to preserve all persons with any means that are reasonable. In some cases this might mean killing a murderer as both a form of restraint and of reparation. Locke seemed unaware that within one paragraph he had shifted from the "right" of one to punish another to the "power" of one to punish another. He admitted one might question if it is right to punish by death. He replied, "Each transgression may be punished to that degree and with so much severity as will suffice to make it an ill bargain to the offender, give him cause to repent, and terrify others from doing the like."[59] The doctrine that "in the state of nature every one has the executive power of the law of nature" is, Locke admitted, a "strange doctrine."[60] He had stumbled upon "inconveniences of the state of nature," and he admitted that "civil government is the proper remedy for the inconveniences of the state of nature, which must certainly be great where men may be judges in their own case."[61]

Therefore human beings in the natural state, despite being "free, equal, and independent,"[62] by unanimous consent make a community "with a power to act as one body, which is only by the will and determination of the majority."[63] The act of the majority passes for the act of the whole. "And thus every man, by consenting with others to make one body politic under one government, puts himself under an obligation to every one of that society to submit to the determination of the majority and to be concluded by it; or else this original compact, whereby he with others incorporates into one society, would signify nothing, and be no compact, if he be left free and under no other ties than he was before in the state of nature."[64]

One might ask, Locke admitted, why anyone in the state of nature—"absolute lord of his own person and possessions, equal to the greatest, and subject to nobody"[65]—would part with freedom and be subject to control of a government. Locke finally confessed he used the words "right" and "power" loosely. Though everyone has the right of freedom in the state of nature, "the enjoyment of it is very uncertain and constantly exposed to the invasion of others."[66] Specifically, three things lacking in the state of nature are supplied by a political society: (1) an "established, settled, known law," (2) a "known and indifferent judge," and (3) a "power to back and support the sentence when right, and to give it due execution."[67]

> Thus mankind, notwithstanding all the privileges of the state of nature, being but in an ill condition while they remain in it, are quickly driven into society.

> Hence it comes to pass that we seldom find any number of men live any time together in this state. The inconveniences that they are therein exposed to by the irregular and uncertain exercise of the power every man has of punishing the transgressions of others make them take sanctuary under the established laws of government and therein seek the preservation of their property. It is this makes them so willingly give up every one his single power of punishing, to be exercised by such alone as shall be appointed to it amongst them; and by such rules as the community, or those authorized by them to that purpose, shall agree on. And in this we have the original right of both the legislative and executive power, as well as of the governments and societies themselves.[68]

Locke's philosophical importance is that he brought into one system the Platonic doctrine of social contract and the Aristotelian insight of social instinct. His historical importance is that his ideas shaped the American Revolution, the American Declaration of Independence, and the American Constitution.

Scheler and the State

One other Western social philosopher should be mentioned, Max Scheler (1874–1928). Thomas Hobbes presented social contract without social instinct; Scheler presented social instinct without social contract. He characterized doctrines that attempt to base the nature and existence of human community on human contracts as "perverted."[69] He explained community in three propositions. The first is that the human being is inherently social: "The being of a man is just as originally a matter of being, living and acting 'together' as a matter of existing for himself."[70] All human beings for whom we have any historical documents lived in communities, and all we have ever experienced live in communities. "Where there is an 'I' there is a 'we,' or 'I' belong to 'we.'"[71] The second is what Scheler called the "sociological proof" of God: "the idea of communion of love and spirit with an infinite spiritual person who at the same time is the origin, founder and sovereign Lord of all possible spiritual communities as of all actual communities on earth."[72] The third is that "each individual is not responsible solely for his own character and conduct . . . but each individual (likewise every comparatively restricted community) is also responsible to God . . . for everything of moral bearing in the character and proceedings of the larger corporate selves of which he is an integral part."[73] Every individual is "co-responsible for the collective guilt and collective merit which accrue to his community as a unit and integer, not as an 'aggregate' of the individuals called its 'members.'"[74]

Hindu Views

There is no argument for human sociality nor is there any discussion of a social contract in Indian philosophical writings, but the assumption throughout is that the human being is a social being.

One evidence for sociality in the ancient tradition is the view first found in the *Ṛg Veda,* advanced in the *Upaniṣads,* and thoroughly analyzed by the Advaita Vedāntins that the real self is the *Ātman* or Universal Self rather than the *jīva* or particular self. The more one stresses one's commonality with others the more one realizes one's true nature. The *Ṛg Veda* presents the dual nature of human beings in a poetic metaphor: "Two birds associated together, and mutual friends, take refuge in the same tree: one of them eats the sweet fig; the other, abstaining from food, merely looks on."[75] The tree here is the human body and the birds are the two selves. The relationship suggests that the soul rests temporarily in the body. The bird that eats the figs is the self that participates fully in the physical life. It is involved in eating, drinking, sleeping, enjoying, suffering, and dying. It enjoys all the fruits of the bodily life, and identifies itself with the body. This is the *jīva.* The self that observes the activities of the individualizing self does not censure the *jīva* for attaching itself to the body, but it sees through the blind enjoyments and needless sufferings experienced by the bodily self. This self knows that the body and the body's self is *māyā,* and it knows that the *Ātman* is *Sat* because this self is *Ātman.* The word *social* does not do justice to the oneness of the *Ātman* nature of humanity, but any word that suggests manyness does grave injustice to the *Ātman* concept.

Other evidence for sociality is found in the four goals of Hindu *sādhanā: artha* (the material principle), *kāma* (the pleasure principle), *dharma* (the moral principle), and *mokṣa* (the religious principle). *Dharma,* which is translated as "duty" or "obligation," is the principle of social restraint brought to bear especially upon *artha* and *kāma.* Hinduism contends that we live in a world in which the satisfaction of our own needs and wants must take into consideration the needs and wants of other persons. The human life is divided into four periods (*āśramas*) with special *dharmas* for each period: *Brahmacarya, Gṛhastha, Vānaprastha,* and *Sannyāsa.* The first is the life of the student with duties of obedience to parents and tutors. The second is the life of the householder with duties to spouse and children. The third is the life of service to one's community. And the fourth is the retirement period in which one should express appreciation of the great scholars and saints by growing in the realms of mind and spirit. These duties and responsibilities have been elaborately spelled out in the *Dharma Śāstras,* the Law Scriptures of Hinduism.

A third evidence of sociality in Hindu India is the principle of nonviolence (*ahiṁsā*). The metaphysical insight upon which the morality of *ahiṁsā* is built is that of the unity of all living beings. Ananda K. Coomaraswamy has written, "The heart and essence of the Indian experience is to be found in a constant intuition of the unity of life, and the instinctive and ineradicable conviction that the recognition of this unity is the highest good and the uttermost freedom."[76] This compassionate concern for the well-being of others takes a wide variety of forms. Sometimes it is defined negatively, as in not harming another, not interfering with another, not killing another. Others have interpreted it positively, as in actively assisting others. Adherents range from the many different types of vegetarians—from those who will not eat beef to those who will not eat any food associated with animal life including milk, butter, cheese, and honey—to the many different types of pacificists—from those who will not serve in a war to those who will not kill insects. However *ahiṁsā* is implemented, it is based on the conviction that all living creatures are part of the great community of life.

A fourth evidence is implicit in the doctrine of *saṁsāra,* namely, all living forms are so related that the *jīva* can migrate into any animal or plant.

A fifth evidence is the very complicated form of social organization known as caste (*varṇa*). The evaluations of caste are as divergent as are its forms. S. Radhakrishnan and Charles A. Moore state, if not with approval at least without disapproval, of the orthodox systems of Indian philosophy, "In different degrees they adhere to the rules of caste,"[77] but Prime Minister Indira Gandhi in her 1982 Independence Day message celebrating the thirty-fifth anniversary of Indian independence said, "We have to fight against various impediments in the paths of progress. This fight is not against any individual or group, but against the forces of communalism, casteism and regionalism." Mrs. Gandhi's view of caste was that it divides the nation. Other Indians see caste in conflict with the democratic stress on human equality: "The challenge to Hindu society, which has now come to the final stages of a decisive issue, arises from the conflict between the equality conception of democracy and the inequality conception of caste."[78] But another view is that it provides recognizable places for everyone in a community with clearly marked privileges and responsibilities.

Ṛg Veda 10:90 describes a Cosmic Man, which may stand prototypically for the body politic in which Brahmins come from the mouth, Kṣatriyas from the arms, Vaiśyas from the thighs, and Śūdras from the feet. This chapter is probably a late addition to the *Ṛg Veda,* but the division of the community into scholars and priests, rulers and warriors, merchants and traders, and manual laborers was probably an ancient division. The clear implication is that each part is essential for the whole.

The term *caste* has become fixed for the fourfold classification of Hindus, although it is a misleading word. It comes from the Portuguese word *casta* (unmixed race). A Hindu caste is not a pure race. Caste is but one of several ways of classifying Hindus. Others are *jāti* (craft or vocation), *gotra* (an ancestral line going back theoretically to Vedic seers), and *kuṭumba* or *kula* (a joint or extended family based on blood and marriage). The Sanskrit word that has been mistranslated as "caste" is *varṇa. Varṇa* means color, but it does not refer to the color of skin or hair. Rather certain colors came to be associated with certain virtues: white (wisdom), red (courage), yellow (wealth), black (physical strength). These virtues were sought seriatim by scholars, soldiers, merchants, and laborers.

The principle that differentiates *varṇas* is purity or cleanliness. Originally it probably had to do with the rituals performed to appease the gods. Ceremonial purity was then judged by exactness in the preservation of the oral tradition. A properly recited *sūkta* (prayer) was pure; an improperly recited one was impure. Since the sacrifices and prayers were offered for the entire community, the community itself was impure if an error was made in the ritual. Purity came to be regarded as a community commodity. But not all priests were pure—some made errors in the ritual. So, although the notion of purity or cleanliness came to be associated with the Brahmins, some Brahmins were less pure than others. Hence, the view arose that purity is likely to be found among the Brahmins, less likely among the Kṣatriyas, still less likely among the Vaiśyas, and very unlikely among the Śūdras. Superimposed upon this was the view that the Brahmins, Kṣatryias, and Vaiśyas because of their greater purity could be allowed to study the *Vedas* and undergo a ceremonial second birth upon completing religious studies. The Śūdras, because of their greater impurity, were not allowed to study the *Vedas*. They became known as the "once-born." Later—the time cannot be established—a fifth group was identified as those not within the *varṇa* system. They have been called the outcastes. They are outcastes not in the sense of being cast out of the community, but as being outside of the four-*varṇa* system. Those within this group were assigned such tasks as collecting garbage, cleaning toilets, washing clothes, disposing of dead animals, making shoes, and barbering. Although they are not within the caste system, they contribute to the purity and cleanliness of the community in very practical ways. Without their activities the community would indeed be impure.

Thus a very complicated *varṇa-jāti* system has evolved in India. The concept of purity governs such matters as whom one can marry, with whom one can eat, whom one can touch, whom one can sit beside. The caste system is not unique to India, but it is probably more complicated in India than anywhere else in the world. Other caste systems include medieval Europe's division of society into lords, vassals, and serfs, Iran's division of Atharvas, Rathestas, Vastria Fasouyantas, and Huiti, and Islam's division into Sayed, Mughal, Sheikh, and Pathan. T. S. Wilkinson, a Christian and a professor of sociology at Nagpur University in India, has called attention to a caste system among Christians in modern India: "The most outstanding feature of Indian society is its caste hierarchy. Caste is so much in the air that members of religious groups that otherwise denounce caste yet follow its proscriptions and prescriptions, consciously or unconsciously."[79] He describes certain members of the urban Christian churches of India as "the Brahmins of the Church."

Buddhist Views

Buddhist views on human sociality are extremely puzzling. The historical Buddha is believed to have taught the doctrine of *anātman,* the doctrine that there is no self. If there are no selves, then it makes no sense to speak of the compassion of one self for another. Yet the Buddha stressed the importance of being compassionate toward others. Moreover, he created the *Saṅgha,* the order of monks and nuns. The three essentials of Buddhism, which are traditionally called "The Three Jewels," are the Buddha, the *Dharma* (teachings), and the *Saṅgha.*

The two great branches of Buddhism—the Theravāda and the Mahāyāna—differ radically as to the human paradigm. In Theravāda Buddhism the ideal Buddhist is the solitary monk called the *arhat,* who is expected "to wander alone like a rhinoceros." But in Mahāyāna Buddhism the ideal Buddhist is the *bodhisattva,* who out of great compassion for other selves—whom he in his wisdom knows have no reality—vows to postpone his own *parinirvāṇa* in order that his merit may be made available for the liberation of these nonreal selves. If one ignores the metaphysical puzzles of Buddhism and considers Buddhism only in its ethical aspects, one concludes that Buddhism has through the centuries been very influential in promoting good will, tolerance, and friendship.

Chinese Views

Chinese philosophy is best understood as Confucianism modified by Taoism. Two composite writings—the *Analects,* which is traditionally assigned to Confucius, and the *Tao Teh Ching,* which is traditionally assigned to Lao Tzu—are the primary sources of information. The former is a textbook of insights in political philosophy; the latter is the work of the loyal opposition. To understand Confucius we should keep in mind that he approved of the ancient Chinese emphasis on the family, that he extended these moral principles to the state, and that he modified them by shifting them from their original aristocratic basis to an egalitarianism.[80] Lao Tzu argued that the good life must be one that is liberated from much of conventional morality with its emphasis on social conformity so that humans may live spontaneously in a physical universe characterized by the harmony of two interacting forces, one passive (*yin*) and one active (*yang*).

By the sixth century B.C. the family was the distinguishing feature of Chinese society. Confucius accepted and rejoiced in this fact. As H. G. Creel has said, "From one point of view, Confucianism might be defined as the philosophy of the Chinese family system."[81] The Chinese family has been called "the joint family," but the term *joint* misrepresents the unity of the traditional Chinese family. It had no joints; it was a unit. "The organic family" would be a better designation. The members of the family were living tissues of the whole organism, which functioned for the life and health of the family. The emphasis was not on the members of the family but on the relationships. The important relationships were father-son, eldest brother-younger brothers, husband-wife, and elders-juniors. Confucius extended the familial relations to the state, and therefore he added another relationship—rulers-ruled. He called the five pairs of mutual obligations "the Five Relationships." He wished to see the unity of the organic family enlarged to the unity of the political state.

The principal virtue of the organic family was the devotion of children to parents, and, since Chinese society was for centuries patriarchal, the relationship singled out paradigmatically was that of son to father. The symbol of filial piety (*hsiao*) consists of the symbol for old with the symbol for son placed below as though in support of the former. A disciple remarked to Confucius, "In my town there is one so upright that when his father stole a sheep, he, the son, testified against him."[82] In other words, justice is blind. But Confucius rebuked him, "The upright folk in my town differ from this. The father in such a case would conceal the son, and the son would conceal the father. Uprightness lies therein."[83] Justice is duty to parents and to children.

Marriage in China at the time of Confucius was not arranged for the purpose of procreation, but for the support of the older generation and for the continuation of worship of ancestors. A young man upon taking a wife did not leave his family. The son, married or unmarried, held no personal property. The cohesiveness of the Chinese family is indicated by the fact that the *Erh Ya*, the oldest dictionary of the Chinese language, contains over one hundred terms for family relations for which there are no English equivalents. As long as a father lived the son did not attain his majority, and the same was true for the younger sons with respect to their eldest brother. A female's devotion was transferred at marriage from her parents, or eldest brother—or some cases eldest male relative—to her husband and his parents. She, like her husband, held no personal property and was expected to turn over to her parents-in-law all gifts that might be given to her. The family was a unit in which the father or eldest brother was the unquestioned head, receiving complete obedience and deference, and in turn showing humane consideration to others in the family. It was upon this secure base that Confucius constructed his ethic. The genius of Confucius was in recognizing the strength of the family in Chinese society and in building upon this an ethic that translated the style and significance of family relationships into the political sphere and into the perfection of the character of the person. According to a later Confucian work , Confucius once said, "Filiality begins with the serving of our parents, continues with the serving of our prince, and is completed with the establishing of our own character."[84]

Confucius did not praise family loyalty and leave to the individual the form this loyalty might take. He said that *li* was the means by which family relations were to be expressed, and also that *li* was the objective measure of family loyality. The concept of *li* originally referred to a religious sacrifice, although it denoted not the sacrifice itself but the ritual in the sacrifice. The term was then extended to proper conducting of the ritual, and finally to the proper way of doing anything regarded worth doing. *Li*, therefore, referred to ethical behavior insofar as it could be objectively measured. The emporor's yearly sacrifice on the Altar of Heaven was controlled by *li* , and so was the daily life of the family.

Who bowed first, who entered a room first, the coarseness of mourning garments, table etiquette, and so on, were matters controlled by *li.* When Confucius emerged as a teacher in his early thirties he was already an authority on ceremony. His followers were assistants in ceremonies in noble households. They were easily identified by their broad-sleeved robes, bright round-feathered hats, and square-toed shoes.

Confucius has been criticized as a ceremonial prig who believed that all was right as long as the ceremony was correct. This criticism does not do justice to Confucius. In the chaotic times in which he lived the rediscovery of order had to begin with the obvious overt order of ceremony, ritual, convention, and etiquette. He saw *li* as a restraint on the lax and unpredictable behavioral patterns in Chinese society at the time. It was not enough to tell the son "honor your father." Confucius believed it necessary to spell out exactly the form that the honoring should take. "It is the style that is important," he said.[85] *Li* is the style of moral acting, the way to act righteously. But *Li* is more than ceremony. It is the way of doing what the situation demands. *Li* is external order, and in China as in our won times a formally correct act can be devoid of moral worth. It may be show without meaning, ceremony without emotions, or acts without attitudes. One's behavior can belie one's emotions. But consider a hypothetical society in which people love each other but have not learned to speak words of endearment, to hold hands, to put arms around each other, to kiss, and to engage in other love-expressing acts. Or consider a society that is losing the emotions of goodwill and love, in which chaos, fear, greed, and disorder claim the lives of the people. This was the society in which Confucius lived. How could he help this society? Could he begin by commanding "Love one another"? Confucius believed that the more practical approach was to begin by saying, "Here is how one expresses love. Here are the rituals, ceremonies, and rites by which our affection for each other can be expressed." He was following the sensible psychological principle that by engaging in the acts appropriate to the emotions of good will and love the emotions will be fostered.

Li is the external criterion for judging morality. But Confucius was aware of the danger of a formality uncoupled with inner reality. He knew that the act without the attitude is bare. Hence he also taught the necessity of the emotional component of the completely moral act, which he expressed in the conception of *jen.* The Chinese character of *jen* consists of the symbol for man and the symbol for two, thus it represents two human beings living in harmony. Whereas before Confucius *jen* meant the harmony of ruler and subjects, Confucius modified it to indicate the harmony of any two people. Confucius placed such importance on *jen* that the term appears 105 times in the *Analects.*[86] Translations of the term include "benevolence," "virtue," "humanity," "humaneness," "true manhood," "human heartedness," "man-to-man-ness," "manhood at its best," "hominity," "goodness," and "love." If *li* be thought of as morality in its external dimension, *jen* may be considered morality in its internal dimension. It is a composite virtue rather than a specific one. As with *li* Confucius expanded the meaning of *jen* from its original meaning of kindness of rulers to subjects to universal human benevolence. *Jen* describes the virtue that honors humanity, and *li* the virtue that honors ceremony.

While it is correct to think of *li* as external virtue and of *jen* as internal virtue, this distinction ought not to be pressed, for it separates what Confucius wanted to keep together. Perhaps a better distinction is that *jen* is virtue in its universality and *li* is virtue in its particularity. But this also runs into trouble, for *jen* has both universal and particular elements. *Jen* is active good will or love for humanity as expressed toward individual people, but humanity is not to be loved in the same manner in each instance. The *jen* of father to son honors humanity in the son, and the *jen* of son to father honors humanity in the father; but *jen* for the father is humaneness to the son, and *jen* for the son is faithful loyalty to the father. Confucius, in other words, held that we should love all people—but not in the same way. He taught a love that makes distinctions. This was a hotly argued point among his followers. The controversy has often been described as all-embracing love versus discriminating love. Confucius taught that all-embracing love of humanity requires differences in the manner of loving among different people. This involves his important notion of the equality of all men. The first task a child received in the classical education in Confucian China was to write the sentence "Men are alike in nature, but through practice they become different." The alikeness of men to which Confucius referred was not their sameness as good or evil but rather that all could and should aspire to the status of Superior Man (*chün-tzü*), a person who attains the level where *jen* and *li* are in perfect harmony. "Manhood-at-its-best is no remote ideal! We have only to desire it and straightway it arrives."[87]

The principle of *jen* was Confucius's way of affirming that the human being is a social animal. There is no humanity except in society. Each person must practice *jen* first with the near and the familiar, and through this simple and immediate beginning move to the fulfillment that is the love of all mankind. Confucius said, "Show affection to my parents, then to other people's parents, and then to the parents of all people in the world. Only then will my *jen* form one body with all parents."[88]

Jen is always an activity. *Jen* is doing, not contemplating. *Li*, of course, is also an activity. The difference is that *jen* connotes the act-qua-motivation and *li* the act-qua-structure. *Jen* is not a state of mind but a principle to be put into practice. It is the efficient cause, the generative principle, of virtue per se. This is why Confucius talked so much about it. Yet *jen* remains that something-I-know-not-what in Confucian ethics that is the inner, universal, creative source of ethical value. *Jen* may be felt, but never adequately defined. Probably the best "definition" from the *Analects* is a collection of simple commanding aphorisms: "When away from home act as respectfully as you would toward an important guest; handle the people as respectfully as you would the grand sacrifice. Do not do to others what you would not desire yourself."[89]

The Democratic Quest

The minimal meaning of democracy is a form of social and political organization in which the adult members of the community share in making decisions pertaining to the life of the society. The word *democracy* comes from the Greek words *dēmos* (people) and *kratéin* (to rule). However, the word *dēmos* in classical Greece denoted only the poor of the population. Socrates in *The Republic* reminds Glaucon and Adeimantos that "democracy . . . comes into being when the poor conquer."[90] Aristotle wrote, "Wherever men rule by reason of their wealth, whether they be few or many, that is an oligarchy, and where the poor rule, that is a democracy."[91] The adjective *democratic* may describe a form of government, a form of the state, a form of industry, a philosophy of life, or a personal characteristic. We shall use it here to describe a form of government. What are the forms of government of which democracy is one kind? Plato said there are five: aristocracy, oligarchy, timocracy, democracy, and tyranny. Aristotle said there were six: monarchy, aristocracy, polity, tyranny, oligarchy, and democracy. Much of Western political philosophy has been variations on the themes set by Plato and Aristotle.

Abraham Lincoln began his address at the dedication of the Gettysburg National Cemetery in 1863 with praise of a nation "conceived in liberty, and dedicated to the proposition that all men are created equal" and ended with the hope that a "government of the people, by the people, for the people" might not perish from the earth. By these prepositional phrases he meant rules that represented the will of the people, rulers elected by the people, and rules for the benefit of the people. This formula provides a schema for distinguishing the principal forms of government: (1) Who makes the policies? (2) Who selects those who carry out the policies? (3) For whose benefit are the policies designed? Lincoln's expression helps distinguish five main classes of government and fifteen subclasses:

1. Theocracy: of God, by God, for God.
2. Tyranny: of one person, by one person, for one person.
3. Aristocracy: of a few people, by a few people, for a few people.
4. Pluralocracy: of a plurality of the people, by a plurality of the people, for a plurality of the people.
5. Pantocracy: of all the people, by all the people, for all the people.[92]

Perhaps there are other forms of government. Monarchy is not listed, but, as

Plato said, it can be included as a form of aristocracy. Anarchy is not listed because it is the rejection of all government. Democracy is not listed because almost every form of government has been defended by someone as democratic.

A theocratic form of government is one whose constitution, magistrates, or being whom it is said to benefit is considered divine. The Vatican is an example of a theocracy.

A tyranny or despotism is a form of government in which one person sets the rules, or rules alone, or rules for his or her own benefit.

An aristocracy is a form of government in which a few of the more powerful, or more wealthy, or those descended from a royal family establish the constitution, or control the government, or rule for their own benefit.

A pluralocracy (or pluralarchy) is one in which a plurality, that is, a group having the largest membership, determines policies, or carries out policies, or establishes policies for its own benefit.

A pantocracy (or polyarchy) is one in which everyone sets the rules, or carries them out, or sets rules for the benefit of everyone. Some of the first English settlements in America were governed in this fashion. New England town meetings are remnants of this pattern of government. During the seventeenth and eighteenth centuries many small utopian societies in America were pantocracies, such as, Bohemia Manor, Woman in the Wilderness, Ephrata, Harmony, Zoar, Hopewell, New Harmony, the many Shaker villages, Shaneateles, Brook Farm, Bethel, Aurora, Amana, Oneida, and Icaria. Today there are more than two thousand communes in the United States. Perhaps the best known is Koinonia, which was established by Clarence and Florence Jordan near Americus, Georgia, in 1942.

There are theoretically one hundred and twenty-five possible variations of these basic forms of government; a community might select as its basic polity rules that the members believe came from a divine or semidivine source, such as the *Torah*, the *Koran*, *The Bhagavad Gītā As It Is* by Swami A. C. Bhaktivedanta, or Mao Tze-tung's *The New Democracy* and *On People's Democratic Dictatorship*, as its magistrates the members of an hereditary aristocracy, and as its goal the mutual benefits of all members of the community.

A political organization is democratic in the degree to which the citizens are free and equal. Freedom and equality in social contexts are both negative and positive. Negative freedom consists in the removal of barriers and constraints on the life and thought of citizens. A negative freedom is commonly indicated as a "freedom from." Positive freedom is the provision for citizens to express their will and to act in accord with their preferences. A positive freedom is commonly indicated as a "freedom for" or a "freedom to." A tariff on imports is a negative freedom protecting the industrialists of a country from undue competition. Provisions for voting are positive freedoms.

Negative equality consists in the removal of barriers to the equality of the life and opportunities of citizens. Positive equality is designed to promote equalities, rather than to eliminate inequalities. A graduated tax structure is an effort to negate inequalities. University scholarships for lower income students is an affirmative effort to promote equalities.

The relationship of liberty and equality remains a puzzling one. Are all human beings free, and therefore equal; or are they equal, and therefore free? In a nation all can be made equal only by denying the liberty of some, or all can be made free only at the cost of the equality of some. Equal freedom for pike and minnow means death for the minnow. The American Revolution was conceived in a desire for liberty. It was not for equality that Patrick Henry declared he was ready to die—"Give me *liberty* or give me death." Yet the authors of American Declaration of Independence gave priority to equality: "All men are created *equal.*" Thomas Jefferson in his original draft stated that freedoms are derived from equality: "All men are created equal, and from that equal creation they derive rights inherent and inalienable, among which are the preservation of life and liberty and the pursuit of happiness." But his colleagues struck out the words "from that equal creation they derive" and substituted the phrase "they are endowed by their Creator with," thus breaking the logical relationship between assumed equality and derived rights with a pious reference to deity. (In the final draft, perhaps through an error in copying, the word "inalienable" became "unalienable.") The French Revolution was primarily an effort on the part of the members of the third estate to obtain equality of voting privileges with the members of the first and second estates, the nobles and clergy. Their motto—"Liberty, Equality, Fraternity"—was interpreted by Henri Bergson as follows: democracy "proclaims liberty, demands equality, and reconciles these two hostile sisters by reminding them that they are sisters, by exalting above everything fraternity. Looked at from this angle, the republican motto shows that the third term dispels the oft-noted contradiction between the two others, and that the essential thing is fraternity."[93] The Universal Declaration of Human Rights adopted by the United Nations General Assembly in 1948 dodges the issue of the priority of liberty or equality by simple affirming that "All human beings are born free and equal in dignity and rights." The preamble to the constitution of India, avoiding any declaration of natural human freedoms or equalities, states that India seeks to secure for all its citizens "equality of status and opportunity."

Freedoms and equalities may be conferred upon or denied to either individuals or groups. A democratic state is concerned for the freedom and equality not only of individual citizens but also of groups within the state. This is the rationale for laws forbidding restrictions upon, denials of opportunities for, or persecution of any individual by reason of sex, race, religion, color, caste, national origin, or membership in any political party, social group, cultural organization, assembly, and so forth. This aspect of democracy is indicated by such expressions as "to promote the general welfare," "the right to assemble," and "to ensure that a nation's gains are mass gains."

By considering negative-positive, individual-social, and liberty-equality choices, eight possible kinds of democracy can be indicated:

1. negative individualistic egalitarian democracy
2. positive individualistic egalitarian democracy
3. negative socialistic egalitarian democracy
4. positive socialistic egalitarian domocracy
5. negative individualistic libertarian democracy
6. positive socialistic libertarian democracy
7. negative socialistic libertarian democracy
8. positive socialistic libertarian democracy

Plato on Democracy

Democracy first rose as theory and practice in the Western world in ancient Greece. Neither Plato nor Aristotle was greatly impressed by democracy as a form of government. According to the Platonic taxonomy democracy is a stage between timocracy and tyranny. A state becomes a democracy through the "insatiate desire" of the poor to become wealthy.[94] When the poor, who are many, overthrow the rich, who are few, they establish the rule of freedom: "the city is full of freedom and liberty of speech, and men in it may do what they like."[95] This, for the order-minded Plato, is the great defect of democracy. It has no constitution, since it is a collection of constitutions: "All sorts of constitutions are there; and if anyone wants to fit up a city, as we have been doing, it is only necessary for him to go to a city governed by a democracy, and choose whatever fashion of constitution pleases him, as if he had come to a bazaar of constitutions."[96] In a democracy, added Plato, no one rules, goes to war, keeps the peace, or obeys any law unless he or she wishes. It's "a lovely, heavenly life, while it lasts."[97] Democracy is "a charming form of government, full of variety and disorder, and dispensing a sort of equality to equals and unequals alike."[98] But it is the love of freedom that is its undoing. Social order vanishes. Everything but liberty is disregarded. "The father gets into the habit of behaving like the son and fears his own children, the son behaves like a father, and does not honour or fear his parents, 'must have liberty' he says."[99] Teachers fear pupils, and pupils despise teachers. "Old men give way to the young; they are all complaisance and wriggling, and behave like young men themselves so as not to be thought disagreeable or dictatorial."[100] Socrates adds that in democracy there is equality between men and women.[101] Even animals assume democratic liberties and equalities: "Horses and asses, if you please, adopt the habit of marching along with the greatest freedom and haughtiness, bumping into everyone they meet who will not get out of the way; and all the other animals likewise are filled full of liberty."[102]

The citizens of a democracy finally divide into three classes: the drones, the rich, and "the people." The drones are the dominant class. They conduct all business of state. The rich take no care for the state, but devote all time and energy to acquiring wealth. The drones regard them as their "fodder." The third and largest class are the handiworkers. In the conflicts among drones, the rich, and "the people" the latter find a protector who in the struggle becomes a tyrant. Thus ends the miserable state of excessive equality and liberty.

Aristotle on Equality

According to Aristotle the basis of a democratic state is equality—the equality of freedom—not the equality of birth, or virtue, or wealth: "Democracy . . . arises out of the notion that those who are equal in any respect are equal in all respects; because men are equally free, they claim to be absolutely equal. Oligarchy is based on the notion that those who are unequal in one respect are in all respects unequal; being unequal, that is, in property, they suppose themselves to be unequal absolutely."[103] He said of democratic states that "equality is above all their aim"[104] Yet Aristotle was not thoroughly consistent in this claim; for example, "The basis of a democratic state is liberty. . . . Every citizen, it is said, must have equality, and therefore in a democracy the poor have more power than the rich, because there are more of them, and the will of the majority is supreme. This, then, is one note of liberty which all democrats affirm to be the principle of their state."[105] He was very critical of this theory. Democracies of the "more extreme type," he said, have produced this "false idea of freedom."[106] "For two principles are characteristic of democracy, the government of the majority and freedom. Men think that what is just is equal; and that equality is the supremacy of the popular will; and that freedom means the doing what a man likes. In such democracies every one lives as he pleases, or in the words of Euripides, 'according to his fancy.' But this is all wrong; men should not think it slavery to live according to the rule of the constitution; for it is their salvation."[107]

Democracy in its "truest form," said Aristotle, is based upon "the recognized principle of democratic justice, that all should count equally; for equality implies that the poor should have no more share in the government than the rich, and should not be the only rulers, but that all should rule equally according to their numbers. And in this way men think that they will secure equality and freedom in their state."[108] But it will not work. Those who want equality without recognizing inequalities reminded Aristotle of the fable of Antisthenes about the rabbits who claimed equality with the lions. In the fable the lions retorted, "Where are your claws and teeth?"[109] "All men think justice to be a sort of equality,"[110] said Aristotle.

> But there still remains a question: equality or inequality of what? Here is a difficulty which calls for political speculation. For very likely some persons will say that offices of state ought to be unequally distributed according to superior excellence, in whatever respect, of the citizen, although there is no

> other difference between him and the rest of the community; for that those who differ in any one respect have different rights and claims. But, surely, if this is true, the complexion or height of a man, or any other advantage, will be a reason for his obtaining a greater share of political rights.[111]

The problem of government, according to Aristotle, is the problem of establishing equality among unequals. Justice is a sort of equality, but "equality or inequality of what?"[112] "All men cling to justice of some kind, but their conceptions are imperfect and they do not express the whole idea. For example, justice is thought by them to be, and is, equality, not, however, for all, but only for equals. And inequality is thought to be, and is, justice; neither is this for all, but only for unequals."[113]

Aristotle enumerated six forms of government: three true forms, namely, kingship, aristocracy, and what he called "polity" or "the constitutional form"; and three perverted forms, namely, democracy, oligarchy, and tyranny. Yet Aristotle, perhaps in revolt against his idealistic master, held that attention ought to be given to the possible, albeit perverted, forms rather than to some lofty ideal that admittedly will never become reality until philosophers are kings—a euphemistic way of saying "Probably never."[114] The word *perverted* is too strong. What he had in mind is that these are the forms of government in which it is easy for the rulers to rule for private interest rather than for the public good.

Democracy is that form of government that "arises out of the notion that those who are equal in any respect are equal in all respects; because men are equally free, they claim to be absolutely equal."[115] It is not good to organize a state exclusively on the democratic principle of equality or on the oligarchic principle of inequality. The evidence for this claim is that neither lasts.[116] Yet "democracy appears to be safer and less liable to revolution than oligarchy,"[117] and therefore Aristotle preferred democracy to oligarchy or tyranny, although democracy is less perfect in theory than kingship, aristocracy, and polity.

In the *Politics*[118] Aristotle distinguished five forms of democracy: (1) All persons share alike in the government. It is based "strictly on equality." (2) Rulers are elected according to a property qualification, but a low one. (3) All the citizens who are under no disqualification share in the government, but the law is supreme. (4) There is no disqualification of citizens. All citizens share in the government, but still the law is supreme. (5) The supreme power is located not in the law but in the majority opinion of the citizens. While these five forms are not altogether clear and distinct, one can see that they represent various interpretations of the principle of equality. But there are two kinds of equality, said Aristotle: numerical and proportional. Numerical equality is sameness in number or size, such as the excess of three over two is numerically equal to the excess of two over one. Proportional equality is the equality of ratios, as in four exceeds two in the same ratio that two exceeds one, namely the half.[119] The democratic principle—those who are equal in one thing ought to have an equal share in all—and the oligarchic principle—those who are unequal in one thing ought to have an unequal share in all—are both "perversions."[120] A balance must be found so that both numerical equality and proportional equality are employed in the state.[121] This would seem to imply, although Aristotle did not say so, that the best possible form of government is what might be called an oligarchical democracy or a democratic oligarchy.

Aristotle, in an interesting passage in the *Politics*,[122] illustrated the problem of implementing equality among unequals. Imagine a state with thirty citizens, ten rich and twenty poor. An issue is brought to a vote in which the ten rich are divided with six in favor and four against, and the twenty poor are split with five in favor and fifteen against. That means a head count of eleven in favor of the measure and nineteen against the measure. But to decide the issue on that basis assumes that equality means numerical equality. There must also be a consideration of the qualifications of the citizens to vote on the issue. The qualifications of the eleven may be far greater than that of the nineteen. What should be done? Aristotle was not very helpful. He wrote that "in such a case the will of those whose qualifications, when both sides are added up, are the greatest, should prevail."[123] If the opinion of the nineteen and the opinion of the eleven are equal in qualification, then it might as well be decided by lot. He concluded this fascinating passage with the comment that the theory of human equality is difficult, but the application of the theory is still more difficult. "Although it may be difficult in theory to know what is just and equal, the practical difficulty of inducing those to forbear who can if they like, encroach is far greater, for the weaker are always asking for equality and justice, but the stronger care for none of these things."[124]

In the midst of his discussion of revolutions Aristotle offered some sage advice about governments in general. In discussing how true the forms of government shift into the perverted forms, he noted that "when men are equal they are contented."[125] He then showed some of the problems that arise when either rich or poor claim more for themselves than is good for the state as a whole. "The only stable principle of government is equality according to proportion."[126] He wrote that in order that oligarchies and aristocracies not deteriorate the rulers ought to be on good terms with both the enfranchised and the unenfranchised.[127]

Those who are excluded from governing ought not to be maltreated. All should be treated "in a spirit of equality."[128] He added, "The equality which the friends of democrary seek to establish for the multitude is not only just but likewise expedient."[129] He advised that in a democracy tenure of office be limited to six months so that all of equal rank may share in ruling. This is a good plan even for oligarchies and aristocracies inasmuch as it prevents ruling from falling into the hands of certain families. Long terms of office will turn oligarchies and democracies into tyrannies.[130] Laws must provide against anyone having too much power, whether that power come from friends or money.[131] Anyone who has too much power "should be sent clean out of the country."[132] Every effort should be made to increase the size of the middle class—the class between the rich and the poor—and thus put an end to revolutions that arise form inequality.[133]

Mill on Liberty

John Stuart Mill considered his essay *On Liberty* his finest work. It is one of the best defenses of civil or social liberty in any language. It appeared first as a brief article in 1854 and, after much revision and enlargement, as a small book in 1859. The issue discussed in the essay—"the nature and limits of the power which can be legitimately exercised by society over the individual"[134]—is, wrote Mill, "A question seldom stated, and hardly ever discussed in general terms, but which profoundly influences the practical controversies of the age by its latent presence, and is likely soon to make itself recognized as the vital question of the future."[135]

Mill did not indicate why he had concluded that civil liberty was soon to become a crucial issue, but one can surmise he was aware that Karl Marx was busy in the library of the British Museum writing his appeals to workers to rise against the bourgeoisie. Mill wrote that the issue "has divided mankind almost from the remotest ages; but in the stage of progress into which the more civilized portions of the species have now entered, it presents itself under new conditions and requires a different and more fundamental treatment."[136] The full therapy was yet to be fashioned. Mill noted that whereas in ancient times the struggle was between subjects and government, the problem had shifted to a struggle with a new form of tyranny—"the tyranny of the majority." "Protection . . . against the tyranny of the magistrate is not enough, there needs protection also against the tyranny of the prevailing opinion and feeling, against the tendency of society to impose, by other means than civil penalties, its own ideas and practices as rules of conduct on those who dissent from them."[137] The establishment of "a limit to the legitimate interference of collective opinion with individual independence . . . is as indispensable to a good condition of human affairs as protection against political despotism."[138]

When may a government, a society, or any group impose its will on an individual? When may an individual be justly denied freedom of thought and action? Mill's answer is "one very simple principle," namely, "to prevent harm to others."

> The object of this essay is to assert one very simple principle, as entitled to govern absolutely the dealings of society with the individual in the way of compulsion and control, whether the means used be physical force in the form of legal penalties or the moral coercion of public opinion. That principle is that the sole end for which mankind are warranted, individually or collec-

> tively, in interfering with the liberty of action of any of their number is self-protection. That the only purpose for which power can be rightfully exercised over any member of a civilized community, against his will, is to prevent harm to others. His own good, either physical or moral, is not a sufficient warrant. He cannot rightfully be compelled to do or forbear because it will be better for him to do so, because it will make him happier, because, in the opinions of others, to do so would be wise or even right. These are good reasons for remonstrating with him or reasoning with him, or persuading him, or entreating him, but not for compelling him or visiting him with any evil in case he do otherwise. To justify that, the conduct from which it is desired to deter him must be calculated to produce evil to someone else. The only part of the conduct of anyone for which he is amenable to society is that which concerns others. In the part which merely concerns himself, his independence is, of right, absolute. Over himself, over his own body and mind, the individual is sovereign.[139]

The "appropriate region of human liberty" in a democratic society, according to Mill, consists of three freedoms: (1) freedom of thought, (2) freedom of tastes and pursuits, and (3) freedom of assembly.

> It [the region of human liberty] comprises, first, the inward domain of consciousness, demanding liberty of conscience in the most comprehensive sense, liberty of thought and feeling, absolute freedom of opinion and sentiment on all subjects, practical or speculative, scientific, moral, or theological. The liberty of expressing and publishing opinions may seem to fall under a different principle, since it belongs to that part of the conduct of an individual which concerns other people, but, being almost of as much importance as the liberty of thought itself and resting in great part on the same reasons, is practically inseparable from it. Secondly, the principle requires liberty of tastes and pursuits, of framing the plan of our life to suit our own character, of doing as we like, subject to such consequences as may follow, without impediment from our fellow creatures, so long as what we do does not harm them, even though they should think our conduct foolish, perverse, or wrong. Thirdly, from this liberty of each individual follows the liberty within the same limits, of combination among individuals; freedom to unite for any purpose not involving harm to others; the persons combining being supposed to be of full age and not forced or deceived.[140]

Mill offered four grounds for freedom of opinion and freedom of expression of opinion. He summarized his arguments in the following manner:

> First, if any opinion is compelled to silence that opinion may, for aught we can certainly know, be true. To deny this is to assume our own infallibility. Secondly, though the silenced opinion be an error, it may, and very commonly does, contain a portion of truth; and since the general or prevailing opinion on any subject is rarely or never the whole truth, it is only by the collision of adverse opinions that the remainder of the truth has any chance of being supplied. Thirdly, even if the received opinion be not only true, but the whole

> truth; unless it is suffered to be, and actually is, vigorously and earnestly contested, it will by most of those who receive it, be held in the manner of a prejudice, with little comprehension or feeling of its rational grounds. And not only this, but, fourthly, the meaning of the doctrine itself will be in danger of being lost or enfeebled, and deprived of its vital effect on the character and conduct: the dogma becoming a mere formal profession, inefficacious for good, but cumbering the ground and preventing the growth of any real and heartfelt conviction from reason or personal experience.[141]

His paean on the value of free expression of opinion is often quoted:

> If all mankind minus one were of one opinion, mankind would be no more justified in silencing that one person than he, if he had the power, would be justified in silencing mankind. Were an opinion a personal possession of no value except to the owner, if to be obstructed in the enjoyment of it were simply a private injury, it would make some difference whether the injury was inflicated only on a few persons or on many. But the peculiar evil of silencing the expression of an opinion is that it is robbing the human race, posterity as well as the existing generation—those who dissent from the opinion, still more than those who hold it. If the opinion is right, they are deprived of the opportunity of exchanging error for truth; if wrong, they lose, what is almost as great a benefit, the clearer perception and livelier impression of truth produced by its collision with error.[142]

Mill's emphasis was largely on the loss society suffers in stifling opinion, rather than on the impact such persecution might have on the individual; both society and the individual suffer when an opinion is silenced. "Who can compute what the world loses in the multitude of promising intellects combined with timid characters, who dare not follow out any bold, vigorous, independent train of thought, lest it should land them in something which would admit of being considered irreligious or immoral? . . . No one can be a great thinker who does not recognize that as a thinker it is his first duty to follow intellect to whatever conclusion it may lead."[143]

Mill held that men should not be as free to act upon their opinions as they should be to express their opinions. But the principle of doing harm to others holds in both cases: "Acts, of whatever kind, which without justifiable cause do harm to others may be, and in the more important cases absolutely required to be, controlled by the unfavourable sentiments, and, when needful, by the active interference of mankind."[144] Still, "it is the privilege and proper condition of a human being, arrived at the maturity of his faculties, to use and interpret experience in his own way. It is for him to find out what part of recorded experience is properly applicable to his own circumstances and character."[145] This is because it is human nature to grow: "Human nature is not a machine to be built after a model, and set to do exactly the work prescribed for it, but a tree, which requires to grow and develop itself on all sides, according to the tendency of the inward forces which make it a living thing."[146]

Mill summarized his essay in two maxims, which he said "together form the entire doctrine": (1) "the individual is not accountable to society for his actions in so far as these concern the interests of no person but himself," and (2) "for such actions as are prejudicial to the interests of others, the individual is accountable and may be subjected either to social or the legal punishment if society is of opinion that the one or the other is requisite for its protection."[147]

The Marxian Challenge

Karl Marx (1818–1883) challenged the democratic principle,[148] holding that freedom in the economic sphere creates gross inequality between two classes of people created by the economic system. These are the workers and the property owners—the proletariat and the bourgeoisie. Marx, holding throughout his life as a guiding maxim "Nothing human is alien to me," labored for the realization of economic and political conditions in which all men and women could attain their true humanity.

Marx's distinction between proletariat and bourgeoisie was strikingly similar to that made by Jesus between the poor, whom he called *'am hā'rets* (the people of the land), and the rich. He said, "Blessed are you poor, for yours is the kingdom of God"[149] and "It is easier for a camel to go through the eye of a needle than for a rich man to enter the kingdom of God."[150] But there was a difference between Jesus and Marx. Jesus advised obedience to the state. Marx called upon workers to rebel, to throw off their chains, and to create a system that would have no classes. Christendom, however, has often chosen as the Christian social message Paul's admonition that servants obey masters (consider Ephesians 6:5, Colossians 3:22, and Titus 2:9) rather than Jesus' revolutionary warning, such as "Do not think that I have come to bring peace on earth; I have not come to bring peace, but a sword."[151] Marx held that the ultimate goal of philosophical wisdom should be to change the social structure.[152]

Marx foresaw a death struggle between the haves and the have-nots, between the propertied owners of the means of production and the nonpropertied workers. Since in his opinion the current economic system prevented both proletarians and bourgeois from attaining their true humanity, he advocated a proletarian revolution that would eventuate in the ideal classless society.

The heart of Marxism is its fourfold analysis of the alienation of proletarians. Workers in industrialized societies, argued Marx, are engaged in "alienated labor": they are separated from the product of their labor. Many cannot even identify the product they make. Instead of rejoicing in the completion of an article of value to fellow human beings, they perform a routine task such as pushing a lever in an assembly line. They have no satisfaction in the product of their labor. Their compensation is money—"the alienated essence of man's work and existence."[153] Money as "the universal and self-sufficient value of all things"[154] is the capitalistic measure of value foisted upon the workers.

A second alienation is the separation of the industrial workers from the natural world. The workers in factories in the nineteenth century often saw little sunlight and had little opportunity to enjoy the delights of field and stream.

A third alienation according to Marx is social alienation. A human being is what he is, not what he has. But in the capitalistic economy the proletarians have been brainwashed by the bourgeoisie. They have appropriated the view that the real nature and the real value of the human being is measured by the bank account rather than by artistic creation, mechanical skill, philosophical acumen, literary proficiency, verbal competence. Capitalistic evaluations are imposed upon the working class by the property owners, alienating the human being from essential humanity. Workers must struggle to maintain existence. They have no time to cultivate their capacities, possibilities, and talents. Their work demeans their humanity. It would be interesting to determine Marx's reaction to the all too common situation today in which workers working thirty to forty hours per week spend most of their spare time in front of a television set!

The fourth alienation is the self-alienation of the worker. Marx wrote that the worker "does not fulfil himself in his work but denies himself, has a feeling of misery rather than well-being, does not develop freely his mental and physical energies but is physically exhausted and mentally debased. . . His work is not voluntary, but imposed, *forced labour*. It is not the satisfaction of a need, but only a *means* for satisfying other needs."[155] The worker "in work . . . does not belong to himself but to another person."[156]

The cure for human alienation, according to Marx, is a revolt of the workers against the capitalists. He foresaw a violent, although brief, revolution. Following the revolution would be a period of dictatorship of the proletariat. Eventually the state would "wither away," and there would emerge the utopia of a "classless society."

This is not the place to summarize what has happened to Marxism since the life of Karl Marx, but perhaps it is sufficient to refer to two types of Marxism: (1) a modified, dogmatic, revisionistic Marxism developed in Russia by such leaders as Lenin and Stalin to suit a country that was not experiencing a proletarian revolution; and (2) a guide to avoiding dictatorships of the proletariat and one-party systems in China, India, and in many Third World countries. The impact of Marx-the-humanist remains a vital force in modern society.

Democracy in the East

Democracy in the East is largely a late twentieth-century development modeled after Western democracies. Unfortunately, Eastern philosophers have not been noticeably active in this area of the philosophical spectrum. India, the first of the rising democracies of the Orient, received independence from the British on 15 August 1947. The preamble to the constitution of India begins "We the people of India, having solemnly resolved to constitute India into a sovereign democratic republic and to secure to all its citizens: *Justice:* social, economic and political; *Liberty* of thought, expression, belief, faith and worship; *Equality* of status and of opportunity; and to promote among them all *Fraternity* assuring the dignity of the individual and the unity of the Nation . . . " Part 3 of the constitution of India lists the "Fundamental Rights," the first being the "Right to Equality": "The State shall not discriminate against any citizen on the grounds of religion, race, caste, sex, place of birth or any of them." Section 17, which abolishes untouchability, raises the delicate issue of the relationship between civil law and social custom. The other rights are "Right to Freedom," "Right against Exploitation," "Right to Freedom of Religion," "Cultural and Educational Rights," "Right to Property," and "Right to Constitutional Remedies." Three Indian philosophers who have been deeply concerned with the political dimension are S. Radhakrishnan, the great historian of Indian philosophy and the first president of the nation, Sri Aurobindo, the founder of the ashram at Pondicherry, and M. N. Roy, who has written extensively on communism.

China in 1949 split into the Chinese People's Republic, which occupied the mainland, and the Chinese Nationalist Republic, which established itself on the island of Taiwan, formerly known as Formosa. Mainland China became a Communist dictatorship under Mao Tse-tung, and remained communistic until the gradual weakening of the Communist Party beginning in 1972. Earlier in the twentieth century China had begun to break from her traditional Confucian moorings. In 1911 Sun Yat-sen led a successful rebellion against the Manchu rulers and had himself established as first president of the Republic of China. This was followed in 1917 with a literary revolution led by Ch'en Tu-hsiu, a professor at the National University in Peking. He and his followers, believing that Confucian orthodoxy was the greatest obstacle to Chinese life and thought, organized the New Culture Movement with the battle cry "Down with K'ung and Sons."[157] He referred to the Confucian concept of *li* as a "cannibalistic doctrine." Hu Shih, who joined the anti-K'ung movement, advocated the complete Westernization of Chinese culture. Chiang Kai-shek in opposition founded the New Life Movement in 1934 supporting the Confucian doctrines of *li* (propriety), *yi* (righteousness), *lien* (integrity), and *ch'ih* (honor).

During the Communist rule on the mainland Fung Yu-lan, the best-known Chinese philosopher of the twentieth century, embraced Communism. Liu Wu-Chi wrote in 1955,

> It is an uncomfortable thought to all worshippers of authority that the K'ung dogma, which was so strongly entrenched in the human mind in the past

> centuries, should now be in danger of being stripped of its power and prestige by the people's court. In spite of . . . attempts at its restitution, it now appears almost certain that the day will never dawn when the K'ung orthodoxy will regain its strong hold on the intellectual life of the Chinese nation. The former adoration of the intelligensia is over, and gone with it is the Master's authority and influence. The younger generation, brought up in the days of Down-with-K'ung-and-Sons Movement, will never look at Master K'ung with the same eyes of awe and respect as did their ancestors. It is indeed epoch-making that the greatest idol humanity has ever built should now be in the process of being dethroned, if not broken![158]

Changes within mainland China since 1972 suggest that Liu may have been unduly pessimistic about the future of Confucianism.

Japan has been a democracy since 1946. One of the most remarkable involvements of philosophers in politics was that of D. T. Suzuki, who opposed Japan's part in World War II while living in Japan during the war.

Beyond the Nation

Nation is a very difficult concept to define, as indicated by the vague and cautious definition offered in *Webster's New International Dictionary*: "A people connected by supposed ties of blood generally manifested by community of language, religion, and customs, and by a sense of common interest and interrelation."

The concept of a national state appeared first in the West in *The Prince*, a small book written by Niccolo Machiavelli in 1514, in which he pleaded with Lorenzo de'Medici to unite the Italian states and free all Italy from the attacks by northern barbarians:

> Italy is waiting to see who can be the one to heal her wounds, put an end to the sacking of Lombardy, to extortion in the Kingdom and in Tuscany, and cleanse those sores which have now been festering for so long. See how Italy beseeches God to send someone to save her from those barbarous cruelties and outrages; see how eager and willing the country is to follow a banner, if only someone will raise it. And at the present time it is impossible to see in what she can place more hope than in your illustrious House, which, with its fortune and prowess, favoured by God and by the Church, of which it is now the head, can lead Italy to her salvation. . . . Let your illustrious House undertake this task, therefore, with the courage and hope which belong to just enterprises, so that, under your standard, our country may be ennobled, and under your auspices what Petrarch said may come to pass:
>
> Vertue 'gainst fury shall advance the fight,
> And it i' th' combate soone shall put to flight:

For th' old Romane valour is not dead,
Nor in th' Italians brests extinguished.[159]

The concept of a modern nation is thus less than five hundred years old. During the twentieth century many questions are being raised about the worth of the national ideal. A group of Western nations at the close of World War I, recognizing the dangers inherent in the doctrine of national sovereignity, established the League of Nations and the World Court to aid in the solving of international conflicts, and after World War II the United Nations was established on 24 October 1945 to promote world peace and human dignity. Democracy is a method of bringing about social change through discussion, compromise, and consensus. The concept of a nation appears to be linked with conflicts, aggressions, and wars. Both world wars resulted in a rebirth of hope that nations could settle differences peacefully. The meliorative accomplishments of these international organizations must not be minimized, but the fact remains that they operate within the framework of nationalistic mentalities. Each nation retains its sovereignity, remains an independent entity manifesting self-righteousness, and still engages in acts for which a person would be punished by incarceration or execution. Patriotism still demands doing for one's nation that which if done for another nation is called treason.

Each nation maintains a standing army as protection against every other nation—and this, in the opinion of Kant, is a major cause of war: "For they incessantly menace other states by their readiness to appear at all times prepared for war; they incite them to compete with each other in the number of armed men, and there is no limit to this. For this reason, the cost of peace finally becomes more oppressive than that of a short war, and consequently a standing army is itself a cause of offensive war waged in order to relieve the state of this burden."[160] It is anomalous that the political state, which according to Hobbes is created to escape that "miserable condition of war," is the institution that fosters wars. Nations, according to Daniel Lang, are "essentially mechanisms for the practice of large-scale violence."[161] He adds, "Perhaps nations will have to be supplanted as objects of patriotism—they are not verities; there was a time, centuries ago, when they were unknown. But if nations are here to stay, then their managers will do well to remember that each of their subjects carries a private vision of his country's value; the more this is discounted, the more scrutiny will the managers attract. It is not enough to die for one's country; one must also want to live in it."[162]

Europeans, according to José Ortega y Gasset, are discovering they cannot think nationally:

> For the first time, the European, checked in his projects, economic, political, intellectual, by the limits of his own country, feels that those projects—that is to say, his vital possibilities—are out of proportion to the size of the collective

> body in which he is enclosed. And so he has discovered that to be English, German, or French is to be provincial. He has found out that he is "less" than he was before, for previously the Englishman, the Frenchman, and the German believed, each for himself, that he was the universe. This is, to my mind, the true source of the feeling of decadence which to-day afflicts the European.[163]

Bertrand Russell submitted that to preserve the nation is to commit genocide: "Nationalism is in our day the chief obstacle to the extension of social cohesion beyond national boundaries. It is therefore the chief force making for the extermination of the human race."[164] And the philosophical zoologist Lewis Thomas adds, "Nations have themselves become too frightening to think about."[165]

Meanwhile similar thoughts were troubling intellectuals in India. Rabindranath Tagore on 2 March 1921 wrote to his friend C. F. Andrews, "We have no word for 'Nation' in our language. When we borrow this word from other people, it never fits us."[166] Nationalism is foreign to the tradition of India. According to *The Cambridge Shorter History of India*, "Foreign domination was nothing to peoples with no consciousness of nationality."[167] However, add the authors, things began to change after 1818 as the Indians began to face a common enemy—the British. Tagore wrote, "Even though from childhood I had been taught that idolatry of the nation is almost better than reverence for God and humanity, I believe I have outgrown that teaching, and it is my conviction that my countrymen will truly gain their India by fighting against the education which teaches them that a country is greater than the ideals of humanity."[168] Tagore warned against "the fierce self-idolatry of nation-worship"[169] and "the bondage of nationalism."[170] The nation is "the survival of that part of man which is the least living."[171] Nations do not create, rather "they merely produce and destroy . . . they crowd away into a corner the living man who creates."[172] In the growth of nationalism "man has become the greatest menace to man."[173] Nationalism is a thing of "gigantic vanity and selfishness."[174] He saw one ray of hope: the Age of Nationalism is "only a passing phase of civilization."[175]

Aurobindo Ghose (1872–1950) in his youth regarded nationalism as a religion, but he began to have doubts as he watched the movement progress to independence from the British. He warned that India might be nationalized and industrialized out of all recognition. He issued an Independence Day declaration on 15 August 1947 in which, while rejoicing in India's liberation from the British, cautioned that nationhood should be only a step toward more valuable governmental organizations: "But an outward basis is not enough; there must grow an international spirit and outlook, international forms and institutions must appear, perhaps such developments as dual or multilateral citizenship, willed interchange or voluntary fusion of cultures. Nationalism will have fulfilled itself and lost its militancy and would no longer find these things incompatible with self-preservation and the integrity of its outlook."[176]

The view that nationalism must pass into internationalism has not been foreign to the West. According to Cicero, when Socrates was asked his nationality he replied "Universian." The urgency that forces internationalism is war. Nuclear armaments is the catalyst. The future depends largely upon how human beings deal with the problem of war. Harrison Brown argues that there are only three patterns for the future. One is that human beings may develop a worldwide free industrial society in which they can live in reasonable harmony with their natural environment and with each other. Brown adds that unfortunately the possibility of this happening is rather low. If human beings are unable to abolish war, then either they will revert to an agrarian existence, a barter culture in which the hand of each is against all others, or they will establish a completely controlled, collectivized industrial society. Neither is desirable, but unless human beings can solve the problem of war they cannot be avoided.[177]

Mortimer J. Adler said there are only four possible world conditions: (1) a plurality of independent, sovereign states that enter into alliances with one another by treaty, which is the present condition; (2) a league of independent nations that may or may not include all nations and that may or may not be supported by alliances; (3) a world community including all peoples under world government, federal in structure; or (4) a world state that consists of a world community under government that is not federal in structure.[178]

Bertrand Russell thought that a world state is the only condition under which man can prosper in the future: "For it is only in the direction of an organized world State that the human race can develop unless it abandons scientific technique, and it will not do this except as the result of a cataclysm so severe as to lower the whole level of civilization."[179]

But only a few observers think an international state may replace national states. One of these is Roderick Seidenberg: "It is not unlikely that, before the present century will have run its course, we shall be privileged to witness the crystallization of this idea; and in time internationalism may well reach the same degree of development, of internal co-ordination and integration, that we now associate with the idea of nationalism."[180]

One reason for doubt is the resistance to world government from patriotic organizations, as when the Veterans of Foreign Wars of the United States formulated the following mandate at its national convention in Miami, Florida, 21–26 August 1949:

> Be it Resolved, By the 50th Annual National Convention of the Veterans of Foreign Wars of the United States, we hereby declare that we are unalterably opposed to any program which would entail the surrender of any part of the sovereignty of the United States of America in favor of World Government.

In opposition to this view consider the words of Tagore written in 1941, the year of his death. He had been saddened almost unendurably by the outbreak of war between the British and the Nazis, yet out of this agony he wrote,

I had at one time believed that the springs of civilization would issue out of the heart of Europe. But today when I am about to quit the world that faith has gone bankrupt altogether. . . . As I look around I see the crumbling ruins of a proud civilization strewn like a vast heap of futility. And yet I shall not commit the grievous sin of losing faith in Man. I would rather look forward to the opening of a new chapter in his history after the cataclysm is over and the atmosphere rendered clean with the spirit of service and sacrifice. Perhaps that dawn will come from this horizon, from the East where the Sun rises. A day will come when unvanquished Man will retrace his path of conquest, despite all barriers, to win back his lost human heritage.[181]

5

The Self and Values

The self discovers and creates in all four worlds. It discovers a world of sun, moon, stars, mountains, plains, rivers, and lakes, and creates mythologies and sciences to account for their origins and operations. It discovers a world of earth, air, fire, water, plants, and animals, and creates dwellings, clothing, tools, and means of transportation. It discovers itself as the product of two human bodies, and forms families, clans, tribes, communities, states, and nations. It discovers a world of clay, stone, metal, and wood, and designs works of art. It discovers a world of joy and grief, satisfaction and frustration, and success and failure, and creates religion to explain, meliorate, celebrate, purge, and solve the mysteries of existence. Creativity is prized in all cultures. In the Hebrew myth of creation recorded in the first chapter of Genesis the refrain "God saw that it was good" is repeated seven times. "It" probably refers both to the act of creation and to the created entities: light, heaven, earth, plants, heavenly bodies, water creatures, earth creatures, human beings.

The human life is the pursuit of truth, beauty, goodness, and holiness. Scientists seek value-free facts. Artists seek beauty. Moralists seek goodness. Religionists seek holiness. But each human being is scientist-artist-moralist-religionist, and each human being decides consciously or unconsciously which has priority in his or her life.

Art and religion constitute the world of human enrichment. Human existence is possible without literature, music, dance, sculpture, and painting, and also without religious faith, ritual, sacrament, and ceremony, but such a life would be an impoverished one. Susanne K. Langer, noting "the striking indifference of the uneducated masses to artistic values," comments, "In past ages, these masses had no access to great works of art; music and painting and even books were the pleasures of the wealthy; it could be assumed that the poor and vulgar would enjoy art if they could have it. But now, since everybody can read, visit museums, and hear great music at least over the radio, the judgment of the masses on these things has become a reality, and has made it quite obvious that great art is not a direct sensuous pleasure."[1] Langer's claim that "the poor and the vulgar" are deficient in appreciation of aesthetic values because they do not go to orchestra concerts, visit art galleries, and read Dante and Shakespeare is not fair to those who appreciate folk music, village dancing, and primitive art. The case of religion is more complicated, since the word religion has many different denotations, such as participation in acts of formal corporate worship, animism, magical practices, appreciative attitudes toward the natural world, membership in an institution celebrating specific values, morality tinged with emotion.

Art and religion are created to overcome loneliness, to add values, to communicate feelings, to produce pleasure, to reduce fears, to relieve tension, to establish wholeness, to solve a wide variety of problems. But, as is always the case in human affairs, new problems are created in solving old ones. One of the tasks of the philosopher is to examine the problems solved and the problems created in the creative process.

A flaw in the four six-week East-West Philosophers' Conferences at the University of Hawaii in 1939, 1949, 1959, and 1964 was that only one paper was presented on art. This probably indicates that the organizers of the conferences were thinking of philosphy in a Western sense even while planning the conferences, that is, a philosophy focused on science and logic rather than on the love of nature and the appreciation of art. Van Meter Ames, the author of that one paper—"Aesthetic Values in East and West"—began his remarks with the admission that "many Western philosophers have not taken art seriously."[2]

The Indian philosopher Mysore Hiriyanna explains that the neglect of the study in art among Indian philosophers stems from the belief that the pursuit of beauty in art cannot directly minister to the attainment of the final goal of life.[3] Chinese philosophers have much to say about art. Japanese philosophers do not—perhaps because they are too busy living art to talk about it.

The Nature of Values

There are three ways of talking about values: (1) "I like X" or "X has value for me," (2) "X has value" or "X possesses value," and (3) "X is a value." These three are the relational, the attributive, and the substantive.

Philosophers who concentrate on the relational nature of value maintain that values are dependent on both subject and object. Value judgments are expressions of the desires, the interests, and the preferences of a subject for an object. "X is valuable" means "X is valued." That in which no one is interested or to which every one is indifferent cannot be a value. Value is identical with preference. Of course that which no one prefers under any circumstances cannot be valuable to anyone, but there is something peculiar about a theory of value that excludes the possibility of an object, action, or idea that one ought to value even though at the present time it is valued by no one. Is it unreasonable to contend that even though persons do not like the music of Beethoven they ought to like it? Is it meaningless to say during a time when no one likes Beethoven's music that it still is good music? Can something that is not yet a reality be valuable, such as a world government? Such questions are raised by those who believe that the relational theory of value is inadequate.

Those philosophers who assume that the only proper form in which to express values is "X has value" regard value as an attribute or quality. Values for them are independent of subjects. An object may be valuable even though no one values it. Philosophers who hold to the objective theory of value are frustrated because there is no logical disproof of the subjectivist's contention. Hence, they must support their assumptions in nonrational ways. For example, G. E. Moore offers the following defense:

> "No one," says Prof. Sidgwick, "would consider it rational to aim at the production of beauty in external nature, apart from any possible contemplation of it by human beings." Well, I may say at once, that I, for one do consider this rational; and let us see if I cannot get any one to agree with me. Consider what this admission really means. It entitles us to put the following case. Let us imagine one world exceedingly beautiful. Imagine it as beautiful as you can; put into it whatever on this earth you most admire—mountains, rivers, the sea; trees, and sunsets, stars and moon. Imagine these all combined in the most exquisite proportions, so that no one thing jars against another, but each contributes to increase the beauty of the whole. And then imagine the ugliest world you can possibly conceive. Imagine it simply one heap of filth, containing everything that is most disgusting to us, for whatever reason, and the whole, as far as may be, without one redeeming feature. Such a pair of worlds we are entitled to compare: they fall within Prof. Sidgwick's meaning, and the comparison is highly relevant to it. The only thing we are not entitled to imagine is that any human being ever has or ever, by any possibility, can, live in either, can ever see and enjoy the beauty of the one or hate the foulness of the other. Well, even so, supposing them quite apart from any possible contemplation by human beings; still, is it irrational to hold that it is better that the beautiful world should exist, than the one which is ugly? Would it not be well, in any case to do what we could to produce it rather than the other? Certainly I cannot help thinking that it would; and I hope that some may agree with me in this extreme instance.[4]

C. E. M. Joad in less elegant fashion wrote, "Yet, although it [the subjective theory] cannot be disproved, I maintain that it fails to make provision for the undoubted fact that we all of us do think that it is better that an uncontemplated Madonna should exist than an uncontemplated cesspool."[5] Those who hold that value is a quality would agree that this is not an irrational belief. Beauty is that which is, regardless of the fact that it may be in a world completely unperceived and unperceivable. Of course those who believe that values can be values only when valued contend that it is irrational to affirm that an unperceived and unperceivable thing is beautiful.

Still other philosophers believe that one is not talking about values unless one is able to say "X is a value." The other two forms, "I like X" and "X has value," are ways of talking about things that are valued or things that are valuable, but not about values. These forms refer to instrumental or extrinsic values, but such are values only because they are means to the attainment of true values, intrinsic values. Value is the name we give to those abstractions that are the norms of evaluation. Values are the universals that particulars instance—to state this Platonic view Platonically. A moral act is good when it is an instance of Good; a painting is beautiful because it reflects Beauty; an equation is true if it participates in Truth. Goodness, Beauty, and Truth—not acts, paintings, and equations—are correctly called values. Values are valuable in and for themselves. They are finalities in relation to which anything can be said to be valuable. No reasons can be given why they are values. They are the presuppositions of all evaluation. For example, it would be absurd to say that happiness is a value because people feel better when they are happy, or because it fosters better human relationships, or because it increases the flow of gastric juices. Happiness is a value, and that is all that can be said about it. That desirable activities flow from happiness is irrelevant to the value status of happiness itself. Value is conceived by these philosophers to be a unique, objective, independent entity, rather than a dependent quality or relation. The most telling charge that those who hold the narrower views of the nature of value, that value is a relation or a quality, can bring against the substantive view is the charge of hypostatization. However, the substantivists have one undeniable advantage over their opponents, namely, any ultimate delineation of the nature of value is concerned only with intrinsic value, since all instrumental values are means to the attainment of intrinsic values.

The substantive theory of value opens another interesting controversial issue about the nature of value. According to the substantive theory the value components of valued acts and objects cannot be analyzed. One cannot identify what it is in a situation that makes the situation valued. But can value be broken down into its component parts? Can one discover the essence of value?

Since we have already mentioned that for some thinkers value is unanalyzable, and therefore indefinable, let us consider this view first. G. E. Moore is an outstanding exponent of this position. "If I am asked 'What is good?'" says Moore, "my answer is that good is good, and that is the end of the matter. Or if I am asked 'How is good to be defined?' my answer is that it cannot be defined, and that is all I have to say about it."[6] Good or value is a simple notion, just as yellow is a simple notion. There can be no proposition about good that analyzes it into its parts, for it has no parts. Good may be defined with an "arbitrary verbal definition," that is, according to a use to which one may wish to put the word, or good may be defined with a "verbal definition proper," that is, according to the way most English-speaking people use the word, but good is indefinable in a real sense, for good "is not composed of any parts, which we can substitute for it in our minds when we are thinking of it."[7] Good and yellow are notions "out of which definitions are composed and with which the power of further defining ceases."[8] But many philosophers are not satisfied with such an explanation of the nature of value. They attempt to analyze value into elements such as pleasure, interest, usefulness, fitness, normativeness, and requiredness.

One of the most obvious answers to the question is that anything is valuable in so far as it causes pleasure. This is the hedonic theory of value. Jeremy Bentham (1748–1832) defined this theory as follows: "By utility is meant that property in any object, whereby it tends to produce benefit, advantage, pleasure, good, or happiness, (all this in the present case comes to the same thing) or (what comes again to the same thing) to prevent the happening of mischief, pain, evil, or unhappiness to the party whose interest is considered: if that party be the community in general, then the happiness of the community; if a particular individual, then the happiness of that individual."[9] This definition may seem broad and loose, but that would be the nature of any definition offered to explain all value experiences by one psychological state. Bentham later wrote that even ascetics are seeking pleasure: if any one were to ask ascetics why they punish themselves they would reply,

> You are to know, that for every grain of pain it costs us now, we are to have a hundred grains of pleasure by and by. The case is, that God loves to see us torment ourselves at present: indeed he has as good as told us so. But this is done only to try us, in order just to see how we should behave: which it is plain he could not know, without making the experiment. Now then, from the satisfaction it gives him to see us make ourselves as unhappy as we can make ourselves in this present life, we have a sure proof of the satisfaction it will give him to make us as happy as he can make us in a life to come.[10]

This quotation illustrates the generalizations that frequently mark the writings of the hedonists. The hedonistic principle that the pleasure state is the only case of a thing liked, that all human action is directed to the pursuit of pleasure, is often supported by this type of reasoning.

Those who find hedonism inadequate call attention to the fact that even if it is granted that pleasure always accompanies the value experience, it does not follow that all acts are done solely for the sake of pleasure. One might point out that breathing accompanies all value experiences, but no one would claim that humans are solely motivated by the desire for the activity of breathing. Is it nonsense to affirm that a person may derive pleasure from an experience that is not good? In other words, a standard of value is required by which acts and objects that may give pleasure can be evaluated with reference to another criterion. This is a charge to be brought against any theory of value that assumes that "I value X" is equivalent to "X is valuable."

A third theory of value—the interest theory—has been described as the twentieth-century counterpart to nineteenth-century hedonism. The theory is associated with Ralph Barton Perry and his epoch-making book, *General Theory of Value,* in which he, after identifying interest as a state, act, attitude, or disposition of favor or disfavor, defined value as "the peculiar relation between any interest and its object, or that special character of an object which consists in the fact that interest is taken in it."[11] Perry's theory has bothered many, because for him the object of an interest is a value, not the satisfaction of the interest in the object. Many find it strange that the attainment or the lack of attainment of the object of interest has nothing to do with value. Yet on this issue Perry clearly stated, "Attainability and security in and of themselves have nothing to do with value."[12] This would mean that unrequited love is no less valuable than love that wins the object of its affection. According to this theory there are no incorrect or mistaken interests or erroneous judgments of value. Perry cannot hold that there are certain objects that ought to be chosen. With the interest theory one cannot differentiate between the value of interest in burglary and of interest in charitable acts. The fact is, say the critics of the interest theory, a subject's interest in an object is neither necessary nor sufficient for the object to be valued. But on the credit side, this theory gives human beings the important opportunity to create new values, and thereby increase the totality of value in the universe:

> The silence of the desert is without value, until some wanderer finds it lonely and terrifying; the cataract, until some human sensibility finds it sublime, or until it is harnessed to satisfy human needs. Natural substances or the by-product of manufacture are without value until a use is found for them, whereupon their value may increase to any degree of preciousness according to the eagerness with which they are coveted. There is no entity that can be named that does not, in the very naming of it, take on a certain value through the fact that it is selected by the cognitive purpose of some interested mind. As interests grow and expand, multiplying in number and extending their radius through experience and imagination, the store of cosmic values is enriched and diversified.[13]

Value is also expressed in such verbal forms as "valuable for" and "good for." This is the fitness or usefulness theory of value. Those who hold this view insist that the value situation has three factors: (1) the object of value, (2) the subject for whom it is valuable, and (3) the end or purpose with reference to which it is valuable. For example, a pocket knife well adapted for cutting wood is a good knife. As George Herbert Palmer has written,

> When is it a good knife? Why, a knife is made for something, for cutting. Whenever a knife slides evenly through a piece of wood, unimpeded by anything in its own structure, and with a minimum of effort on the part of him

> who steers it, when there is no disposition of its edge to bend or break, but only to do its appointed work effectively, then we know that a good knife is at work. Or, looking at the matter from another point of view, whenever the handle of the knife neatly fits the hand, following its lines and presenting no obstruction, so that it is a pleasure to use it, we may say that in these respects also the knife is a good knife. . . . Its goodness always has reference to something outside itself, and is measured by its performance of an external task.[14]

Sometimes persons designate fitness in value expressions, but in so doing they are expressing an instrumental value, not an intrinsic value, the value we are seeking to define. Furthermore, the object of value might be useful for some purpose that is not good at all; it might be used to achieve an evil end; for example, the knife might be used as an instrument of murder. For these reasons the fitness theory alone cannot be accepted as an adequate key to the essence of value.

A fifth theory of value—the typical theory—has the merit of attempting to define the nature of intrinsic value. The verbal expression of this theory is "good of its kind." An act or an object is said to be good when it embodies all that could be expected for the most complete representation of the sort of thing it is. A good pumpkin is one that sets forth the full pumpkin nature, and a good whipping is a whipping that leaves nothing to be desired! A good pumpkin need not be one that is good for making pumpkin pie, nor need a good whipping be one that compels the wayward child to behave in an approved manner in the future. Rather, as Palmer says, "what seemed to be intended was that all the functions constituting the things talked about were present in these instances and hard at work, mutually assisting one another, and joining to make up such a rounded whole that from it nothing was omitted which possibly might render its organic wholeness complete."[15]

But this theory is too broad. Everything is a good instance of something. A horrible example of humanity may be one of the best examples of imbecility, or inebriety, or schizophrenia. Physicians speak of a good case of pneumonia or tuberculosis. A standard of values is needed by which acts and objects are evaluated. The typical theory might also be called the normative theory. For every object and every act there are certain rules or principles by which its value can be measured. The moralist might appeal to the Ten Commandments, or the Sermon on the Mount, or the Noble Eight-Fold Path, or the Constitution of the United States, or natural law. The artist appeals to principles of versification, harmony, rhythm, and balance. While admitting that one cannot imagine all artists and all moralists would ever agree on the norms of beauty and goodness, there must be some standards, say the supporters of this theory, by which Shakespeare is evaluated as a greater poet than Edgar A. Guest, Ludwig van Beethoven as a better musician than Stephen Foster, Gandhi as a man of higher morality than Caligula.

What is the essence of value—is it pleasure, or interest, or usefulness, or normativeness? Or is value undefinable and unanalyzable? Must an adequate theory of value include elements from all of these theories? At least it is certain that no one of these five theories, or any of the other theories mentioned, has been universally accepted.

Another problem of the nature of values is the locus or place of value. Is value located in the valuing subject, in the valued object, or in the relation of subject and object? Do silver and gold possess value in themselves, or do they have value because humans desire them? Is the Mona Lisa good art independent of any judgment of its art value? Is truth-telling right in itself, or is it right because we in our civilization call it right? Is love of others right because God demands it, or does God demand it because it is right? According to the objective theory of the locus of value, things, actions, and ideas are valuable whether or not they are valued by someone. According to the subjective theory things, actions, and ideas are valuable only when they are valued by someone. Thus one who holds to the objective theory of value believes that the statement "X is valuable even though no one values it" is a meaningful statement; whereas advocates of the subjective theory contend that such a statement can be neither true nor false—it is self-contradictory. Valuable for the objectivist means "ought to be valued," valuable for the subjectivist means "is valued."

The subjectivist believes that the objective theory of value is inadequate in that it does not do justice to the relative character of all evaluations. The objectivist counters that gold is more valuable than bread. Little gold will buy much bread. However, the subjectivist adds that a person lost in the desert would gladly trade gold for a crust of bread and a drink of water. Evaluations are made with reference to the needs and desires of the subject. There are some occasions in which normal evaluations do not apply. Jacob took advantage of Esau on such an occasion.[16] Values, says the subjectivist, are nothing but preferences of a subject. One person prefers brown bread, port, jazz, and winter, while another prefers white bread, sherry, classical music, and summer. The subjectivity of individual evaluations is expressed in the aphorism, "One man's meat is another man's poison." As is usual with proverbs, there is another proverb that expresses the other point of view: "What is sauce for the goose is sauce for the gander." The subjectivist also points out that the different evaluations of groups are evidences of the subjectivity of values. Chinese music is din to Western ears. Slavery was defended by moralists two hundred years ago. The fashions of twenty years ago seem odd today. Subjectivity thus becomes a reason for relativism—the position that all valuations are relative to local times, places, and cultures.

Some philosophers thinks it is a misleading simplification to assert that values are located solely in the object or solely in the subject. Value is a total relationship between a valued object and a valuing subject. C. J. Ducasse, for example, defines beauty as "that property of an object which consists in capacity of the object to cause pleasure in a subject who contemplates it. Beauty, that is to say, is a character of some objects, but a relational character of them—the character, namely, that consists in their having to certain minds (subjects) the relation just described. The question whether beauty is objective or subjective is thus exactly parallel logically with the question whether poisonousness is objective or subjective."[17] The subjectivist would admit that an object may be said to be the locus of value in the sense that it is an object that *is* preferred by a subject, but not that an object *ought* to be preferred by a subject. The objectivist would admit that a subject may be said to be the locus of value in that there can be no relationship without a subject. The objectivist is mainly anxious to deny that the subject's preferences create value. From the objective point of view value is that aspect of a thing that arouses a preference in a subject. From the subjective point of view value is the preference of a subject for an object. The objectivist and the subjectivist are wrong only when each claims that his point of view is the only correct point of view, say these middle-of-the-roaders. Stephen C. Pepper, pointing out that in beauty "conditions both of an impersonal and a personal nature must be fulfilled,"[18] adds that the view may be called *contextualism*.

Principles for the Classification of Values

Philosophers make an important contribution to the understanding of values by suggesting how values may be classified. Twelve principles have been offered for value classification.

One is the classification of values according to subscribership to the value. Who holds it to be a value? Values may be subscribed to by either individual persons or by groups. Much of what is meant by individuality is the value to which a person subscribes. Some of the values classified according to the groups that support them are familial values, professional values, vocational values, community values, and national values. A classic example of difference in value subscribership is the antithesis between the values commonly held by property owners and by wage earners as stated by the sixth congress of the Communist International in 1928:

> The ultimate aim of the Communist International is to replace world capitalist economy by a world system of Communism. . . . A Communist society will abolish the class division of society, i.e., simultaneously with the abolition of anarchy in production, it will abolish all forms of exploitation and oppression of man by man. . . . The abolition of private property and the disappearance of classes will do away with the exploitation of man by man. Work will cease to be toiling for the benefit of a class enemy; instead of being merely a means of livelihood it will become a necessity of life: want and economic inequality, the misery of enslaved classes, and a wretched standard of

> life generally will disappear; the hierarchy created in the division of labour system will be abolished together with the antagonism between mental and manual labour; and the last vestige of the social inequality of the sexes will be removed.[19]

National axiological stereotypes are well known: the English have no sense of humor, Germans are philosophical, the French are great lovers, Indians are mystics, Americans value only money, Japanese are overly polite, Chinese are superstitious. A reliable way to compare the value preferences of peoples of various nations is difficult to formulate.

An American sociologist, Thomas M. Kanto, has compared the annual per capita expenditure of the central governments of several Western nations in support of what he calls "High Culture."[20] He discovered the following amounts:

Austria	$11.40
West Germany	8.30
France	1.50
Italy	1.24
Netherlands	.80
United Kingdom	.40
United States of America	.10

Kanto adds that this gloomy picture of government support of "high culture" in the United States must be balanced by the fact that "the American culture market remains by far the largest in the world. Never before in history has a continental civilization of hundreds of millions of people engaged so massively in the consumption of High Culture. The hundreds of millions of classical records, library check-outs, concert, opera, ballet and theater tickets, museum admissions, musical instruments, and books sold annually testify to the continued vigor of High Culture in America."[21]

Values can also be classified according to the objects to which the value applies. Thing values are desirable features of inert objects. For example, gems are classified according to purity, brilliance, hardness, refraction, luster, and color. Automobiles are valued according to speed, style, gas consumption, resale value, and horsepower. Environmental values refer to desirable features of the natural world, such as beauty of the landscape, fertility of the soil, and purity of the water. Personal values are prized aspects of individual persons, such as beauty, bravery, intelligence, good temper, and sense of humor. Group values are the desirable relationships between the individual and the group, such as mutual trust, solidarity, and respect. Societal values are the valued arrangements of the society, including equality before the law, economic justice, provision for the infirm and the elderly, and fair taxation.

A third classification refers to the nature of the value itself. What is the nature of the benefit it brings? Some things are valued because they are enjoyed for their own sakes; others are valued because they are a means of avoiding what one does not value. The former can be called positive values; the latter are negative values. Candy is enjoyed because its flavor is pleasurable. Ether and morphine are not pleasant, yet their use makes possible surgery without pain. The ancient Epicureans were so troubled by the pains and anxieties that plague mankind that they conceived of pleasure itself as freedom from pain in the body and trouble in the mind. Modern hedonists are more inclined to believe that the absence of pain is not the same as the presence of pleasure. There does seem to be a difference between not being unhappy and being happy. Perhaps the truth is that the neutral state of the Epicureans—*ataraxía*—would not be counted as happiness by modern hedonists.

Values can also be classified according to whether the benefit they yield is an activity or a product. Aristotle wrote that "a certain difference is found among ends; some are activities, others are products apart from the activities which produce them."[22] The goal of winning a race may be called an activity as end; the prize given for winning is the product as end. In the next sentence Aristotle says, "Where there are ends apart from the actions, it is the nature of the products to be better than the activities." However, much concern for the product is not always approved. The person who does a job for the love of doing a good job will be praised more than the person who does a job for the love of the money he receives at the completion of the job. William Lyon Phelps of Yale University used to say, "If Yale did not pay me for teaching, I'd pay Yale for the privilege of teaching." There are still people in the world who regard their vocation as a service to others, rather than as merely a means of earning a living. James Ramsay Ullman closes his volume on mountaineering, *High Conquest,* with this explanation of why men climb mountains: "It is not the summit that matters, but the fight for the summit; not the victory, but the game itself."[23] Those who regard life as a great adventure are more likely to value the activity than the products of the activity.

The benefit at issue may also be classified according to a wide variety of classes: material values: warm clothing, dry shelter, good food; physical values: health, restful sleep, satisfying sex experiences; economic values: financial security, productiveness; moral values: honesty, sense of fair play, charitableness; social values: courtesy, friendliness, willingness to forgive; psychological values: peace of mind, self-esteem, joy in living; political values: justice, freedom, equality before the law; vocational values: sense of fulfillment in one's work, success, professional recognition; intellectual values: intelligence, clarity, logical precision; aesthetic values: beauty, balance, symmetry, harmony; religious values: the sacred, piety, at-homeness in the universe, salvation. Scaling these values according to height or preference constitutes a philosophy of life.

A fourth classification is according to who benefits. Some values are egocentered, such as success, comfort, privacy; others are oriented to others, such as the immediate family, the joint family, an organization that one joins, the community, the profession to which one belongs, the nation, the family of nations, the next generation, humankind at large.

A fifth classification is according to the intensity of the value. How great is the benefit? How strong is the urge to seek and possess the value? Moralists, artists, and religious leaders often lament that the so-called higher values have the lowest psychological appeal. Great books of devotion like Augustine's *Confessions* and Thomas à Kempis's *The Imitation of Christ* are filled with lamentations that inordinate affections and earthly desires intrude upon the mystic's devotions. The Greek and Roman stoics advised their followers to live vigorously, assume full citizenship responsibilities, and endure the hardships of life without complaint. "Be like the promontory against which the waves continually break, but it stands firm and tames the fury of the water around it," said Marcus Aurelius.[24] The epicureans, on the other hand, recommended a life of peaceful calm attained by avoiding all that might disturb one's inner poise. Epicurus said, "The most unalloyed source of protection from men, which is secured to some extent by a certain force of expulsion, is in fact the immunity which results from a quiet life and the retirement from the world."[25]

A sixth manner of classifying values is according to the duration of the benefit. A choice is sometimes made between a short intense satisfaction and a long mild satisfaction. Should an ice cream cone be eaten slowly to make the pleasure last as long as possible, or should it be eaten quickly in order to have the most intense pleasure? According to Aristotle a good man "would prefer a short period of intense pleasure to a long one of mild enjoyment, a twelve-month of noble life to many years of humdrum existence, and one great and noble action to many trivial ones."[26] Rousseau said that "life is not breath but action, the use of our senses, our mind, our faculties, every part of ourselves which makes us conscious of our being. Life consists less in length of days than in the keen sense of living."[27] John G. Neihardt agreed:

> Let me live out my years in heat of blood!
> . . . .
> Give me high noon—and let it then be night!
> Thus would I go.[28]

But Robert Browning preferred a longer, milder life:

> Grow old along with me
> The best is yet to be,
> The last of life, for which the first was made.[29]

Values may also be classified according to the propinquity of the benefit. Will the desired results appear immediately, or are the returns in the distant future? The choice is often between eating or keeping one's cake. Aesop's fable of the grasshopper and the ant addresses this theme. Should one spend money for present enjoyments or save for retirement years? Augustine confessed that as a young man he resolved the problem of present pleasures and future morality by praying "Grant me chastity and continency, but not yet."[30] Some religions dwell on the choice between enjoyments of the mortal state and the anticipated enjoyments of the postmortal state.

An eighth classification is based on the purity of the value. Is the benefit one that is mixed with disvalue, or is it relatively free from disvalue? Every value has a price tag. There appear to be few bargains. Wealth and position bring worries, responsibilities, and cares that do not disturb the poor and obscure person. "Uneasy lies the head that wears a crown."[31] Epicurus wrote, "It is better to be free lying upon a pallet, than to have a golden couch and a rich table and be full of trouble. . . . I spit upon luxurious pleasures not for their own sake, but because of the inconveniences that follow them."[32]

A ninth way of classifying values is according to their attainability. How certain is the realization of the expected benefit? Walter Lippmann in *A Preface to Morals*[33] argued that a common cause of human unhappiness is aspiring for that which cannot be attained. He advised limiting one's desires to what one will attain. The flaw in the advice is that one cannot know in advance what is attainable. Some nations, for example, Russia and India, break down their aspirations into five year plans on the assumption that vehicles hitched to stars ought to be equipped with odometers to measure the progress toward goals.

Another classification is on the basis of the sharability or nonsharability of the benefits. Spinoza, contending that the goods of life can be divided into those that can and those that cannot be shared with other people, pled for the pursuit of the sharable goods inasmuch as the attainment of these does not prevent others from similar attainment. A determination to learn all that can be known about Homer does not in any manner prevent another person from also learning about Homer. But a desire to collect Chippendale furniture does conflict with another's similar desire. David Grayson in his delightful book *Great Possessions* recounts his forages into his neighbor's posted fields to purloin pleasant sights, fragrant odors, and the songs of birds—fruits of the fields that the legal owner of the land had never harvested. Grayson observes that "real possession is not a thing of inheritance or of documents, but of the spirit."[34]

An eleventh means for classifying values is the distinction between intrinsic values and extrinsic values. Some acts are valuable in themselves; others are valuable because they are instrumental for the attainment of intrinsic values. One may drink a cooling beverage because one enjoys its flavor, or because one seeks to overcome drowsiness, to quench thirst, or to alleviate a headache. Although the distinction between intrinsic values and extrinsic values is often confused, some are quite clearly one or the other; for example, the extrinsic value of money is far greater than its intrinsic value. A serious problem arose in England when the copper in the penny became worth more than the purchasing power of the coin. The value of music is largely intrinsic, although it also aids digestion, performs a catharsis of the emotions, serves as background for television programs, promotes religious responses, and aids in psychiatric therapy. Plato distinguished intrinsic goods, extrinsic goods, and those that are both intrinsic and extrinsic: "For tell me—do you think that there is a kind of good which we should be glad to have for its own sake alone, not because we desire what comes from it? . . . And again one kind that we love both for its own sake and for what comes from it? . . . And do you see a third kind of good which athletic sports belong to, and to be cured by treatment when sick, and the art of healing, and the other ways of making money?"[35] Aristotle defined the highest value of life in terms of its intrinsic characteristics: "If, then, there is some end of the things we do, which we desire for its own sake (everything else being desired for the sake of this,) and if we do not choose everything for the sake of something else (for at that rate the process would go on to infinity, so that our desire would be empty and vain,) clearly this must be the good and the chief good."[36] Wealth, he added, is regarded by many as the goal of their lives, but they make a grave error in identifying a means as an end, for wealth "is merely useful and for the sake of something else."[37]

The twelfth classification has to do with fruitfulness. Will the value produce other values? Some values mushroom into other values. A chance meeting, a smile, or a remark overheard have changed the course of personal and, in some cases, national history. Abraham Lincoln saw a slave sold from the auction block and resolved he would some day strike a blow at the slave trade. The Roman Empire became Christian because Emperor Constantine thought he saw a sign in the clouds. Augustine's life was changed by overhearing a child singing a song. But other events are sterile—no values stem from them. The same event may be sterile for one person and fruitful for another. Others witnessed the selling of slaves, heard children singing, and saw signs in the heavens, but for them these led to no significant values.

6

The Self in the Aesthetic World

Both the word *aesthetics* and the branch of philosophy designated by that word were introduced by Alexander Baumgarten (1714–1762), a minor German rationalistic philosopher. He reasoned that since there are three basic values—the true, the good, and the beautiful—and since there are three faculties of the soul corresponding to these values—reasoning, willing, and feeling—there must be three disciplines. Logic is the science of reasoning, and ethics is the science of willing, so there must be a science of feeling. He chose the Greek term *aisthētikós* (perceptible) for this science. The choice was not a happy one. Baumgarten believed that sensation is the locus of beauty. While this is true for ordinary sense experiences like the taste of an apple, the sound of bird calls, and the color of flowers, it is not true for art objects. The beauty of a painting or a concerto is more than sensed sight and sound. Susanne K. Langer observed that "great art is not a direct sensuous pleasure." She added, "There is a strong tendency today to treat art as a significant phenomenon rather than as a pleasurable experience, a gratification of the senses."[1] The term *aesthetics* has continued to be used by Western philosophers to designate the study of values associated with beauty. Beauty is assigned as a value to both nature and art, that is, to both natural objects and art objects. They are said either to possess aesthetic values, according to the objective theory of value, or to possess the potentiality to arouse aesthetic values, according to the subjective theory of value. Naturally beautiful objects are discovered. Artificially beautiful objects are created. The latter are created by value-perceiving beings as a means of self-expression and as a means of communication with other value-perceiving beings. This guarded language leaves open the question whether lower animals, birds, and insects produce art forms, since art in this treatment is limited to the works of human beings.

The Nature of Aesthetics

Art is the human language of aesthetic values. Melvin Rader writes, "Art is thus fundamental to the whole enterprise of living as a means of self-expression, communication, and creation."[2] This description may be misleading, suggesting that art has three separable functions. Art might better be described as expression-communication-creation, that is, as creative activity that expresses the artist's attitudes, emotions, values, thoughts, ideals, tastes, desires, hopes, faith, and prejudices in a manner that appeals to, communicates with, stimulates, arouses, satisfies, and impresses other people.

Art criticism is judgment of a work of art. The critic decides whether the work—a painting, a sculpture, a play, a building, a poem, a musical composition, a flower arrangement—is good or bad as art. Terms such as *beautiful*, *integrative*, *realistic*, *formal*, *romantic*, and *impressionistic* are the tools of art criticism. The critic judges art in three contexts: (1) Does the work of art appear to express what the artist had in mind? (2) What is the impact of the work of art on the viewing public? (3) Has the artist shown skill, technique, creativity, mastery, and freshness in use of materials?

Aesthetics considers the language about aesthetic values, what is meant by *beauty, truthful, unified, impressionistic,* and so on when applied to art objects by artists, by art critics, and by the viewing public. This language may be used to discuss the aesthetic values of nature and natural objects, or the aesthetic values of art objects. There is no special term for the former, but the latter is known as philosophy of art. Aesthetics, like any branch of philosophy, is an effort to attain wisdom or understanding; in this case the area in which understanding is sought is the world of beauty. Aesthetics is not designed to increase one's feeling for beauty or appreciation of art. If such a result occurs, it is entirely accidental. Aesthetics, according to DeWitt H. Parker, "is an effort to obtain in a clear general idea of beautiful objects, our judgments upon them, and the motives underlying the acts which create them—to raise the aesthetic life, otherwise a matter of instinct and feeling, to the level of intelligence, of understanding."[3]

Aestheticians appear to enjoy self-flagellation. For example, Clive Bell began his important work *Art* with these words: "It is improbable that more nonsense has been written about aesthetics than about anything else: the literature of the subject is not large enough for that. It is certain, however, that about no subject with which I am acquainted has so little been said that is all to the purpose."[4] The article on aesthetics in *Philosophy—A to Z* begins, "Hardly any other philosophical discipline rests upon such uncertain presuppositions as aesthetics does. Like a weathercock 'it is turned sharply about by every philosophical, cultural, and scientific-theoretical gust of wind.'"[5]

The chief question of aesthetics or, more sharply, of philosophy of art is "What is art?" The answers given fall into three classes: imitation, form, and expression.

Art as imitation has had a long career in Western culture. It survives in the question often asked by visitors to art galleries: "What is it supposed to represent?" Those who attend a symphony concert may be especially pleased to recognize a thunderstorm, a battle, a rippling brook, or a clash of human emotions in the music. In the West the theory of art as imitation stems chiefly from Plato. According to his analysis in *The Republic,* there are three forms of objects. His example is a bed. "Here are three different beds: one is the nature of things, bedhood, which we would say God made. . . . And one that the carpenter made. . . . And one that the painter made."[6] There is one and only one Form of bedhood: "God, then, whether it was his will, or whether some necessity was upon him not to complete more than one in the nature of things, at any rate God made one only, that very Bed which a bed really is; two or more such were not made by God and never shall be, world without end."[7] The carpenter is not a maker of the Bed, but of a bed. He makes many beds, and each bed is an imitation of the Bed. The painter and the poet likewise make beds, but theirs are imitations of the imitation of the Bed. Painters and poets are imitators "in the third generation from nature."[8] They are crafters of appearances. Aristotle would say that their "bed" does not function as a bed. One cannot sleep on the bed portrayed in Van Gogh's "The Artist's Room in Arles."

According to Plato: "The imitative art is a long way from truth, and, as it seems, that is why it reproduces everything, because it touches only a part of each, and even that an image."[9] Artists, poets, and musicians, as copyists, never get to reality and never reach the truth: "We may take it, then, that all the poetic company from Homer onward are imitators of images of virtue and whatever they put in their poems, but do not lay hold of truth. Indeed, as we said just now, the painter will fashion an apparent cobbler, although he knows nothing of cobbling himself, nor do his viewers, who judge from the colours and shapes. . . . The maker of the image, the imitator, as we say, knows nothing of the real thing, but only the appearance."[10] "The imitative art is an inferior uniting with an inferior and breeding inferior offspring."[11] Therefore, concluded Plato, with the exception of "hymns to the gods and encomiums of the good,"[12] all imitative arts must be banished from the ideal state. Plato, perhaps in defense of his own consummate aesthetic skills, added, "But let it be said plainly that if imitation and poetry made to please can give some good reason why she ought to be in a well-ordered city, we should be glad indeed to receive her back home, since we are quite conscious of her enchantment for us. Yet to betray the truth as we see it would be very wrong."[13]

A second answer to the question "What is art?" is "Form." Clive Bell, writing in 1913, asked what quality do all works of visual art have in common:

> Whatever it will be, no doubt it is often found in company with other qualities; but they are adventitious—it is essential. There must be some one quality without which a work of art cannot exist; possessing which, in the least

> degree, no work is altogether worthless. What is this quality? What quality is shared by all objects that provoke our aesthetic emotions? What quality is common to St. Sophia, the windows at Chartres, Mexican sculpture, a Persian bowl, Chinese carpets, Gioto's frescoes at Padua, and the masterpieces of Poussin, Piero della Francesca, and Cézanne?

He answered at once, "Only one answer seems possible—significant form. In each, lines and colours and relations of forms, stir our aesthetic emotions. These relations and combinations of lines and colours, these aesthetically moving forms, I call 'Significant Form;' and 'Significant Form' is the one quality common to all works of visual art."[14]

Other aestheticians, such as L. A. Reid, Roger Fry, Ben Shahn, and Susanne Langer, extended the scope of this description to all art forms. But DeWitt H. Parker was the Western philosopher of art who fully and carefully analyzed what is meant by aesthetic form. In *The Analysis of Art*[15] he differentiated six general principles or characteristics of aesthetic form: (1) organic unity, (2) theme, (3) thematic variation, (4) balance, (5) evolution, and (6) hierarchy. The principle of organic unity or unity in variety means that every element in a work of art is necessary, all necessary elements are present, and no elements not necessary are present. The unity is threefold: the materials are unified, the work is an expression of the whole being of the artist, and the enjoyment of the work confers a wholeness upon the spectator. The principle of the theme is that "there is some one (or there may be several) preeminent shape, color, line, melodic pattern or meaning, in which is concentrated the characteristic value of the whole."[16] The theme is signified by such terms as theme in music, line in architecture and sculpture, inflection in poetry, design in carpets, and plot in novels. According to the principle of thematic variation the theme must be elaborated and embroidered. Parker identified four types of thematic variation: (1) recurrence of the theme; (2) transposition of the theme, as when a melody is transposed to another key or tempo; (3) alternation of the theme, such as at least two different transpositions of the theme; and (4) inversion of the theme, such as an inverted melody or a reversed curve. The fourth principle of aesthetic form is balance, the equality of opposing or contrasting elements. In a painting a threefold balance is sought: horizontal, perpendicular, and diagonal. The principle of evolution is "the unity of a process when the earlier parts determine the later, and all together create a total meaning."[17] The clearest examples are the introduction of characters, the stage of complication and climax, and the unraveling of the complication in a drama; but even in nontemporal arts, such as painting, there is an evolution in that the eye is led to focus first on one part of the work and then move to other parts. The principle of hierarchy is the species of organization of elements in the thematic variation, balance, and evolution. Parker writes, "Any quality whatever—large size, unusual brightness, richness of elaboration, central position, fullness of meaning—that attracts the attention to itself more strongly than the attention is attracted to other elements, creates relative dominance."[18]

Art as expression has been the dominant theory in the West for more than a century. Walter Pater concluded his "Essay on Style" (1888) with the statement that "all beauty is in the long run only fineness of truth, or what we call expression." According to Alan Tormey, "it would be only a slight exaggeration to claim that from the close of the eighteenth century to the present 'expression' and its cognates have dominated both aesthetic theorizing and the critical appraisal of the arts."[19] Melvin Rader wrote in 1935, "The most significant artists and critics of this century . . . reject all theories of mere imitation. They recognize, implicitly if not explicitly, that art expresses values and does not simply manipulate matter or reproduce facts."[20] Rader added, "When we say that art expresses values, we simply mean that it expresses the precise qualities that excite one's preferences—the enchanting features of a certain landscape, or the repugnant aspects of a certain personality. We might accordingly define an artistic value, actual or potential, as any quality in a work of art successfully designed to excite the appropriate liking or disliking."[21]

To define art as expression recognizes that art is not imitation and not form. But what does art express? Emotions? Illusion? Play? Isolation? Spirit? Will? Pleasure? Intuition? Empathy? Detachment? Cultural values? Religion? Mystical experience? Admitting that expression in art is "a difficult thing to become clear about," Melvin Rader and Bertram Jessup wrote,

> What then does art express? What does it mean? . . . Art is not expression merely of what the facts are in the world and human experience, but very much more; it is the expression of how the individual artist feels, and if his feelings are normal, how we too feel about facts and experience—how we feel about mountains, love, patriotism, sorrow, joy, adventure, death, a bowl of fruit, an assortment of bottles, an old woman's face. . . . Only when the subjective and objective poles are united and the value is embodied in a work of art, is the process complete.[22]

One of the important aspects of the definition of art as expression is that it relieves the aesthetician of the onus of defending every art object as beautiful. That which is expressive may be beautiful, but only in some metonymical sense. Rembrandt's self-portraits, Picasso's "Still Life," Munch's "Anxiety," Picasso's "Guernica," and Dali's "Apparition of Face and Fruit-dish on a Beach" are not beautiful in any customary use of that much-used term, but each is a powerful expression of values. The ideal of modern art, said Rader, is "to express values, not to imitate or passively respond."[23] Hence, "a work of art is not the record of a bare matter of fact, but the projection of the artist's inspiration, his emotions, preferences, or sense of values. . . . Thus art is the expression of values, isolated, unique, and ideal."[24]

Another advantage of defining art in terms of expression of values is that it resolves some of the conflicts between facts and values. "Thus we must look to art to express the values of science, just as, conversely, we must look to such sciences as esthetics and archeology to record the facts of art."[25] "Science describes facts; art expresses values. It would *seem,* therefore, that science has a collective and impersonal character that art lacks. Science deals with the more permanent, public, and universal elements of experience; art with the more fleeting, private, and particular elements. Science, it may be said, is social, art individual."[26] Rader qualified his statement (as if in anticipation of C. P. Snow's "two worlds") by pointing out what seems to be the case is not fully correct, since there is both a community of scientists who function in a world of description and a community of artists who function is a world of appreciation.

> Although art is obviously a mode of self-expression, it also is social. Just as there is a community of scientists engaged in the coöperative search for facts and using the language of description as their instrument, so there is a community of artists engaged in the coöperative search for values, and using the language of appreciations as *their* instrument. Just as scientific discourse is the language of descriptions, so artistic expression is the language of appreciations. Art is the expression of values, both individual and social.[27]

This brings the artist back into society.

Twentieth-century philosophers of art, who begin with a critical attitude toward Plato's moral judgments on artists, may find they agree with Plato. For example, Rader concluded his introduction to the first edition of his *A Modern Book of Esthetics* with these words:

> Thus art participates in the total joy of existence, and esthetics becomes the indispensable aide of social engineering. Any philosophy of art that hopes to stand must recognize the need of such an alliance. The esthetician must join with the scientist, the engineer, and the social idealist, igniting mind against mind in the conflict and coöperation of thinking. "Self-expression," as a concept, will then seem less important than "social collaboration." The self will no longer be conceived in separate abstractness, parted off from the rest of the world and thereby impoverished. The way for the artist to secure a great and profound self, it will be realized, is through the establishment of sympathetic relations to other things, and especially to other personalities.[28]

Art in Japanese Culture

Western aestheticians usually make passing references to beauty in nature, and then turn to what they obviously regard as the more important beauty, beauty in art. A typical example is the opening paragraph of the fifth edition of Rader's *A Modern Book of Esthetics:*

> A natural object, such as the song of the meadowlark, has esthetic qualities; and therefore esthetics, which is the theory of esthetic objects and experiences, applies both to natural objects and to works of art. In appreciating the latter, we respond not only to sensuous qualities and forms but also to technical, psychological, and cultural values—to the *human* expressiveness of the works. The writers represented in the present anthology have a great deal to say about natural objects, but their main emphasis is upon art; and it is art that I now wish to discuss.[29]

Clive Bell likewise made a distinction between beauty as applied to natural objects and beauty as applied to art objects:

> Does anyone feel the same kind of emotion for a butterfly or a flower that he feels for a cathedral or a picture? Surely, it is not what I call an aesthetic emotion that most of us feel, generally, for natural beauty. I shall suggest, later, that some people may, occasionally, see in nature what we see in art, and feel for her an aesthetic emotion; but I am satisfied that, as a rule, most people feel a very different kind of emotion for birds and flowers and the wings of butterflies from that which they feel for pictures, pots, temples and statues.[30]

The rationale for the difference, according to Bell, is that the function of art is to transport us "from the world of man's activity to a world of aesthetic exaltation. For a moment we are shut off from human interests; our anticipations and memories are arrested; we are lifted above the stream of life. The pure mathematician rapt in his studies knows a state of mind which I take to be similar, if not identical."[31] The representative element in a work of art is always "irrelevant" said Bell.[32] A painting of a peasant working in the fields may arouse in the spectator sympathies for the poor, but that cannot be the intent of the artist.

The distinction between nature and art, which seems so clear to Bell, may not be made by the Japanese. What would Bell say about the Japanese love of flower arrangements and the traditional links between the Japanese house and garden? Would he call the two famous gardens at Kyoto—the natural Tenryu-ji garden and the rock and sand Ryoan-ji garden—works of nature or works of art? Claude Chidamian says of the Japanese, "Nowhere on earth have men lived so close to nature." He adds that "nowhere else on earth has nature shown such bewildering variety and awesome majesty to capture the heart of man."[33] Chidamian asks with respect to natural beauty, "Is it any wonder that the Japanese have sought to hold fast to this never-ending source of inspiration, tried to picture its sublimity in their art, its simplicity in their flower arrangements, its vastness in their miniature potted trees?"[34]

An examination of the cultivation of dwarf potted trees called *bonsai* is an excellent avenue to understanding the aesthetics of the Japanese, a people whose "great genius lies in little things."[35] Bonsai culture renders nature almost indistinguishable from art. Chidamian writes,

> From gardens, fields, and mountains, from the wind-swept crags above the sea, plants for bonsai are carefully chosen. Pines, juniper, maple, and many more—naturally dwarfed plants gnarled and twisted by weather and privation—they are skillfully dug and their roots pruned and prepared for shallow pots scarcely large enough to hold them. Choosing the right containers for bonsai is as important as selecting the right plants.

He adds

> Once the plant and container have been chosen the bonsai is firmly potted, thoroughly watered, and carefully sheltered until it becomes reestablished. . . . Actually few of the trees or shrubs collected are so well shaped that they need not be trimmed and trained before they can make good bonsai. And it is this technique that makes bonsai culture an art. It is difficult to describe the skill and sensitivity of the master artisan as the plants come to life at his touch.[36]

The goal is to create an illusion of a little tree

> so perfectly proportioned in every leaf, twig, and branch, its roots and trunk so realistically gnarled and twisted that anyone who sees it will forget that it is only a miniature. . . . That's the magic of bonsai. Using the highest skills of the gardener, the eye of a painter, the touch of a sculptor, the bonsai maker perfectly recreates a scene from nature that can be held in the palm of one's hand. For bonsai are not simply potted plants to be appreciated for their beautiful foliage and flowers, but works of art as suggestive and appealing as sculpture, poetry, and painting.[37]

The idea of bonsai, like so much that is now referred to as typically Japanese, was borrowed from China. For centuries the Chinese had forced flowering trees and shrubs to bloom as part of the pageantry of the lunar new year, had used potted trees to decorate courtyards, and had piled stones and rocks to represent distant mountain scenery; but it was the Japanese who in probably the fourteenth century fused these ideas in order to turn their gardens into miniature mountains, rivers, and trees. Until the nineteenth century the dwarf trees were called *hachi-no-ki* (trees in pots), but the name was changed about one hundred years ago to distinguish these works of art from mere potted plants. The Japanese borrowed two Chinese characters—*p'en tsai* (planted in a shallow vessel)—that, according to Japanese pronunciation, became *bone sigh*.

Zen Buddhism and tea were imported from China to Japan in 1191 by Eisai, the founder of the Rinzai sect, the sect that uses the *koan* and sudden enlightenment. The Soto sect, which emphasizes meditation, spiritual discipline, and moral conduct, was founded by Dogen, the pupil of Eisai. During the Ashikaga period (1333–1573), a time of great enthusiasm for things Chinese, Rinzai and

Soto priests advised the shoguns as to which arts and art objects should be added to the Japanese court. Accordingly, in the words of Hugo Munsterberg, "Many elements of Japanese culture which today seem typically Japanese—flower arrangement, landscape gardening, the tea ceremony, *sumi-e* (ink painting), the cult of the subdued, the love of simplicity and understatement—were all borrowed from Chinese Zen during the Ashikaga period. Over the centuries, however, they have become such an integral part of Japanese culture that they are no longer felt to be foreign or, for that matter, even particularly Zen."[38]

Sen-no-Rikyu (1521–1591), the creator of the classical tea ritual (*cha-no-yu*), held that the basic principles of the ceremony are harmony, reverence, purity, and silence. Zen introduced into painting a rough spontaneity that is manifested in *sumi-e suiboku* (water and ink style), in *p'o-mo* (spashed ink style), and in the use of a brush made of straw or shredded bamboo rather than the conventional hair brush. The seventeen-syllable poem known as *haiku* is also a Zen development.

Zen introduced and helped develop in Japan a distinct way of creating and appreciating a work of art. D. T. Suzuki, in discussing a painting of a hibiscus, wrote,

> The secret is to become the plant itself. But how can a human being turn himself into a plant? Inasmuch as he aspires to paint a plant or an animal, there must be in him something which corresponds to it in one way or another. If so, he ought to be able to become the object he desires to paint. The discipline consists in studying the plant inwardly with his mind thoroughly purified of its subjective, self-centered contents. This means to keep the mind in unison with the "Emptiness" or Suchness, whereby one who stands against the object ceases to be the one outside that object but transforms himself into the object itself. The identification enables the painter to feel the pulsation of one and the same life animating both him and the object. This is what is meant when it is said that the subject is lost in the object, and that when the painter begins his work it is not he but the object itself that is working and it is then that his brush, as well as his arm and his fingers, become obedient servants to the spirit of the object. The object makes its own picture. This spirit sees itself as reflected in itself. This is also a case of self-identity.[39]

Art in Chinese Culture

The Chinese, like the Japanese, have for generations felt a closeness to nature that they express in the term *T'ien-tao* (the Way of Heaven). According to *T'ien-tao* the human being is expected to live with no more struggle than water seeking lower levels, or plants growing and flowering, or stars silently moving in their courses. But the Chinese, unlike the Japanese, also have a long tradition of discussion of the nature and function of aesthetic forms and experiences.

Art, for Confucius, was primarily ceremony (*li*). According to the *Analects* Confucius was one who could not stand "a ceremonious act which is not carried out respectfully."[40] The artistry of life was to be manifested in the proper rituals. Much of the ritual dealt with the child-parent relationship: "While the parents live, serve them according to the rites. When they die, bury them according to the rites and make offerings to them according to the rites. . . . If for the three years [of mourning] a man does not change from the ways of his father, he may be called filial."[41] Belief in the presence of the spirits and the gods was secondary to the exact performance of the religious ceremonies: "Make your offerings to the ancestors as though they were actually present in person; make your offerings to the divinities as though they were actually present in person."[42] When a certain man told Confucius he wished to discontinue the custom of sacrificing sheep to announce to ancestors the beginning of a new month, Confucius rebuked him, "You are in love with the sheep; I, with the ceremony."[43] Confucius observed all the externals of etiquette; he was "ceremonious to the highest degree." He was "pleasant and agreeable" at home, "frank and firm" at court, and "respectful to the point of allowing nervousness to show" before the prince, because these were what the situations required.[45] But we miss the point if we suppose Confucius was satisfied with externalities. The admonition "Assign proper roles with the rites. Provide unity with music"[46] must be qualified by "By rites we certainly don't mean gems and silks! And by music we certainly don't mean bells and drums! These are merely the externals!"[47] Confucius believed that if the external rituals and ceremonies were kept the appropriate emotions would follow. Art for him was both structure for the expression of the correct social relationships and catalyst for the correct social emotions. Charles Hampden-Turner was thinking of Confucian China when he wrote, "We cannot understand Chinese art unless we see it as moral symbolism."[48]

Taoism has always stressed the simple, the unadorned, the primitive in Chinese art. Since according to Taoism fundamental reality cannot be expressed in words, an appeal is often made to paintings. The models for art according to Taoism are water, the valley, the female, and the infant. The "uncarved block"(*p'u*) is the symbol for nature unspoiled by art.[49] Students of Chinese painting have constantly pointed out that the viewer is expected to focus attention on the unpainted portions. The lines depicting mountains, trees, and clouds are not drawn to call attention to themselves but to indicate where to stop looking at the unpainted surfaces. The more important part of a painting is the unpainted part.

The Chinese believe that art is an expression of the inner spirit and that the spontaneous flow of the brush should be an expression of the untrammelled mood of the artist. The phrase used often by Chinese aestheticians is "taking off clothes and squatting down bare-backed." The expression comes from a story told of Chuang Tzu:

When Prince Yüan of Sung was about to have a portrait painted, all official painters came, bowed, and at the royal command stood waiting, licking their brushes and mixing their ink. Half of them were outside the room. One official came late. He sauntered in without hurrying himself, bowed at the royal command and would not remain standing. Thereupon he was given lodging. The prince sent a man to see what he did. He took off his clothes and squatted down bare-backed. The ruler said, "He will do. He is a true painter."[50]

The best method for achieving the spontaneity preferred in Chinese art was described by Shih-t'ao (1641–c. 1717) as "the method of no-method":

Again it is said, "The perfect man has no method." It is not that he has no method, but rather the best of methods, which is the method of no-method. For there is expediency besides the principle, and flexible development besides the "method." One should know the principle and its flexible adaptation in expediency as one should know the method and apply it flexibly. For what is painting but the great method of changes and developments in the universe.[51]

Shih-t'ao added that artists must reply to those who would demand they imitate the master artists, "I am as I am; I exist. I cannot stick the whiskers of the ancients on my face, nor put their entrails in my belly. I have my own entrails and chest, and I prefer to twitch my own whiskers. If sometimes by chance I happen to resemble someone, it is he who happens to come to me, and not I who try to be his death. This is the way it is. Why should I model myself upon the ancients and not develop my own forte?"[52] According to Shih-t'ao the method by which artists are expected to express themselves in their own way is the method of cosmogony, which may be called the one-stroke (*i-hua*) method:

In the primeval past there was no method. The primeval chaos was not differentiated. When the primeval chaos was differentiated, method (law) was born. How was this method born? It was born of one-stroke. This one-stroke is that out of which all phenomena are born, applied by the gods and to be applied by man. People of the world do not know this. Therefore this one-stroke (*i-hua*) method is established by me. The establishment of this one-stroke method creates a method out of no-method, and a method which covers all methods.[53]

Lin Yutang said of the *K'u-kua Ho-shang Hua-yu-lu* (Sayings of Friar Bitter-Melon), from which the above three selections are taken, "It is completely original and shows a psychological insight into the process of artistic creation not found elsewhere in Chinese literature. In style, it is archaically beautiful, terse and taut with meaning, and very difficult to render into English. But of all Chinese essays on art, this is the most profound ever written, both as regards content and style."[54]

Shih-t'ao even detailed the technique of the one- stroke method of no-method, namely, wrist control.

> For if the wrist is infinitely flexible and responsive, then the drawing goes in different ways. If the brush is quick and sure, then the forms take definite shape. When the wrist is firm, the drawing is sure and expressive, and when it is flexible, it darts and dances and soars. Or with a perpendicular position, the strokes strike the paper squarely without showing the tip of the brush. Or it may incline and make possible many graceful dragging lines. When it moves fast, it gathers force; when it moves slowly, there is a meaningful dip and turn. When the wrist moves, unconsciously inspired, the result is true to nature, and when it changes, the result can be weird and fantastic. When the wrist is gifted with genius, the painting is beyond the work of human minds, and when the wrist moves with the spirit, the hills and streams yield up their souls.[55]

Chang Yen-yüan, a ninth-century aesthetician, described the talent of the artist Wu Tao-tse as nature working through the artist's brush:

> Someone may ask, How could he draw bows and knives and columns and beams without a ruler or guiding line? The reply is that he did it by full concentration of his mind. Nature seems to work through his brush. This has been described as the idea going ahead of the brush so that when the strokes are completed, the concept remains. . . . a man who thinks deliberately how to paint misses it by so doing, while one who deliberates on his brush-lines achieves a drawing without trying. His lines flow naturally, spontaneously, in an inexplicable manner, far beyond what can be achieved by rulers and guiding lines.[56]

The one word that describes the correct state of mind of the artist, wrote Shen Tsung-ch'ien (fl. 1781) is *ease:*

> It is like the pattern of ripples formed by a passing wind, or the carefree lifting of clouds from a recess in a high mountain. Beauty emerges where the brush touches the paper, and the paper moves in harmony with the beauty of the scene. One moves the other, responds to the other, and the beauty of nature is captured. When this happens, all considerations of texture, veins and arteries may be forgotten and yet they will be found to be all there. This comes from daily occupation with the heart and mind and with actual practice, and when the moment of beauty comes, the artist can trace it on paper naturally and without too much thinking.[57]

The goal of the Chinese artist is to attain a freshness (*sheng*) that transcends artistic mastery (*shu*). A controlled mastery (*yüan-shu*) does not reveal itself; an uncontrolled mastery results in easy familiarity (*lan-shu*, literally "overcooked"). For this reason the artist was often advised to be blunt (*chuo*) rather than skillful. Chao Meng-fu (1254–1322) described this freshness as a simple crudeness best denoted by the word *ku-yi*. Lin Yutang translates *ku-yi* as "antique spirit." He explains, "The 'antique spirit' is a term hard to define, but generally refers to sparseness in design, a certain 'crude' or 'primitive' (*chuo*, literally 'stupid') touch in brush-strokes, the use of pale blue-green, dull reddish-brown and bronze colours, and above all, simplicity and restraint."[58] According to Chao Meng-fu,

> The important thing in a painting is the antique spirit (*ku-yi*). A painting may be very well done, and yet be worthless if the antique spirit is lacking. People today only think of delicate lines and fresh colours and call themselves competent artists. They fail to see that in the absence of the antique spirit, all kinds of trouble start, and the work will not be worth looking at. My paintings seem to be simple and crude, but those who understand know that they are akin to the antique way, and are therefore good. I can explain this only to those who understand.[59]

The danger of which the Chinese artists were—and still are—aware is that of attaining prettiness rather than blunt, primitive simplicity. When this happens, the sixteenth-century artist Ku Ning-yüan advised that the artist take a walk:

> When one is not equal to painting, the best thing is to take a stroll alone. Perhaps one will encounter nothing, or perhaps one will come across an odd piece of rock, or a dried-up branch, a small pool, or a sparse wood. These things lie about, unwanted by anybody. But they are pieces of nature, totally unlike what is seen in pictures. One should give them a cool, careful look and try to catch that indefinable quality wherein lies the expression of life. This is like poets jotting down lines to be incorporated in verses later.[60]

The role of painting in Chinese culture was summarized by Chang Yen-yüan as follows: "Painting completes culture, helps human relations, and explores the mysteries of the universe. Its value is equal to that of the Six Classics and, like the rotation of the seasons, stems from nature; it is not something handed down by tradition."[61] "Six Classics" (*Liu Yi*) refers to the body of literature regarded by Chinese as their heritage purporting to come from pre-Confucian times. These include the *I Ching* (Book of Changes), the *Shu Ching* (Book of History), the *Shih Ching* (Book of Odes), the *Li Chi* (Book of Rites), the *Ch'un Ch'iu* (Spring and Autumn Annals), and a book on music that has been lost. Chang Yen-yüan's statement about painting should be expanded to denote all the arts. In other words, art updates the classical heritage preserved in the sacred books such that the wisdom and values incarcerated in the ancient scrolls become a living, immediate, and personal experience.

Art in Indian Culture

There is no word for art in the Sanskrit language.[62] The nearest equivalent is *śilpa,* which means "variegated" or "diverse." The term was used to denote skills in the broadest sense: painting, horsemanship, archery, cooking. Ananda K. Coomaraswamy has warned,

> "Art in India" and "art" in the modern world mean two very different things. In India, it is a statement of a racial experience, and serves the purposes of life, like daily bread. Indian art has always been produced in response to a demand: that kind of idealism which would glorify the artist who pursues a personal ideal of beauty and strives to express himself, and suffers or perishes for lack of patronage, would appear to Indian thought far more ridiculous or pitiable than heroic. . . . In India, the same qualities pervade all works of any given period, from pottery to architecture, and all are equally expressive: the smallest fragment of a textile portrays the same as the most elaborate temple. In other words, there are no distinctions of fine and applied or decorative art and no unsurmountable barrier dividing the arts of the folk from the canonical arts. Indian art has always an intelligible meaning and a definite purpose. An "art for art's sake," a "fine" or useless art, if it could be imagined, would only have been regarded as a monstrous product of human vanity.[63]

V. S. Naravane must have been thinking of what Coomaraswamy called " 'art' in the modern world" when he wrote that in India "the philosopher and the artist seem to inhabit two different planets."[64] *The Cultural Heritage of India,* a work published in 1937 in three volumes by the Ramakrishna Mission Institute of Culture in Calcutta, enlarged to four volumes and revised in 1953, 1956, 1958, and 1962, and to which a fifth volume was added in 1978, contains no essay on art. Other Indian intellectuals have a different opinion about art in India. Vasudeva S. Agrawala writes, "The spiritual and religious content of India's creative genius has found full and perfect expression in her aesthetic creations."[65] Radhakamal Mukerjee states, "Indian art has been through the centuries a sensitive organ of the Indian man's progressive apprehension of total Reality."[66] And Sishil Kumar Saxena contends, "Traditional Indian aesthetics conceives of every art as a pathway to the Ultimate."[67] The German Indologist Heinrich Zimmer agreed with the position of Agrawala, Mukerjee, and Saxena. He began his book *The Art of Indian Asia* with this eloquent statement: "Indian art, besides documenting the history of a majestic civilization, opens a comparatively simple, delightful way into the timeless domain of the Hindu spirit; for it renders in eloquent visual forms the whole message that India holds in keep for mankind."[68]

Like art in any culture, Indian art is associated with the world of the senses, the world of color, form, sound, touch, taste, and odor. If that world is negated, then art has but a secondary role in human existence. In the framework of world-negation (as contrasted to world-affirmation) art may produce the artifacts of worship, the building to house the gods, and the modes of worship, but it does not enter into the clarification of the meaning of the gods and their worship. Art is an ornament, not a necessity of the good life. But if the world of the senses is prized either for its own sake or for what it reveals about the reality it manifests, then art has a primary role in the life of man. Hindus have been divided on this issue for centuries, and the split remains. For example, Vasudeva S. Agrawala said in 1964, "The essential quality of Indian art is its preoccupation with things of the spirit."[69] But N. K. Devaraja wrote in 1967, "The claim . . . made by both the admirers and the detractors of Indian culture that the people here were highly religious, and therefore otherworldly, is both spurious and unreasonable. It cannot be substantiated by any kind of objective evidence. . . . All the varieties of fine arts, including dance and painting, formed an essential part of popular Hinduism."[70]

These divergent views of art in India grow out of an unresolved conflict within Hinduism regarding the reality and value of human life in the physical world. One of the most one-sided assessments of Hinduism has been that of Albert Schweitzer, who in his volume *Indian Thought and Its Development* argued, "Indian thought in its very nature is so entirely different from our own because of the great part which the idea of what is called world and life negation plays in it."[71] Schweitzer may have indicated the source of his bias in the preface when he observed that he first became acquainted with Indian thought through reading the works of Schopenhauer. Moreover, he admitted at the close of the book, "We Europeans have inherited from Schopenhauer and Deussen a tendency to give too little attention to the ideas of world and life affirmation which are found in the Upanishads."[72] He also recognized that both Rabindranath Tagore and Aurobindo found world and life affirmation in the *Upaniṣads.*[73] Movements such as hedonic Cārvāka, dualistic Sāṁkhya, erotic Tantra, and integral yoga are embarrassments to those who think Hinduism ascetic, otherworldly, restrictive, and pessimistic. To maintain balanced thinking about Hinduism, the student must remember that the culture that produced the great body of Vedic literature also produced delightful folk tales like the *Pañchatantra,* works on kingship like the *Artha Śāstra,* and volumes on the techniques of sexual love like the *Kāma Sūtras.*

To put the matter flatly and without argument: there are two Hinduisms. One looks upon human life as a weary cycle of births and deaths from which the individual longs to but cannot escape until *karma* has been exhausted. The other regards human existence as a state envied by the gods in which the individual has open before him or her the possibility of almost unlimited realization and fulfillment. (The authors of the ancient ethical treatises assumed that only males could attain the ideal human condition. Women were advised to pray that they be born a male in the next incarnation! Today, however, the role of women in Hindu society is changing rapidly.) The human ideal in the ancient ethical texts is either that of the *ātmansiddha* or the *nāgaraka*. The *ātmansiddha* is one who has paid all debts to gods, ancestors, society, family, and previous incarnations, and who now awaits final absorption into the Absolute. The *nāgaraka* is the man of the world, the man who is handsome, healthy, rich, and above all accomplished in the sixty-four skills auxiliary to the goal of being a complete lover. This form of Hinduism appears in the erotic sculptures on temples such as those at Khajuraho and in the thousands of tantric texts. The distance between the *nāgaraka* and the *ātmansiddha* may be indicated in that males aspiring to the former state were advised to pass semen every third day, wheras those aspiring to the latter state were advised to pass semen only when a child was desired. Agehananda Bharati, a European who adopted Hinduism, wrote in 1964, "I have yet to meet an Indian-born scholar who stands squarely by the tantric tradition. . . . The official Indian culture, formulated by Vivekananda and his numerous admitted or unadmitted followers, by Gandhi and Radhakrishnan, keep tantrism well outside the ken of permissible interests."[74] Bharati ignored Aurobindo, who in the first half of this century developed a magnificent system that covers both the *ātmansiddha* and *nāgaraka* ideals. Aurobindo stated humans' reason for existence as follows: "To find and embody the All-Delight in an intense summary of its manifoldness, to achieve a possibility of the infinite Existence which could not be achieved in other conditions, to create out of Matter a temple of the Divinity would seem to be the task imposed on the spirit born into the material universe."[75] The two Hinduisms are illustrated in the two Indians best known to Western people: Mahatma Gandhi and Jawaharlal Nehru. Gandhi represented the life and ideals of the villager. Loin cloth and spinning wheel were symbols of his hope that India would become an independent nation of self-supporting villages. Nehru, with his fascination for airplanes and with an omnipresent nonutilitarian red rose in his buttonhole, represented the urban ideal. India still stands between the primitive age and the atomic age.

Two theories of the function of art correspond to the two Hinduisms. One is the ornamentation theory. According to this theory, the function of art is to decorate an otherwise plain object. Indians lavishly decorate doors and wall panels, roofs and gates of temples, city arches, manuscript margins, taxis and lorries, horns of bullocks, jewelry, even their feet. "The Indian idea is that only things covered with ornaments are beautiful," wrote Heinrich Zimmer.[76] The other theory of the function of art may be called the empathetic theory. According to this theory the purpose of art is to elicit a sympathetic response in the spectator. This empathy varies from a fleeting feeling of harmony with the aesthetic object to the full absorption expressed in the Upaniṣadic *tat tvam asi*.

Since there are two Hinduisms and two theories of the function of art in India, it is not surprising to find a number of attitudes toward art and aesthetic objects in Hindu Indian culture. Seven may be distinguished. Two of these are variations of the ornamentation theory of art and may be called the hedonic theory and the excess energy theory. The other five attitudes are variations of the empathetic theory of art. The seven may be identified as (1) *kāma,* (2) *līlā,* (3) *māyā,* (4) *yoga,* (5) *anubhāva,* (6) *pramāṇa,* and (7) *sādhanā.* The word *kāma* is translated "desire," "enjoyment," or "pleasure." It refers especially to sexual pleasures. In Indian literature it is used in three ways: as a cosmic force at the heart of creation, as a principle for the perpetuation of the race, and as a weakness of human nature and an obstacle to liberation. According to *Ṛg Veda* 10. 129. 4, *kāma* aroused "That One Thing" to the production of the cosmos. Kāma in mythology is an impish ever-youthful god armed with bow, arrow, hook, and noose. His weapons symbolize the four aspects of the art of love: to confuse, to submit, to paralyze, and to subdue. *Kāma,* according to the Hinduism that interprets *mokṣa* as escape, impedes the wayfarer on the road to salvation; but according to the Hinduism that interprets *mokṣa* as realization, *kāma* is the zest that makes life worth living. According to this second evaluation, *kāma* objects have the characteristic known as *chārutā* (pleasing). They promote *bhukti* (enjoyment). The paradigm is the *nāgaraka,* the town man, the man of the world. In the literature of Hinduism his life is thoroughly prescribed: he cleaned his teeth and scraped his tongue daily, anointed his body every other day, had coitus with his mistress every third day, shaved his beard fourth day, cut his fingernails every fifth day, shaved his entire body every tenth day, had an enema every twelfth day, took a laxative every thirtieth day, had a phlebotomy every six months. All these were done in order that hedonic satisfactions, especially those of sex, be intense.

Lists of *kāma* skills enumerate as many as 528 subjects in which *nāgarakas* were supposed to be proficient. The most well-known of these lists is a group of sixty-four skills found in the *Kāma Sūtra* of Vātsyāyana. According to this fourth-century writing, both lover and beloved were expected to be dilettantish in performing and adept in conversing about the sixty-four skills. They can be classified into eleven groups: major fine and applied arts, such as dancing, drama, music, painting, architecture, medicine, alchemy; philosophical arts, such as logic, systematic philosophy, psychology; social arts, including mathematics, , economics, politics, history, weights and measures, navigation; military arts, such as archery, tactics, charioteering; literary arts, such as poetry, etymology, grammar, lexicography, rhetoric, penmanship; handicrafts; including goldsmithing, blacksmithing, carpentry, pottery, weaving; agricultural arts, such as metallurgy, horticulture, animal breeding and training; the urbane arts, such as etiquette, field sports, parlor games, gambling, festival celebrations; magical arts, including juggling, legerdemain, casting of spells, argumentation, divination; arts of personal adornment; arts that pertain to the bedchamber and sexual love. The sixty-four are not skills of voluptuousness, but skills that emanate from the belief that love is too important to be left to chance.

The second function of art, according to the ornamental theory, is *līlā.* *Līlā* means sport that grows out of a sense of exuberance. It is an expression of high spirits, joyousness in existence, and a desire to express the manifold possibilities latent in reality. Aurobindo refers to a unity that can only be manifested in infinite multiplicity: "a real diversity brings out the real Unity, shows it as it were in its utmost capacity, reveals all that it can be and is in itself, delivers from its whiteness of hue the many tones of colour that are fused together there; Oneness finds itself infinitely in what seems to us to be a falling away from its oneness, but is really an inexhaustible diverse display of unity."[77] The theme of the necessary sportive multiplication of a one appears again and again in Hindu theology: "One only fire blazeth forth in various shapes."[78] Agni the fire god is reported to say, "Having, by ascetic power, multiplied myself, I am present in various forms. . . in places where holy rites are performed."[79] Śiva, the god of destruction, has a hundred divine names. Kṛṣṇa multiplied himself in the circle dance in the moonlight at Brindiban so he was as many as the *gopis* (milk maids). According to the *Bhāgavata Purāna* Kṛṣṇa had 16,008 wives. The large numbers in the lore of Hinduism—the number of the Vedic gods is said to be 330 million, the *Gheraṇḍa Saṁhita* claims there are 8.4 million *āsanas* (yogic postures), and in the *Rāmāyana* Rāvaṇa is said to have 150 million elephants and 300 million horses in his army—are not to be regarded as the exaggeration of childish minds but as the workings of the minds of people who delighted in the plurality and diversity of things.

In her architecture, sculpture, music, and painting the ancients of India did not hold back in riches. There was no love of blank spaces. The roofs of the *gopurams* (gateways) in southern India are covered with a wealth of relief sculptures of animals, men, and gods. The temple at Chidambaram has a hall with 984 pillars and a gateway illustrating Lord Śiva in 108 classical dance poses.

The *līlā* or art production was so intense in traditional India that artists specialized to increase their output. In a painting one artist might sketch the outline of the figures, another paint only landscapes, and a third would do the color work on human figures. To do art well was to imitate the lavish productivity of the gods.

A third view of art in India is that art is *māyā*. Both *līlā* and *māyā* are manifestations but, whereas *līlā* production is the free, spontaneous, purposeless, playful manifestation of a creative matrix, *māyā* production is seriously designed creation. The term comes from *mā*, meaning "to measure," "to shape," and "to display." It is used sparingly in the *Upaniṣads*. In *Bṛhad-Āraṇyaka Upaniṣad* 2. 4. 12 a seer says that the real self is like a lump of salt cast into water. The salt is no longer real "as it were," yet when one tastes the water one experiences the salt. The expression "as it were" is a translation of the Sanskrit word *iva,* which is the germ of the idea of *māyā*. *Iva* calls attention here to a being that has shifted its ontological structure from an overt reality to a covert manifestation, from noumenon to phenomenon. Real beings are like that, says the seer. They appear to vanish, but in fact they have only changed their ontological mode.

The early Hindus concluded that if anything has power to change its appearance, then it has magical powers. *Māyā* came to mean the power to conceal, to hide, to create illusory effects. It was *māyā* in this sense that was developed by Śaṅkara in the ninth century. The argument continues as to whether *māyā* means an illusion that is false or a perspective that gives less than the whole. Part of the resolution may proceed by pointing out that Śaṅkara had a purist notion of reality. For him reality meant complete, absolute reality. He designated this by *Sat* (being), and he contended that only Nirguṇa Brahman was *Sat*. At the other end of the ontological spectrum was *asat*. *Asat* was complete, absolute irreality. *Sat* is that which cannot not be; *asat* is that which cannot be. *Asat* is a peculiar sort of "reality"—the reality of irreality. The classic example is the son of a barren woman. *Māyā* was used by Śaṅkara to denote and to connote all that lies between *Sat* and *asat*. *Māyā,* then, is the reality of things that neither absolutely exist nor absolutely nonexist. The world of contingent realities is *māyā*. *Māyā* objects are illusions only to the person who does not understand that they are *māyā*.

With reference to art and aesthetics *māyā* has three aspects. Just as the philosophical notion of *māyā* may have grown out of magic as a form of production, so *māyā* with reference to art meant a way of making things happen. According to an ancient Indian story, a singer was reputed to have the power to create fire by his singing. A king commanded him to give a demonstration. The singer protested, but finally obeyed the king. He did produce fire by singing, but the fuel was his own body and he perished even though he jumped into a river to put out the flames.

A second feature of the *māyā* theory of art is that though art is a form of production, what it produces is inferior. This Platonic view is still held in India by many intellectuals. The artist is a misrepresenter of reality who calls attention from the One to the many, from the Brahman to the world, and from the Self to the selves.

A third view of art as *māyā* is now attaining respectability in India. To a large extent this is the work of Aurobindo. He offered an evolutionary interpretation of the Vedic literature in which he insisted that the manifested pluralities are not an illusory or deceptive manifestation but a necessary manifestation of the One. *Māyā* is the divine art that expresses the real in infinitely varied modes. The artist is a revealer—an instrument of Brahman's necessary pluralization.

Art as *yoga* is a fourth view, which claims either that the ancient mental and physical discipline of the Hindus is carried over into the realm of artistic production or that the development of the disciplines in handicrafts and skills with the expectation that such attitudes and actions will carry over into the pursuit of ultimate concerns. Perhaps the best example of aesthetic discipline is the classical music of India. Music is an excellent subject with which to distinguish discipline in the West from that in India. Western music is played from set compositions. Its discipline is a fixed following of specific notes in sequences indicated by the composer. But the discipline of Indian music is a melody type (*rāga*), such as a series of fixed notes within the octave, and a time measure (*tāla*), such as a series of unstressed beats. Within the framework of the rigidity of *rāga* and *tāla* the Indian musician extemporizes. Whereas the Westerner thinks of freedom as the absence of restraint and of determinism as the presence of rules, the Indian finds freedom in functioning well within the limits set by rules and laws. The master musician functions freely within *rāga* and *tāla*. Hindus discover existentially that the freedoms they enjoyed as infants are not abrogated by the *dharma* placed upon them in the adult world. Freedom in the profoundest and final sense, which is *mokṣa*, is possible only within the confines of *dharma*.

The *yoga* or discipline of art is illustrated by the *ganya-māna* (reckoned measurement) that applies to architecture and sculpture. In Indian sculpture the unit of measurement is the length of the face. The correct height for sculptures of women is seven times the length of the face, eight for men, nine for goddesses, ten for minor gods, and eleven for major gods. Additional canons dictate proportion for the various parts of the anatomy. While this resulted in a stylized sculpture, it also freed the sculptors to do what they wished within the language of the form of their art, that is, to say something about the types of gods or humans so depicted. In architecture rules governed the ratio of heighth and breadth of a building according to the psychological state the building was intended to foster. If the intent was to produce a peaceful, calm effect, heighth and breadth should be equal. If a feeling of stability and assurance was sought, the heighth should be one and a quarter times the breadth. If joy and pleasantness was desired, the heighth should be one and a half times the breadth. Strength and affluence was assured if the heighth was one and three-quarters times the breadth, and a feeling of majesty and loftiness was created by making the building's height twice its breadth.

A fifth view of art in India is that art is emotional empathy (*anubhāva*). *Anubhāva* is not a term of aesthetics in the wider sense, since it refers to an ingredient in works of art rather than in natural objects. One may emotionally empathize with a tree in a painting but not with a tree that grows in the yard. Religious values are found in rivers, mountains, sunsets and sunrises, clouds and stars, but there is no *anubhāva* with respect to such objects. We can only guess why Indians since Vedic times have not had a love affair with nature; perhaps the best guess is that they suffered too much from droughts, floods, heat, cold, dust, and insects to empathize with nature. During at least half of the year the weather of India can be described as uncomfortable. *Anubhāva* holds that all works of art are intended to create in the viewer or listener responsive emotional states. The quality and quantity of response is determined by the relationship between the *guṇas* (properties) of the object and the *dosas* (humors) of the person. Since *anubhāva* denotes the response of a person to an art object, it is not surprising that one term designates the property of the object and another designates the kindred response of the subject. These two terms are *rasa* and *bhāva*.

Rasa is an ancient term denoting the quality of the juice, sap, or pith of an edible object. In the *Ṛg Veda* it used for the juice of the soma plant, for water and milk, and for flavor itself. In the *Upaniṣads rasa* is refers to the flavor of things tasted, but also more abstractly to "the essence of existence."[80] Although *rasa* is often translated "taste" it does not imply any ethical evaluation; there is no good or bad taste. *Rasa* is that in the art object that causes it to be relished, appreciated, and enjoyed. Again, the term *rasa* does not necessarily mean that which gives pain or pleasure, for the emotional response determined by an art object is inadequately described as pleasant or painful. Arousing or stimulating are better terms. If an object does not produce an identifiable emotional response in a prepared recipient, it cannot be an art object. Thus a "poem" that elicits no emotional response in the qualified reader may be said to have no *rasa,* and therefore to be no poem.

Rasa is also used in Indian classical medicine. Here it refers to properties of things that produce six distinct tastes: sweet, salty, bitter, sour, pungent, astringent. The language of art theory borrowed the term from both the Vedic philosophical tradition and Āyurvedic medicine to indicate the mood, emotional tone, sentiment, keynote, temper, and so forth, of a work of art. The *rasas* are applied to painting, music, dance—in fact to any art. *Rasa* in literary criticism is sometimes described as the soul of a poem, a short story, or an essay. The *rasas* are eight in number: erotic, furious, heroic, comic, wonderful, pathetic, disgusting, and terrifying. But to these a ninth is often added, the peaceful. According to some, the peaceful is either the supreme *rasas* or the *rasas* considered collectively. Ananda K. Coomaraswamy refers to the *rasas* as "no more than the various colorings of one experience."[81] Thus *rasa* in the broadest sense seems equivalent to the term beauty (*saundarya*), but specifically a *rasa* is a property that elicits a *bhāva*.

The *bhāvas* are the empathetic responses to the *rasas*. The nine *bhāvas* correspond to the nine *rasas*: love, anger, high-spiritedness, laughter, astonishment, sorrow, disgust, fear, tranquility. The *bhāva* experience is not to be confused with intellectual understanding. It is possible for one to study art for an entire life and never experience *bhāva*. This may account for the already noted tension and misunderstanding between philosophers and artists in India that makes it possible for philosophers to write volumes on Indian culture with no reference to Indian art.

A sixth view of art in India is art as a *pramāṇa* (a method of knowing). According to this interpretation art is a mental activity (*citta-sannā*). In this view artistic creation depends upon the type of mental concentration associated with *yoga,* and artistic appreciation depends upon intellectual universalizing. Indian art depicts the generic rather than the specific. Indian artists draw what they mean, not what they see. They seek to express the essential rather than to copy the model. In fact, the classical sculptors and painters did not work from models; hence the monotony of the paintings of Rādha and Kṛṣṇa, and of the sculptures of gods and heroes. Coomaraswamy says that "the mere representation of nature is never the aim of Indian art. . . . Possibily no Hindu artist of the old school ever drew from nature at all. His store of memory pictures, his power of visualization, and his imagination were for his purpose finer means; for he desired to suggest the Idea behind sensuous appearance, not to give the detail of the seeming reality, that was in truth but *māyā,* illusion."[82] One of the ideals of Indian art is *sādrisya* (similitude), but it is a resemblance between the art object and the species, not between the art object and the natural object. The Indian artist paints the idea not the shape.

Finally, art in India may be a *sādhanā,* a discipline of human endeavors for the realization of ideal goals. In Hindu India everything may seem to be transformable into a means for the attainment of liberation or salvation. Benjamin Rowland has written that "art is religion in India, and religion art. . . . In India all art, like all life, is given over to religion. Indian art is life, as interpreted by religion and philosophy."[83] Rowland is only partially correct; the Hindus who embrace the *nāgaraka* ideal do think of art as a *sādhanā* for the attainment of *mokṣa,* but those who embrace the *ātmansiddha* ideal have serious reservations about such a generalization.

Art in the Western World

The balanced pursuit of the three great values—truth, goodness, beauty—has long been a Western ideal. But beauty has been forced to struggle to maintain equal status with her sisters. Plato banished most poets, artists, and musicians from his utopia. After discussing his planned expurgation of poetry, he apologized: "We will beg Homer and the other poets not to be put out if we strike through such things as these; we do not deny they are good poetry and what most people like to hear, but the more poetical they are, the less we wish our children and men to hear them, those who must be free, and afraid of slavery more than death."[84] Poetry, he wrote, has a power "of harming even the good." Poetry "feeds and waters the passions instead of drying them up; she lets them rule, although they ought to be controlled, if mankind are ever to increase in happiness and virtue." Poetry "is not to be regarded seriously as attaining to the truth."[85] Therefore, the citizen must be protected from the seductions of the artists "for the safety of the city which is within him."[86]

Plato's charge that art must be subordinate to science and morality has dominated much of the life of the arts in the West. When the Western world became largely Christian, the arts of pagan Greece and Rome were frequently retained as mere decoration. Whenever possible, a design would be modified to suit a Christian theme, for example, Hermes carrying a sheep became Christ the Good Shepherd. Later the Protestants—notably the Puritan followers of Oliver Cromwell—destroyed statues, stained glass windows, and other works of art, contending they were violations of the divine commandment not to make graven images. Likewise Islam forbade portrayal of the human form in sculpture.

The "ancient quarrel between art and morals"[87] appeared in Europe in the conflict between the moralism of the pre- and post-Renaissance, church-dominated centuries and the rebirth and revival of art, letters, and learning known as the Renaissance. The Renaissance was a time of freedom of the arts from most of the moral restraints placed upon artists by the church. During the Renaissance beauty did not have to submit to the demands of goodness. Jacob Burckhardt in his famous history of the Renaissance wrote, "The Italians were the first among modern peoples by whom the outward world was seen and enjoyed as something beautiful."[88] Burckhardt added, "To the discovery of the outward world the civilization of the Renaissance added a still greater achievement, in that it was the first to discover and bring to light the full, whole nature of man."[89]

The classic Renaissance statement of human nature is that of Giovanni Pico Della Mirandola (1463–1494):

> At last, the Supreme Maker decreed that this creature, to whom He could give nothing wholly his own, should have a share in the particular endowment of every other creature. Taking man, therefore, this creature of indeterminate image, He set him in the middle of the world and thus spoke to him: "We have given you, Oh Adam, no visage proper to yourself, nor any endowment properly your own, in order that whatever place, whatever form, whatever gifts you may, with premeditation, select, these same you may have and possess through your own judgment and decision. The nature of all other creatures is defined and restricted within laws which We have laid down; you, by contrast, impeded by no such restrictions, may, by your own free will, to whose custody We have assigned you, trace for yourself the lineaments of your own nature. I have placed you at the very center of the world, so that from that vantage point you may with greater ease glance round about you on all that the world contains. We have made you a creature neither of heaven nor of earth, neither mortal nor immortal, in order that you may, as the free and proud shaper of your own being, fashion yourself in the form you may prefer."[90]

But the West was not able to retain this lofty conception of human freedom to "become what you are" (as Pindar said), nor the freedom to seek "beauty bare." The "ancient quarrel" was renewed and is perpetuated today in imprimaturs of the Roman Catholic church, legislation on pornography, movie ratings in the United States, warnings about objectionable language in television programs, censorship of art exhibits and theater productions.

The conflict between art and morality is not the only distinguishing feature of Western art, but because of its longevity and vitality, it merits emphasis. The conflict is between protagonists holding two extreme positions: moralism and aestheticism. Partisans of moralism contend that artists and their works must always be judged by the moral impact they have upon the public. Those who support aestheticism contend that art must be judged solely on aesthetic standards; "art for art's sake" is their motto. They believe that art for moral goals, social causes, or national ideals is a prostitution of art.

One of the most vigorous, emotional, and prejudiced attacks on the "art for art's sake" theory of the role of art in society was made by Leo Tolstoy (1828–1910) in his *What is Art?*:

> In every large town enormous buildings are erected for museums, academies, conservatories, dramatic schools, and for performances and concerts. Hundreds of thousands of workmen—carpenters, masons, painters, joiners, paperhangers, tailors, hairdressers, jewelers, molders, typesetters—spend their whole lives in hard labor to satisfy the demands of art, so that hardly any other department of human activity, except the military, consumes so much energy as this.
>
> Not only is enormous labor spent on this activity, but in it, as in war, the very lives of men are sacrificed. Hundreds of thousands of people devote their lives from childhood to learning to twirl their legs rapidly (dancers), or to touch notes and strings very rapidly (musicians), or to draw with paint and represent what they see (artists), or to turn every phrase inside out and find a rhyme to every word. And these people, often very kind and clever, and capable of all sorts of useful labor, grow savage over their specialized and stupefying occupations, and become one-sided and self-complacent specialists, dull to all the serious phenomena of life and skilled only at rapidly twisting their legs, their tongues, or their fingers.[91]

José Ortega y Gasset in his essay "The Dehumanization of Art" (1948) continued Tolstoy's theme, but in a more restrained manner. He wrote,

> It is not an exaggeration to assert that modern paintings and sculptures betray a real loathing of living forms or forms of living beings. . . . A good deal of what I have called dehumanization and disgust for living forms is inspired by just such an aversion against the traditional interpretation of realities. . . . All peculiarities of modern art can be summed up in this one feature of its renouncing its importance—a feature which, in its turn, signifies nothing less than that art has changed its position in the hierarchy of human activities and interests. . . . Art that has rid itself of human pathos is a thing without consequence—just art with no other pretenses.[92]

Ortega tempered his protest with the recognition that someone must offer a positive view: "a suggestion of another way of art different from dehumanization and yet not coincident with the beaten and worn-out paths."[93]

Clive Bell was one of the chief defenders of formalism, or the "art for art's sake" interpretation. "To appreciate a work of art we need bring with us nothing but a sense of form and colour and a knowledge of three-dimensional space," he wrote.[94] Bell, in a curious attack upon Aristotle's theme that tragic drama is an effort to purge the spectators of fear and pity, added,

> A painter too feeble to create forms that provoke more than a little aesthetic emotion will try to eke that little out by suggesting the emotions of life. To evoke the emotions of life must use representation. Thus a man will paint an execution, and, fearing to miss with his first barrel of significant form, will try to hit with his second by raising an emotion of fear or pity. But if in the artist an inclination to play upon the emotions of life is often the sign of a flickering inspiration, in the spectator a tendency to seek, behind form, the emotions of life is a sign of defective sensibility always.[95]

Rader and Jessup state that "it is a mistake to subordinate the aesthetic to the moral or the moral to the aesthetic."[96] But as yet the West has not established a truce between the good and the beautiful.

7

The Self in the Religious World

We live in four worlds—the natural, the social, the aesthetic, and the religious. Or do we live in one world with four dimensions? Our world is natural-social-aesthetic-religious. Our greatest creativity—most varied, most original, most meaningful—is religion.

The Nature of Religion

Philosophers sometimes study religion by collecting many definitions of religion and then point to inadequacies in the definitions that omit elements considered essential by some religion. If a definition affirms that a religion must include belief in a God, the philosopher may call attention to original Buddhism as a religion without God. This methodology proceeds on the assumption that the denotation of *religion* is Christianity, Judaism, Islam, Zoroastrianism, Hinduism, Jainism, Buddhism, Sikhism, Confucianism, Taoism, and Shinto. These have been called "the eleven great world religions." But such a list raises questions. What about the native religions of African tribes, Eskimos, American Indians, Mongolians, Todas? Are native religions religions? Or are they excluded because they are not great religions, or because they are not sufficiently worldwide in their appeal? Are communism, fascism, and democracy religions?[1] Is any form of nationalism a religion? Can money-making, career-seeking, stamp-collecting, dancing, jogging, and television-viewing be religions? Can one define religion by abstracting a common denominator of religions?

James H. Leuba in his research for *A Psychological Study of Religion*[2] collected forty-eight definitions of religion as "a splendid illustration both of the versatility and the one-sidedness of the human mind in the description of a very complex yet unitary manifestation of life."[3] He found that the definitions fell into three classifications: (1) intellectualistic definitions, such as "the belief in spiritual beings"; (2) affectivistic definitions, such as "the feeling of absolute dependence"; and (3) voluntaristic definitions, such as "pure religion... is this, to visit the fatherless and widows in their affliction." He concluded that a full religion must include something to believe, something to feel, and something to do.

William P. Alston used the definition-examination method in his article on religion in *The Encyclopedia of Philosophy*.[4] He discovered in the definitions what he calls "religion-making characteristics": (1) belief in supernatural beings; (2) distinction between sacred and profane objects; (3) ritual acts focused on sacred objects; (4) moral code believed to be sanctioned by the gods; (5) feelings such as awe, mystery, guilt, and adoration that tend to be aroused in the presence of the sacred objects and during the practice of ritual, and that are connected in idea with the gods; (6) prayer; (7) a world view; (8) a more or less total organization of one's life based on the world view; (9) a social group bounded by the above.[5] Alston's cautious definition of religion—"When enough of these characteristics are present to a sufficient degree, we have a religion"[6]—borders on the ridiculous.

The English word *religion* comes either from the Latin word *religare* (to find, to tie back, to tie up, to make fast) or from *relegere* (to collect, to gather together). The Greek terms closest to *religion* are *theosébeia* (fear of the gods) and *deisidaímon* (fear of demons). The Sanskrit terms that approximate *religion* are *sādhanā* (a disciplined way of life leading to the attainment of ideal goals) and *bhakti mārga* (the devotional path). The Chinese word *chiao* is used for the three religions of China—Confucianism, Buddhism, and Taoism—but in different contexts *chiao* may mean education, culture, or religion. *Pai* is the Chinese term for formal, sophisticated worship, and *chi* denotes primitive sacrificial offerings.

One way to define religion is to examine the usage of the adjective *religious*. The term sometimes designates the condition of being seriously, passionately, and fully concerned about something. One may be said to be religious about working, playing, housekeeping, making love, chewing gum, or filing finger nails. When so used it may be completely unrelated to what is usually meant by *religion*.

Ludwig Wittgenstein (1889–1951), described as "one of the greatest philosophers of our time" and as one whom "numerous philosophers in English-speaking countries would be quite prepared to describe as the greatest,"[7] is an interesting example. Those who knew Wittgenstein intimately agree that "he was not... in any conventional sense a religious man"[8] and that nothing he said or demonstrated "in the class would seem to indicate that he was at all religiously inclined."[9] Yet they continually refer to him as a religious man. Rudolf Carnap compared him to a religious prophet: "His point of view and his attitude toward people and problems, even theoretical problems, were much more similar to those of a creative artist than to those of a scientist; one might almost say, similar to those of a religious prophet or seer."[10] Carnap added that "the impression he made on us was as if insight came to him through a divine revelation."[11] Wolfe Mays makes Wittgenstein appear an Amos or an Ezekiel: "At first I found the man and his manner somewhat strange, and I felt a little scared of him. His prominent staring eyes, intensity of manner, and irritability, which no doubt showed that he was usually at a high level of anxiety, heightened this."[12] Norman Malcolm says, "He did not have 'a sense of humor' if one means by this a humorous view of the world and of oneself. His outlook was grim. He was always troubled about his own life and was often close to despair. He was dismayed by the insincerity, vanity, and coldness of the human heart."[13] J. M. O'C Drury likewise remembers him as a prophetic person: "He made wonder secure. No one had such power to awaken that primitive wonder from which all great philosophy begins."[14] Drury recalled an interesting event: "One evening not long before his death Wittgenstein quoted to me the inscription that Bach wrote on the title page of his *Little Organ Book*: 'To the glory of the most high God, and that my neighbor may be benefited thereby.' Pointing to his own pile of manuscript, he said: 'That is what I would have liked to have been able to say about my own work.'"[15]

His friends were impressed by his seriousness. According to Georg H. von Wright "Wittgenstein's most characteristic features were his great and pure seriousness and powerful intellect."[16] He adds, "He put his whole soul into everything he did."[17] Norman Malcolm says he was more than "a deeply serious philosopher," since he was "pursued and tormented by philosophical difficulties."[18] Malcolm adds, "Wittgenstein's conversation made an overwhelming impression because of the united seriousness and vivacity of his ideas, and also because of the expressive mobility of his beautiful face, the piercing eyes and commanding glance, the energetic movements and gestures. In comparison, someone has remarked, other people seemed only half alive."[19]

Gasking and Jackson report his seriousness in a different manner: "He had a horror of slickness—of philosophical opinions arrived at by any process other than an honest wholehearted strenuous endeavor to find out the truth for oneself."[20] They also state, "He had complete respect for religious people, and for those non-philosophers who do their chosen job and follow their chosen way of life as well as they can. At times he would even try to persuade students who hoped to become professional philosophers to give it up and take a 'decent' job, such as that of a mine manager or a farmer."[21] Gasking and Jackson conclude their article "Wittgenstein as a Teacher": "There are many sorts of human excellence. Not least among them is the excellence of one who devotes his whole life, giving up all else, to the attempt to do one single thing supremely well. That Wittgenstein did."[22] Wittgenstein was a religious person in this minimal sense of the term. But the minimal sense is not enough, according to John Dewey.

In his important book, *A Common Faith,* Dewey argued that "there is a difference between religion, *a* religion, and the religious; between anything that may be denoted by a noun substantive and the quality of experience that is designated by an adjective."[23] He contended that "*a* religion" may be used properly for whatever one may choose to designate by the term, that *religion* as a term for a collection of religions has no precise meaning and therefore ought not to be used, and that *religious* is to denote "attitudes that may be taken toward every object and every proposed end or ideal."[24] Dewey was anxious to explore "the difference between an experience having a religious force because of what it does in and to the processes of living and religious experience as a separate kind of being."[25] "My purpose" he wrote,

> is to indicate what happens when religious experience is already set aside as something *sui generis*. The actual religious quality in the experience described is the *effect* produced, the better adjustment in life and its conditions, not the manner and cause of its production. The way in which the experience operated, its function, determines its religious value. If the reorientation actually occurs, it, and the sense of security and stability accompanying it, are forces on their own account. It takes place in different persons in a multitude of ways. It is sometimes brought about by devotion to a cause; sometimes by a passage of poetry that opens a new perspective; sometimes as was the case with Spinoza—deemed an atheist in his day—through philosophical reflection.[26]

The religious attitude is any attitude in which there is a better, deeper, and enduring relationship. The components of this attitude are accommodation, adaptation, and adjustment. The religious attitude unifies the self and its worlds, while "the essentially unreligious attitude is that which attributes human achievement and purpose to man in isolation from the world of physical nature and his fellows."[27] Perhaps Dewey should have left his concept of the religious attitude in this form, but he could not resist the philosophic urge to expound, offering a definition of the religious in which he slipped from "attitude" to "activity." His definition is: "Any activity pursued in behalf of an ideal end against obstacles and in spite of threats of personal loss because of conviction of its general and enduring value is religious in quality."[28] While Dewey's definition of the religious as attitude and activity successfully separated it, as he intended, "from the supernatural and the things that have grown up about it,"[29] one may wonder if Dewey watered down the term *religious* until it meant little more than dedication, intensity, and commitment. In his zeal to release religious values from "their identification with the creeds and cults of religion,"[30] Dewey may have exceeded his original purpose of clarifying religion, which as he admitted does "involve specific intellectual beliefs."[31]

Other students of religion, while not denying that *religious* can describe a wide variety of experiences, insist that another important kind of experience can be designated "religious experience." For example, Joachim Wach proposed four formal criteria for defining religious experience: (1) a religious experience is the most intense experience of which a person is capable; (2) a religious experience is a total experience of the person, involving mind, affections, and will; (3) a religious experience is a response to what is experienced as ultimate reality; and (4) a religious experience involves an imperative to action that joins religious experience with moral experience and distinguishes religious experience from aesthetic experience.[32] Wach may have overlooked another feature of religious experience, that is, the tension that triggers the experience. This may be a vague feeling—or an intense one—that things are not as they ought to be. This feeling may be an awareness of a fundamental wrongness, dissatisfaction, guilt, conflict, uneasiness, fragmentation, separation, finitude, impurity, lostness, futility, sinfulness, loneliness, anxiety, meaninglessness. This was what Paul Tillich had in mind when he stated, "Religion is the consequent of the estrangement of man from the ground of his being and of his attempts to return to it."[33] But tension is not the full picture; there is also an optimistic note of expectation. David Hume correctly noted the duality of religious motivation when he wrote that "the first ideas of religion arose not from a contemplation of the works of nature, but from a concern with regard to the events of life, and from the incessant hopes and fears which actuate the human mind."[34] The other side of estrangement is the hope for integration, wholeness, restoration, satisfaction, meaning, harmony, and peace.

The Origin of Religion

A fruitful method for understanding religion is to examine its origins. But this cannot be done by observational-experimental methods. Anthropologists generally agree that no people are without a religion; Bronislaw Malinowski unqualifiedly stated, "There are no people however primitive without religion and magic."[35] The claim that a particular religion is the creation of a deity is not worth serious consideration, although it is not uncommon. David James Burrell in *The Religions of the World* wrote, "Christianity, alone of religions, is of divine origin."[26] A curious version of the theory that a religion came to be through divine agency is the view that foreign religions are the fabrication of the devil to snare souls from the true faith. The view is well expressed in Milton's *Paradise Lost.* In the middle of the nineteenth century a French priest returned from a journey into Tibet during which he studied Lamaism. He, finding a startling similarity between the Buddhism of Tibet and Roman Catholicism, concluded that Satan, in anticipation of Christianity, had revealed to these Buddhists an anticipatory counterfeit of Christian doctrine and ritual.[37] In 1882 Max Müller delivered a course of lectures entitled *India: What Can It Teach Us?* at the University of Cambridge. He said that India was the ideal place to study the "true origin" of religion, its "natural growth," and "inevitable decay." The American publishers of these lectures, wishing to make Christianity an exception to Müller's observation, added in a footnote, "This is true of what theologians call natural religion, which is assumed to be a growth out of human consciousness; but the Christian religion is not a natural religion."[38]

George B. Vetter, after noting that the "theories of the nature and origin of religion are numerous and varied, " and that he was unaware "that any serious attempt has ever been made to classify, organize or compare the various theories that have been put forth, other than a very casual designation of three different classes of theories by Hopkins,"[39] presented the following classification:

I. Traditional Philosophical Theories
   1. Religion was created by divinities.
   2. Religion was fashioned to glorify deities.

II. Physiological-Psychological or Instinct Theories
   3. Religion evolved from an univeral religious instinct.
   4. Religion evolved from a religious "sense" found in a few individuals.
   5. Religion developed out of human fears.
   6. Religion developed from the awe humans felt before the natural world.
   7. Religion evolved from social emotions.
   8. Religion evolved from sexual experiences.

III. Psychological Experience and Rationality Theories
   9. Religion developed from human dreams.
   10. Religion grew out of abnormal experiences with drugs.
   11. Religion developed from a specific and unique religious experience.
   12. Religion originated in mystical states.
   13. Religion developed from attempts at redemption from sin and suffering.
   14. Religion began as a product of the human inability to face the unknown.
   15. Religion began as a rational deduction from the facts of the cosmos.

IV. Psychological Development and Frustration Theories
   16. Religion originated as the product of habits acquired in the family situation.
   17. Religion grew out of the disappointments and shortcomings of the world that created belief in a more perfect order.
   18. Religion originated as a product of the felt inadequacies of the human equipment.
   19. Religion evolved from the desire to escape from reality.
   20. Religion began as an embracement of a collective neurosis to save oneself from an individual neurosis.

V. Historical Development Theories
   21. Religion evolved out of animism.
   22. Religion evolved out of animatism.

23. Religion evolved out of the mana concept.
24. Religion grew out of the failure of magic.
25. Religion evolved out of totemism.
26. Religion evolved out of fetishes.
27. Religion evolved out of ancestor worship.
28. Religion began as euhemerism, that is, as the deification of kings and heroes.

VI. Conspiracy Theories

29. Religion began as a creation of the medicine man who discovered the average person could be exploited for the medicine man's own ends.
30. Religion began as an opiate for keeping subject classes distracted from their mundane miseries.

VII. Miscellaneous Theories

31. Religion originated in any excessive or fanatical zeal for causes or beliefs.
32. Religion arose from any social frame of reference and object of devotion.[40]

The more defensible of the theories may be the following:

1. *Animism.* This is the belief that inanimate objects possess living souls. The savage believed that the stick and the stone were not really lifeless; they harbored a spirit or god. The world of the primitive was filled with living spirits both beneficent and malevolent. Animism is seen today in the child whose doll becomes in imagination a real baby, in the machinist who thinks the machine possesses personality, and the person who kicks a rug in retaliation for its having tripped him.The anthropologist E. B. Tylor brought this theory of the origin of religion into prominence.

2. *Totemism.* Totemism is the belief of a community in the ability of an animate object or an inanimate representation of the object to aid the group or individuals of the group. Many American Indian tribes have legends of aid rendered by an animal or bird. Some tribes in Africa worship the lion, believing that the courage of the lion enters into the warriors. The bull was sacred in ancient Egypt; the cow in modern India. The ape, the cat, and the turtle have also been sacred animals. A possible remnant of totemism is the mascot of athletic teams. This theory has been developed by the sociologist Émile Durkheim.

3. *Magic.* J. G. Frazer in *The Golden Bough* (1911) developed the theory that religion is the child of magic. Magic is the attempt of human beings to gain power over the forces believed to be hidden in the world. The medicine man or witch doctor was supposed to be able to conjure forces latent in nature and direct them into channels beneficial to the tribe. Frazer claimed that when human beings failed to control nature by magical means they turned to entreaty, and thus religion was born.

4. *Fear.* Fear as a source of religion in the human race is embodied in some of the theories indicated above, but some scholars have singled it out as the sole cause. In the ancient world Epicurus and Lucretius claimed that religion sprang from human fears and contributed to the increase of fear. David Hume in *The Natural History of Religion* and Lewis Browne in *This Believing World* (1930), to cite two other authorities from varying periods, assert that religion arises from fear of the forces of nature and hope of securing the good will of the gods behind the forces. The fears were often linked with the idea of certain objects being taboo (literally, "prohibited"). Among the Hebrews, for example, the first fruits of the land, the seventh day of the week, women during menstrual periods, and the ark of the covenant were taboo.

5. *Feeling of Need of Cosmic Support.* Others claim that religion from the start was an attempt to persuade the cosmic powers to be friendly. When human beings recognized their own impotence and the greatness of their aspirations, they sought something greater that would support their hopes and ideals and guarantee their realization. Religion is an attempt to maintain confidence beyond that which might be expected on the basis of human strength. Some religious thinkers, however, regard religion so conceived as an unwarranted hunger for cosmic support. They believe a religion that looks for a sign in the skies neglects the real business of religion, which is the promotion of better human relations on earth.

6. *Human Reason.* The deists of the seventeenth and eighteenth centuries believed the core of religion was a set of ideas that had been establised by unaided human reason. This ability of the human reason to formulate a natural religion was regarded as a natural process and therefore religion was assumed to have originated with the appearance of minds.

7. *Search for Ultimate Causes.* Still others have held that religion is one of the ways through which human beings search for the ultimate causes of events in human and cosmic history. Each individual cause is but the effect of an antecedent cause. Transcendent to causal series, it is assumed, there is a first cause, or cause of all causes. Religion is the metaphysical search for ultimate causes.

8. *Worship of Ancestors.* Religion may have grown out of human belief in the survival of the spirits of the dead. Often the ghosts of the deceased were imagined to linger about the household and fields. These ghosts were assumed to have peculiar powers to help those who showed them favor or to hinder those who disregarded them. Dreams about the dead strengthened the belief in survival. Worship of the ghosts through sacrifices was assumed to help win and hold their good will. Later the ghosts were replaced by divinities, and worship continued as a method of appeasement. This theory is chiefly associated with Herbert Spencer.

9. *Respect and Reverence for Heroes and Kings.* A somewhat similar view was that of Euhemerus, a Sicilian writer of the fourth century B.C., who claimed that religion arose from the respect and reverence paid to kings and heroes during

their lives and continued by custom after their deaths. Roman emperor worship and the Japanese worship of the Mikado illustrate this theory.

10. *Perception of the Infinite.* Max Müller and Morris Jastrow claimed that primitives had a dim perception of an Infinite that they could not understand but that they believed was real. The conception probably arose out of conviction that there was more to the universe than could be gained through the senses. Jastrow wrote that "the origin of religion, so far as historical study can solve the problem, is to be sought in the bringing into play of man's power to obtain a perception of the Infinite through the impression which the multitudinous phenomena of the universe as a whole make upon him."[41]

11. *Myth.* Religion may have begun when people took seriously the myths of former generations. For example, the Greek and Norse myths may have been told originally merely as fairy stories but later generations gave credence to them and began to worship the heroes in the myths. The stories of Paul Bunyan and Baron Munchausen might be regarded as myths that did not develop into religion.

12. *Sex.* Sigmund Freud and others have pointed out the close relationship between religion and sex. George Albert Coe, who did not support the theory, named the following facts that give rise to the theory:

> (1) the wide distribution of gods of procreation, of phallic symbols, and of sexual acts as a part of religious ceremonial; (2) the discovery of a sexual factor in mental disorders that take the form of religious excitement, depression, or delusion; (3) the existence of various sects that connect spiritual yearning or perfection directly with sex, either in the way of indulgence or in the way of suppression;. . . (4) the imagery of courtship and marriage that figures so largely mystical literature, together with evidence that sexual sensations and desire, in certain individuals, are a factor in mystical ecstasy; (5) the close connection between conversion experiences and adolescence; (6) the emphasis upon "love" in the Christian religion.[42]

In connection with the fourth point it is interesting to note the subtitle of the famous *New England Primer*: "Spiritual Milk for American Babes, drawn from the Breasts of both Testaments."

13. *Dawn of Social Consciousness.* Edward Scribner Ames regarded religion as "social consciousness" and believed that "The original and perpetual spring of religion is therefore the life activity itself involved in procuring food, caring for young, acquiring, and defending property, and in furthering social welfare."[43]

14. *Cosmic Piety.* Ludwig Feuerbach and Karl Robert Eduard von Hartmann presented the theory that religion grew out of human consciousness of weakness in the presence of the overwhelming majesty of the universe. The starry heavens, lightning, thunder, mountains, plains, and oceans aroused a feeling of awe that has developed into religion. This veneration of natural phenomena, according to the supporters of the theory, may take either a pessimistic or an optimistic world outlook.

Classification of Religions

Another philosophical way to study religion is to attempt to classify the religions of the world. S. Radhakrishnan suggested a distinction based on whether the religious experience or the religious object be stressed: "The religions of the world can be distinguished into those which emphasize the object and those which insist on experience. For the first class religion is an attitude of faith and conduct directed to a power without. For the second it is an experience to which the individual attaches supreme value."[44]

Arnold Toynbee said there are eight faiths in the world today, and they can be divided into those that are the creations of civilizations still living, Confucianism and Hīnayāna Buddhism, and those that are the creations of civilizations no longer living, Zorastrianism, Judaism, Christianity, Islam, Mahāyāna Buddhism, and Hinduism.[45]

Paul Tillich offered a similar classification: the nonhistorical religions, Brahmanism and Buddhism, and the historical religions, that is, Zoroastrianism, Judaism, Christianity, and Islam.[46] A much more interesting and fruitful classification of religions, although not offered as a classification of religions, is Tillich's assertion that humans are in quest of the "New Being" or "New Creation." He wrote, "The message of Christianity is not Christianity, but a New Reality. . . . And we should not be too worried about the Christian religion, about the state of the churches, about membership and doctrines, about institutions and ministers, about sermons and sacraments. . . . The New Creation—that is our ultimate concern."[47] Tillich often quoted St. Paul's words, "Wherefore if any man be in Christ, he is a new creature."[48] He used the term "New Being" both for the hopes and efforts of human beings to realize all their potentialities, which he called "the horizontal direction of the expectation of the New Being,"[49] and for the transcendent illumination that he called the "vertical" direction revealed in the symbols "Messiah," "Christ," "Servant of Jahweh," the "Son of Man," and the "Man from Above."[50] Although Tillich admitted that the expectation is universal, that "the history of the symbol 'Messiah' ('Christ') shows that its origin transcends both Christianity and Judaism, thus confirming the universal human expectation of a new reality,"[51] he continued to claim that the vertical or revelatory direction was exclusively Christian—at least until the final year of his life when, after sharing a seminar on world religions with Mircea Eliade at the University of Chicago, he stated publicly that some parts of his thinking would have been different had he had the benefit of this exposure earlier.

In volume 2 of *Systematic Theology*, in a section titled "Ways of Self-Salvation and Their Failure," Tillich listed alternatives to revelatory religion, that is, religions in which salvation comes as a gift or grace. Although Tillich used the classification to point to the error in any religion that follows the way of self-salvation exclusively, his discussion contains the following excellent classification of religions.

1. Revelatory religions that identify religion and revelation, excluding self-salvation.
2. Self-salvation religions that identify religion and the attempt at self-salvation. The former, said Tillich, "distorts what it has received" and the latter "fails in what it tries to achieve."[52]
3. Legalistic religions that attempt to establish a relationship among human beings and between human beings and gods by means of a law.
4. Ascetic religions that attempt to extinguish desire by eliminating the objects of desire.
5. Mystical religions that, rather than waiting for the moments of ecstasy, attempt to promote them.
6. Sacramental religions that establish rites that must be exactly observed.
7. Doctrinal religions that, in insisting on the importance of right believing, create the "terrible inner struggles between the will to be honest and the will to be saved."[53]
8. Emotional religions that make an effort to promote emotion for its own sake until " 'piety' becomes a tool with which to achieve a transformation within one's self."[54]

Tillich argues that the quest for the New Being is universal, but that the horizontal quest without the vertical revelation results in distortion:

> All ways of self-salvation distort the way of salvation. . . . Actually, even the awareness of estrangement and the desire for salvation are effects of the presence of saving power, in other words, revelatory experiences. The same is true of the ways of self-salvation. Legalism presupposes the reception of the law in a revelatory experience; asceticism, the awareness of the infinite as judging the finite; mysticism, the experience of ultimacy in being and meaning; sacramental self-salvation, the gift of a sacramental presence; doctrinal self-salvation, the gift of manifest truth; emotional self-salvation, the transforming power of the holy. Without these presuppositions, human attempts at self-salvation could not even begin. *Falsa religio* is not identical with special historical religions but with the self-saving attempts in every religion, even in Christianity.[55]

Another philosophical classification of religions may be found in the *Bhagavad Gītā*—"the richest treasure amongst the spiritual possessions of the Hindus."[56] According to Radhakrishnan and Moore it is "a religious classic rather than a philosophical treatise,"[57] yet they included its full text in their *A Source Book in Indian Philosophy*. According to the *Gītā* religion has four primary paths (*mārgas*). Originally *mārga* denoted a path made by wild animals. In time it denoted the path a hunter follows to the lair of a wild animal, and finally *mārga* was used to indicate a path or way that leads to salvation. *Mārga* is closely related to other Sanskrit terms, such as *pada* (step), *yāna* (vehicle), *upaya* (mean), *yaga* (yoko), *āchāra* (rule), *vāda* (thesis). *Mārga* in Hinduism leads to *mokṣa* (liberation from the birth-death cycle) and in Buddhism leads to *nirvaṇa* (extinction of the notion of a self). In a Western framework a *mārga* is a way to salvation, wholeness, psychological integration, or self-perfection.

The *Bhagavad Gītā* is an excellent source of information for those interested in *mārgas*. Although the dramatic context of the *Gītā* is Arjuna's hesitation to enter a battle, the conversation with his charioteer—Lord Kṛṣṇa in disguise—soon turns to the broader question of how one may live a rich and full life. According to the *Gītā* four *mārgas* lead to salvation. These four are presented in many places in the poem. At least once they are listed as four alternatives. This passage, which Indian interpreters regard as the heart of the message, may be translated:

> Anyone who does my work,
> or who seeks to know me,
> or who worships me,
> or who is free from attachment,
> that one comes to me.[58]

The four are: (1) the path of action (*karma mārga*), (2) the path of thought (*jñāna mārga*), (3) the path of devotion (*bhakti mārga*), and (4) the path of psychological discipline (*yoga mārga*). Arjuna, understandably confused by the wealth of paths, asks Kṛṣṇa to select for him the way he ought to go. But Kṛṣṇa refuses. The choice, he says, must be man's, not God's.

> I have expounded the wisdom
> that is most secret.
> You are the one who must ponder it
> and act as you think best.[59]

Arjuna is assured by Kṛṣṇa:

> Whatever path you travel
> is my path;
> wherever you walk
> the path leads to me.[60]

Kṛṣṇa's words are similar to that magnificent advice of Eckhart: "Whatever the way that leads you most frequently to awareness of God, follow that way; and if another way appears, different from the first, and you quit the first and take the second, and the second works, it is all right. It would be nobler and better, however, to achieve rest and security through evenness, in any thing, and not have to delay and hunt around for your special way."[61]

A *jñāna mārga* religion does not proceed by the positive attaining of knowledge, nor by argument, nor by inference from observation and experiment. It proceeds rather on the assumption that by removing barriers self-revealing reality will be manifest. The illumination of self-awareness displaces the darkness of Self-forgetfulness.

A *karma mārga* religion is more than a religion of good works and moral practice. It is also based on the sound principles that acting is often the stimulus that leads to believing, feeling, and knowing. One who fulfills *dharma* (obligation) may discover for whom and to whom it is a *dharma*.

A *bhakti mārga* religion is the way of love and devotion to a chosen god, and it will lead to the obligation to do the will of the god and to understand the nature of the god.

A *yoga mārga* religion is the way of rigorous physical and psychological discipline. *Jñāna* and *bhakti* are ways of thought and feeling which lead to action, and *karma* and *yoga* are ways of action which lead to thought and feeling.

The four ways as presented in the *Gītā* are not only alternative religious paths, but also elements, factors, and stages in the human quest for meaning and significance in life and in the discovery of the ultimate values of existence. Kṛṣṇa therefore tells Arjuna to select a way—an *iṣṭa mārga* (chosen way)—because any way, properly followed, will encompass the values of the other ways. According to Nalini Kanta Brahma the *Bhagavad Gītā* is "a beautiful synthesis of all the divergent lines of thought and practice that have found a permanent footing in the history of the cultural development of the Hindus. . . . In the *Gītā* we find *Karma*, *Yoga*, *Jñāna* and *Bhakti*, in fact, all the different forms of *Sādhanā* that are current. . . . The *Gītā* is primarily the scripture of synthesis, and to force on it sectarian views seems to be an entire mis-interpretation of its spirit."[62]

Hinduism through the centuries has expanded upon the primary four *mārgas* with variations that might be termed "sub-*mārgas*." There are within the general rubric of *karma mārga* such sub-*mārgas* as (1) *dharma mārga* (the way that stresses doing one's duty); (2) *ahiṁsa mārga* (the way of nonviolence); (3) *āśrama mārga* (the way of doing the duties that befall one through the stages of life); (4) *swami mārga* (the way of the priest); (5) *pravritti mārga* (the way of full participation in life); (6) *niṣkama mārga* (the way of acting with no concern for results); (7) *Kriyā mārga* (the way of making places of worship and the artifacts of worship); (8) *akriyā mārga* (the way of nonaction, or cultivation of the passive virtues); (9) *bhoga mārga* (the way of full enjoyment and pleasure both for one's self and for others).

Under *jñāna mārga* are subsumed such *mārgas* as (1) *tarka mārga* (the way of logic, reasoning, discussion, and debate); (2) *dhyāna mārga* (the way of meditation); (3) *syād mārga* (the way based on the notion that things are perhaps so and perhaps not so; the way used in the logic of Jainism); (4) *śūnya mārga* (the way based on the doctrine that all things are empty). *Sūnya mārga* is the way of

Mādhyamika or Śūnyavāda Buddhism. It can be called "the nothingness way," that is, the way of no substance.

The sub-*mārgas* of *bhakti mārga* include (1) *īṣvara mārga* (the way of worshipping a personal god); (2) *iṣṭadevatā mārga* (the way of worshipping a personally chosen deity); (3) *puṣṭi mārga* (a way that is not of human effort, but one that is a blooming of divine grace; the way of "efflorescence."); (4) *upāsana mārga* (the way or prayer); (5) *mantra mārga* (the way of incantations, spells, and recitation of sacred formulae); (6) *yajña mārga* (the way of sacrificial rituals).

Under *yoga mārga* are included such sub-*mārga* as (1) *tapas mārga* (the way of asceticism and self-denial); (2) *deha mārga* (the way of the body, or physical culture); (3) *haṭha marga* (the way of the development of psychological powers of the body); (4) *śilpa mārga* (the way of art creation and art appreciation); (5) *śaḍja mārga* (the way of music creation and musical appreciation); (6) *laya mārga* (the way of stimulation of the *chakras* of the spine); (7) *rāja mārga* (the way of the realization of all possibilities by total control of mind and body; the "kingly" way); (8) *nirodha mārga* (the way of mental restraint until the mind is without objects of perception or conception); (9) *rasavāda mārga* (the way that involves the use of drugs); (10) *samādhi mārga* (the way of trance contemplation; destruction of "all-pointedness" and rise of "one-pointedness"); (11) *tantra mārga* (the way of eroticism); (12) *śava mārga* (the way of meditation on the dead in graveyards and cremation grounds; the "cadaver" way).

The "keynote of the *Gītā*" according to Brajendra Nath Seal is the synthesis of the *mārgas*. Seal writes that "there is Knowledge in Works and Works in Knowledge. . . . Knowledge in Devotion and Devotion in Knowledge . . . Works in Devotion and Devotion or faith in Works."[63] Any path faithfully and fully pursued includes the values of the other paths. I interpret Seal's insight to imply that each person existentially places the *mārgas* in hierarchical order. A *bhakta*, one who follows *bhakti mārga*, ranks the other *mārgas* in second, third, and fourth places in the pursuit of *mokṣa*. Similar rankings are made by the *karmin*, the *jñānin*, and the *yogi*. Hence, there are twenty-four synthetic *mārgas*. When the rankings are expressed in percentages of interest—as they must be—the *mārgas* are practically innumerable. For example, I estimate Gandhi's synthetic *mārga* as 60 percent *karma*, 20 percent *bhakti*, 15 percent *yoga*, and 5 percent *jñāna;* Ramakrishna's as 60 percent *bhakti*, 20 percent *yoga*, 10 percent *jñāna*, and 10 percent *karma*; and Radhakrishna's 70 percent *jñāna*, 20 percent *karma*, 5 percent *yoga*, and 5 percent *bhakti*.

Religious Values

The discussion of religious values in both the East and the West is often marred by a failure to indicate whether the discussion is of the values of religion in general or the values of a specific religion. Argument about the relative merits of individual religions of the world is not on the philosophical agenda, although the philosopher should note that religions claim to offer moral guidance, to provide a faith for living, to motivate human endeavor, to bring salvation, and so on. The philosopher should also note that some claim religions prevent moral growth, limit life choices, restrain human activities, and disintegrate personalities; Solomon Reinach wrote that religion is "a sum of scruples which impede the free exercise of our faculties."[64]

I shall limit consideration of religious values to the chief religious value with respect to the natural world, with respect to the social world, and with respect to the self.

The chief religious value in human relations to the external, physical, natural—and some may wish to add supernatural—world was presented in 1917 by Rudolf Otto in *Das Heilig*. This book went through six editions in its first ten years, and was translated into English in 1923 with the title *The Idea of the Holy*.[65] It is a phenomenological study of religion, that is, an analysis of the data of experience in the subject's existential immediacy. The phenomenologist believes that the question "What do you feel?" is as important as "What do you know?" and "How do you know?" But Otto was not only a phenomenologist, as he indicated in the foreword he wrote in 1923 for the first English translation of *Das Heilig*:

> In this book I have ventured to write of that which may be called "non-rational" or "supra-rational" in the depths of the divine nature. I do not thereby want to promote in any way the tendency of our time towards an extravagant and fantastic "irrationalism," but rather to join issue with it in its morbid form. The "irrational" is to-day a favourite theme of all who are too lazy to think or too ready to evade the arduous duty of clarifying their ideas and grounding their convictions on a basis of coherent thought. This book, recognizing the profound import of the non-rational for metaphysic, makes a serious attempt to analyse all the more exactly the *feeling* which remains where the *concept* fails, and to introduce a terminology which is not any the more loose or indeterminate for having necessarily to make use of *symbols*. Before I ventured upon this field of inquiry I spent many years of study upon the *rational* aspect of that supreme Reality we call "God," and the results of my work are contained in my books, *Naturalistische und religiöse Weltansicht* (Eng. Tr. *Naturalism and Religion*. London, 1907), and *Die Kant-friesische Religions-Philosophie*. And I feel that no one ought to concern himself with the "Numen ineffabile" who has not already devoted assiduous and serious study to the "Ratio aeterna."[66]

Otto examined the feelings an individual has when he says he had an experience of God. Otto admitted this is difficult:

> The reader is invited to direct his mind to a moment of deeply-felt religious

> experience, as little as possible qualified by other forms of consciousness. Whoever cannot do this, whoever knows no such moments in his experience, is requested to read no further; for it is not easy to discuss questions of religious psychology with one who can recollect the emotions of his adolescence, the discomforts of indigestion, or, say, social feelings, but cannot recall any intrinsically religious feelings.[67]

Although religions should take pride in having no lack of conceptions about God, said Otto, these conceptions are predicates of that which cannot be grasped by rational conceptions. The essence of the religious object is non-rational or superrational, and the relationship between that object and a human being "is not exclusively contained and exhaustively comprised in any series of 'rational' assertions."[68] The rational is the way to conceive God, but full understanding of God as the religious object depends upon an understanding of what is involved in the existential immediacy of religious experience. The God-experience has both a rational and an irrational component. The irrational is "the holy." Kant had used the term *the holy* (*das Heiling*) for the completely moral good. Otto agreed, but according to him moral goodness is only part of the connotation. The additional element Otto called "the numinous," a word he coined from the Latin *numen*. *Numen* is closely related to *mana*, a Polynesian term adopted by anthropologists for extraphysical and impersonal power emanating from nature, a power that produces and maintains the order of the universe.[69] The numinous is the heart of the religious experience. It is a unique, psychical experience, not a combination of other experiences. This was what the ancient Greeks had in mind when they spoke of "shuddering" before the image of a god. Students of Otto have compared the feeling to those of a wealthy man who has lost all his friends by death. An American psychologist claimed he had a numinous experience when, after accidentally dropping his glasses while fishing in a deep lake, he found them resting on the anchor of the boat. Otto said the numinous is "creature-consciousness": "It is the emotion of a creature, abased and overwhelmed by its own nothingness in contrast to that which is supreme above all creatures."[70] He also insisted that the experience is the experience of something—the *numen*. The numinous as a value category is evoked by the presence of the *numen*, which is an objective value-reality in the religious object.

The nature of the numinous as feeling response to the *numen* as the object embodying awe-inspiring power can be expressed as *mysterium tremendum*. *Tremendum* refers to the hidden or esoteric that cannot be conceived or understood because it is extraordinary and unfamiliar. *Mysterium* refers to the beyond. The *tremendum* has three components: (1) awefulness, a terror by reason of the absolute unapproachability of the religious object; (2) overpoweringness, the element of might and majesty; and (3) energy or urgency, that which is felt as vitality, will, force, movement, excitement, violence. The components of *mysterium* are "The Wholly Other" and "Fascination." The Wholly Other denotes the beyond in mysticism that leaves the mystic in stupor, blank wonder, absolute amazement, and an astonishment that strikes one dumb. Fascination refers to the elements of entrancement and longing in the numinous experience.

Otto's considerations were made in the context of Judaic-Christianity, but a Hindu feels similar emotions in the presence of images, at the confluence of rivers, on the ghats at Banaras, and even before a *guru*. Taoists, Buddhists, Confucianists, Shintoists, or Muslims also may experience *The Holy* in various aspects of their devotional life.

The chief religious value in human relations to the social world is peace. According to the Hebrew prophets a time is coming when there shall be a "Prince of Peace"[71] who will inaugurate a period of history when wild animals will no longer prey on each other—"And the wolf shall dwell with the lamb, and the leopard shall lie down with the kid; and the calf and the young lion and the fatling together"[72]—and wars will end—"They shall beat their swords into plowshares, and their spears into pruning-hooks; nation shall not lift up sword against nation, neither shall they learn war any more."[73] Christians believe that Jesus the Christ was that Prince of Peace, pointing out that his birth was announced by an angelic proclamation of peace on earth, he preached a message of love, and he departed with a benediction of peace—"Peace I leave with you; my peace I give unto you."[74]

In Indian society "*Śanti*" (peace) is a common salutation and farewell. Many Hindu prayers end in mantralike fashion: "*Śanti. Śanti. Śanti.*" The principle of *ahiṃsā* (nonviolence or harmlessness) is a basic moral principle of Hinduism, Jainism, and Buddhism that has been applied in various ways, such as vegetarianism, nonslaying of animals, pacificism, passive resistance, and acts of charity. The following from the *Sutta-Nipata* is characteristic of all of Buddhism and Jainism, and of much of Hinduism:

> May creatures all abound
> in weal and peace; may all
> be blessed with peace always;
> all creatures weak or strong,
> all creatures great and small;
> creatures unseen or seen,
> dwelling afar or near,
> born or awaiting birth,
> —may all be blessed with peace![75]

The chief value of religion with respect to the self is salvation. This emotionally laden term has at least three meanings: metaphysical, moral, and psychological. The metaphysical meaning is that a human being does not cease to exist at death. To be saved in this sense means to be preserved.

The moral meaning is that an individual can be saved from the judgment and the punishment that rebellious and immoral acts deserve. Christianity has assigned to the Christ the role of atoning for human sins, that is, restoring the at-one-ness between the human and the divine, but it has never reached an agreement as to how the atonement works. At least five types of theories have been offered. According to the ransom theories, those who had rebelled against God and had not recognized his sovereignty in their lives were held captive in hell by a satonic figure known as the Devil. The Devil agreed he would release the captives upon receipt of a suitable consideration, namely, the Son of God. This is the meaning of the phrase in many of the early Christian creeds, "he descended into hell." However, according to the story the Devil was outwitted, since upon releasing the captives he found he was unable to hold the Christ in hell—"He arose from the dead." One of the most ingenious of the ransom theories was the fishhook theory of Rufinus of Aquileia (c. 400):

> The purpose of the Incarnation . . . was that the divine virtue of the Son of God might be as it were a hook hidden beneath the form of human flesh . . . to lure on the prince of this age to a contest; that the Son might offer him his flesh as a bait ad that then the divinity which lay beneath might catch him and hold him fast with its hook . . . Then as a fish when it seizes a baited hook not only fails to drag off the bait but is itself dragged out of the water to serve as food for others; so he that had the power of death seized the body of Jesus in death, unaware of the hook of divinity concealed therein. Having swallowed it, he was caught straightway; the bars of hell were burst, and he was, as it were, drawn up from the pit, to become food for others."[76]

A second class of theories of atonement known as the satisfaction theories was later introduced. Anselm in the eleventh century claimed only a *deus-homo* (god-man) could pay the debt owed to God as a satisfaction of divine outrage at human sinfulness. Penal substitution theories—the third class—were popular at the time of the Protestant Reformation. According to these theories the crucifixion was the punishment that penal justice required, which Christ suffered in substitute of the sinner. A fourth type, the governmental theories, held that Christ was not punished for the sins of humanity, but he as the Son of God endured the sufferings that God the righteous ruler accepted as vindication of his honor lost in the wayward behavior of his special creation to whom he had granted free will. A fifth class consists of moral influence theories. These theories were developed in Christianity as a reaction against the legalism of the other four theories. According to the moral influence theories the crucifixion and death of the Christ were not intended to remove obstacles to divine forgiveness, but were part of a divine plan to bring sinners to repentence and to win their love and devotion.

Although these are the chief types of theories of the atonement developed in Christianity, individual Christians continue to develop new interpretations. J. W. C. Ward has recently offered what might be called a Platonic theory: "As Jesus Christ, the Incarnate pays the debt humanity owes to absolute goodness and unites to Himself all members of the human race who will accept His claim upon their allegiance."[77]

The psychological meaning of salvation is that persons can be cured of the anxiety, frustration, fragmentation, boredom, and disintegration that so often beset beasts aspiring to be God. While Christian poetry and hymnology are filled with assurances of the psychological impact of salvation, it is interesting to find such also in the *bhakti* literature of Hinduism. A poem from Tukārām (1608–1649), a Maratha Vaiṣṇavite, is illustrative:

O save me, save me, Mightiest,
Save me and set me free.
O let the love that fills my breast
Cling to thee lovingly.

Grant me to taste how sweet thou art;
Grant me but this, I pray,
And never shall my love depart
Or turn from thee away.

Then I thy name shall magnify
And tell thy praise abroad,
For very love and gladness I
Shall dance before my God.

Grant to me, Viṭṭhal, that I rest
Thy blessed feet beside;
Ah, give me this, the dearest, best,
And I am satisfied.[78]

Mokṣa in Hinduism can mean an elevation in caste in the next incarnation, escape from reincarnation, a post mortem nonphysical state of identity with celestials, an absorption into the Brahman, a joyous freedom from paying the penalty for one's sins, liberation from turmoil and suffering, or the attainment of a richer and fuller life both mortal and postmortal.

Nirvāṇa is used in two senses in Buddhism. One is the state of enlightenment in which the mortal individual has annihilated from his thinking, feeling, and acting all notions of a self. This is known in Theravāda Buddhism as having attained the *arhat* condition. Mahāyāna Buddhism adds to this negativity of the self the positive side of universal love (*karunā*) for all beings. Such a compassionate being, who gives his earned merit to help others attain the same condition, is known as a *bodhisattva*. The second use of the term *nirvāṇa* is for the cessation of all existence, the ending of rebirths, the condition of being completely extinguished or "blown out." This is sometimes denoted by *parinirvāṇa*. In Mahāyāna *parinirvāṇa* there is the elimination of not only the notion of a self or ego, but also all discriminations and all dualisms, and the recognition that emptiness is the sole truth and sole reality. *Nirvāṇa* in Theravāda is the ending of all desires. *Nirvāṇa* in Mahāyāna is the ending of both all desires and all that can be desired. Perhaps the paradigm of full *nirvāṇa* in Mahāyāna is to think of mirrors mirroring mirrors.

God

The most creative human act is to make gods in the human image. God-creation is also an absurdly arrogant act. The human being, having evolved to the level of self-awareness, assumes that selves like the human self control events in the natural world—and even that the entire universe is governed by a Self. Xenophanes, the first Western philosopher to disclose the natural origin of the gods and to call attention to their anthropomorphic nature, wrote, "The Ethopians say that their gods are snub-nosed and black, the Thracians that theirs have light blue eyes and red hair. But if cattle and horses or lions had hands, or were able to draw with their hands and do the works that men can do, horses would draw the forms of the gods like horses, and cattle like cattle, and they would make their bodies such as they each had themselves."[79] He also pointed out that humans perversely depict the gods as morally inferior: "Homer and Hesiod have attributed to the gods everything that is a shame and reproach among men, stealing and committing adultery and deceiving each other."[80] The god that Xenophanes believed to be the true god was transcendent to human imagination: "One god, greatest among gods and men, in no way similar to mortals either in body or in thought. Always he remains in the same place, moving not at all; nor is it fitting for him to go to different places at different times, but without toil he shapes all things by the thought of his mind. All of him sees, all thinks, and all hears."[81] Diogenes Laertius wrote that Xenophanes was expelled from the city of his birth, Colophon, and lived as a wandering minstrel in Sicily, and perhaps in Italy. We do not know whether his expulsion was due to his criticism of Homer and Hesiod, or for his exposure of the anthropomorphism of the gods, or for his heretically new idea of an abstract concept of deity.

Etymology is not very helpful in understanding the nature of God. The English word *god* may have come from *guth*, an Old Irish word for voice. The Greek *theós*, in addition to its symbolization of the gods of classical mythology, was used for the abstract notion of completeness or fullness, as titles of rulers, and as a term for an authority. The Latin *deus* was probably a transliteration of *theós*. The basic Hebrew root for god is *El* (high one). From this the ancient Hebrews formed *Elohim* (the most high ones); *El Shaddai* (the high one of the mountains, or perhaps the high one with breasts, since the Hebrew word *Shaddai* may have come from the Akkadian work *Shadu*, which meant "breasts"; see Genesis 49:25 for reference to "blessings of the breasts, and of the womb"); *El*

Olam (the everlasting high one); *El Bethel* (the high one of Bethel). They used *JHVH* as the tetragrammation to symbolize their God. This was considered so sacred it was not to be spoken. The Sanskrit word *deva* means "one who gives." The Chinese have used such words as *Shang-Ti* (upper ruler) and *T'ien* (heaven), but the connotation has usually been cosmic order rather than that which other cultures might call a god.

An essential aspect of the concept of god is its designation of personality or selfhood. Thus a theist is one who believes in the existence of a cosmic self sufficiently similar to a human self that the word *self* may be used properly in respect both to the human being and to the universal being. If the notion of self or person is not intended, then one ought not to use the word *god*. This is why the followers of Rāmānuja may correctly refer to Brahman as God, but the followers of Śaṅkara ought not to refer to Brahman as God. An atheist, therefore, is one who denies the existence of a cosmic self, although the atheist (or nontheist) may affirm the reality of an Absolute, a Brahman, a Totality, a One, or a Ground of Being. Monotheism is the belief in one God, ditheism in two gods, tritheism in three, and polytheism in many.[82] Deism is the view that the one god is creator only. Pantheism, which etymologically means "all is God," is sometimes used when terms like *monism* or *absolute idealism* would be more appropriate. Panentheism is the view that God's being includes the physical universe but is not exhausted by the physical universe.

Charles Hartshorne, one of America's leading religious philosophers of the twentieth century, contends there are five major questions relative to the conception of God: (1) is God eternal? (2) is God temporal? (3) is God conscious? (4) does God know the world? (5) does God include the world? He, answering "yes" to all the questions, defines God as "the Supreme as Eternal-Temporal Consciousness, Knowing and including the World."[83] Hartshorne says there are eight alternatives to his view:

1. God as eternal consciousness, neither knowing nor including the world, such as the theism of Aristotle.
2. God as eternal consciousness that knows but excludes the world, such as the classical theisms of Augustine, Anselm, Aquinas, and Leibniz.
3. God as the Eternal beyond consciousness and knowledge, as in the emanationism of Plotinus.
4. God as eternal consciousness, knowing and including the world, such as the classical pantheism of Spinoza and Josiah Royce.
5. God as eternal-temporal consciousness, partly exclusive of the world, such as the temporalistic theism of Faustus Socinus and Jules Lequier.
6. God as eternal-temporal consciousness, partly exclusive of the world, as in the limited pantheism of William James and E. S. Brightman.
7. God as wholly temporal or emerging consciousness, such as the emergent evolutionism of S. Alexander.

8. God as temporal and nonconscious as in the naturalistic empiricism of H. N. Wieman.

Philosophers, in offering and examining arguments for the existence of God, have rarely given sufficient attention to the nature of the God for whose existence the argument is offered. Most of the arguments studied by Western philosophers are for the existence of alternative number two above, that is, a God as eternal consciousness that knows but excludes the world. The three traditional arguments are the cosmological, the teleological, and the ontological.

The cosmological argument begins with the assumption that every event is an effect of a previous event. But if this principle were to apply to everything, then nothing would happen and nothing would be. The productive causes of events could then be traced back infinitely. In such a situation nothing would ever happen because the series of productive events would be endless. So to explain the fact that things are and that events do happen, we must assume a First Cause that lies outside our experience. The First Cause is in one sense never experienced, yet indirectly it is experienced in its effects. Everything that is and everything that happens are effects of this First Cause. The firstness of the First Cause is not a chronological first, but it is first in the sense that it is not caused by something else. The First Cause is the cause of the cause-effect series. God is the term we use to symbolize this First Cause.

The teleological argument begins with the observation that there are evidences of design and order within the world, and proceeds to argue analogously to the design and order of the entire world. As William Paley (1743–1805) stated, a watch implies a watchmaker and a world implies a worldmaker. Aquinas presented the argument in this manner:

> We see that things which lack knowledge, such as natural bodies, act for an end, and this is evident from their acting always, or nearly always, in the same way, so as to obtain the best result. Hence it is plain that they achieve their end, not fortuitously, but designedly. Now whatever lacks knowledge cannot move towards an end, unless it be directed by some being endowed with knowledge and intelligence; as the arrow is directed by the archer. Therefore some intelligent being exists by whom all natural things are directed to their end; and this being we call God."[84]

Western philosophers have probably given far more attention to the three arguments for the existence of God than they deserve. The god established by the arguments is not the god of religious experience. The cosmological arguments attempt to establish the existence of a First Cause, the teleological arguments attempt to establish the existence of a cosmic designer, and the ontological arguments attempt to establish that existence is inherent in the idea of God. But no one prays to first cause, cosmic designer, or idea of God. The ontological arguments, which are often regarded as the jewels of all arguments for God, are probably the worst because they confuse the *fact* of existence with the idea of existence. To establish that the *idea* of God includes the *idea* of existence does not establish that a God, who is more than an idea about God, has existence, which is more than an idea about existence. There is a vast difference between having an idea of a hundred pounds in one's pocket and having a hundred pounds in one's pocket.

One of the most ingenious efforts to offer an alternative basis for belief in God was that developed by William James in a lecture given to a joint meeting of the philosophy clubs of Yale and Brown universities in 1896. He entitled the lecture "The Will to Believe," although he later said it should have been called "The Right to Believe." He described it at the opening of the lecture as "an essay in justification *of* faith, a defence of our right to adopt a believing attitude in religious matters, in spite of the fact that our merely logical intellect may not have been coerced."[85] He said he was defending "the lawfulness of voluntarily adopted faith."[86]

A hypothesis, said James, is "anything that may be proposed to our belief."[87] Hypotheses may be either live or dead. A live hypothesis is "one which appeals as a real possibility to him to whom it is proposed."[88] A dead hypothesis, obviously, is one that has no appeal as a real possibility. A situation in which a choice must be made between hypotheses is known as an option. Options are living or dead, forced or avoidable, momentous or trivial. What should one do when facing an option between A and B in which the option is living, forced, and momentous, and which cannot be settled by appeal to knowledge and reason? There are three possibilities: (1) "A," (2) "B," and (3) "I'll not decide." But since the option cannot be decided on intellectual grounds, and since it cannot be avoided, then the choice among "A" and "B" and "I'll not decide" is a passional choice. Since the choice must be made, and since the choice must be passional, argued James, then would it not be better to decide according to what one wants? The thesis he was defending is this: "Our passional nature not only lawfully may, but must, decide an option between propositions, whenever it is a genuine option that cannot by its nature be decided on intellectual grounds; for to say, under such circumstances, 'Do not decide, but leave the question open,' is itself a passional decision,—just like deciding yes or no,—and is attended with the same risk of losing the truth."[89]

The option James had in mind appears to be belief in the existence of God. He compared his option with Pascal's wager, which he stated in the following manner:

> You must either believe or not believe that God is—which will you do? Your human reason cannot say. A game is going on between you and the nature of things which at the day of judgment will bring out either heads or tails. Weigh what your gains and your losses would be if you should stake all you have on heads, or God's existence: if you win in such case, you gain eternal beatitude; if you lose, you lose nothing at all. If there were an infinity of

> chances, and only one for God in this wager, still you ought to stake your all on God; for though you surely risk a finite loss by this procedure, any finite loss is reasonable, even a certain one is reasonable, if there is but the possibility of infinite gain. Go, then, and take holy water, and have masses said; belief will come and stupefy your scruples,—*Cela vous fera croire et vous abêtira*. Why should you not? At bottom, what have you to lose?[90]

Such a religious faith, said James, "in the language of the gaming table . . . is put to its last trumps."[91] "We feel that a faith in masses and holy water adopted willfully after such a mechanical calculation would lack the inner soul of faith's reality; and if we were ourselves in the place of the Deity, we should probably take particular pleasure in cutting off believers of this pattern from their infinite reward."[92]

James's option is not between intellectual belief and intellectual disbelief in the existence of God but between the pragmatic conditions of living with belief in the existence of God and living without belief in the existence of God. There is no third choice—one either lives with or without the belief. To refuse to choose is to choose to live without belief in God.

> When I look at the religious question as it really puts itself to concrete men, and when I think of all the possibilities which both practically and theoretically it involves, then this command that we shall put a stopper on our heart, instincts, and courage, and *wait*—acting of course meanwhile more or less as if religion were *not* true—till doomsday, or till such time as our intellect and senses working together may have raked in evidence enough,—this command, I say, seems to me the queerest idol ever manufactured in the philosophic cave. Were we scholastic absolutists, there might be more excuse. If we had an infallible intellect with its objective certitudes, we might feel ourselves disloyal to such a perfect organ of knowledge in not trusting to it exclusively, in not waiting for its releasing word. But if we are empiricists, if we believe that no bell in us tolls to let us know for certain when truth is in our grasp, then it seems a piece of idle fantasticality to preach so solemnly our duty of waiting for the bell. Indeed we *may* wait if we will,—I hope you do not think that I am denying that,—but if we do so, we do so at our peril as much as if we believed.[93]

Evil

Evil is a problem for the theist. Only one who believes that the world is under the control of an all-powerful and all-good deity finds the experiences of pain, frustration, suffering, sin, and death a problem demanding solution. Consequently, the reality of evil is an effective weapon with which the atheist can torment the theist.

The problem of evil was formulated in the following manner by Lucius Caecilius Firmianus Lactantius (c. 300):

> God either wishes to take away evils and he cannot, or he can and does not wish to, or he neither wishes to nor is able, or he both wishes to and is able. If he wishes to and is not able, he is feeble, which does not fall in with the notion of god. If he is able to and does not wish to, he is envious, which is equally foreign to god. If he neither wishes to nor is able, he is both envious and feeble and therefore not god. If he both wishes to and is able, which alone is fitting to god, whence, therefore, are there evils, and why does he not remove them?[94]

The theist who accepts the reality of evil must develop a theodicy.

Evil is any event that hampers human development or diminishes human happiness. This definition indicates that evil always refers to human beings. While human carnivorous appetites might be regarded as evil by cows, pigs, and chickens, we assume that only self-conscious beings can distinguish good and evil. The definition also assumes that the development and happiness of human beings has intrinsic worth.

The evils in the world can be divided into moral evils and nonmoral evils. Moral evils are those for which human beings are culpable. Misdemeanor, felony, crime, and sin are some of the terms used to designate various kinds of moral evils. Jesus is reported to have attempted to extend the denotation of moral evil from acts to thoughts and desires: "Ye have heard that it was said, Thou shalt not commit adultery: but I say unto you, that every one that looketh on a woman to lust after her hath committed adultery with her already in his heart."[95] A moral evil in the "heart" would be most difficult to detect and bring to trial.

The nonmoral evils can be classified as natural, physical, intellectual, and metaphysical. Natural evils include droughts, floods, cyclones, earthquakes, mosquitoes, and all the other aspects of nature that may handicap human efforts to live. Human beings have often believed that nature is controlled by malicious spirits that seek our destruction. Physical evils include the pain and suffering experienced in the diseases that rack bodies, destroy minds, and finally produce deaths. The presence of suffering has always been a problem, particularly the apparent unjust distribution of suffering. Intellectual evils are the doubts, perplexities, and errors that disrupt the pursuit of knowledge. Metaphysical evils are the realities that frustrate human activity. The recalcitrance of matter is one. Others are the vast collection of witches, demons, poltergeists, dragons, devils, and so on, with which fertile imaginations have populated the world. The nonmoral evils present serious problems for the theist. How can the theist contend that a universe in which a flood destroys hundreds of innocent lives is still a moral universe? Is it right that rain should fall alike on the just and the unjust? The burden of proof falls on the theist. The theist can offer a rationale for evil by arguing from the nature of God, from human nature, or from the nature of evil.

The explanation of the presence of evil in a theistically religious world may proceed by claiming either that God is less good or less powerful than is commonly supposed. The former contends that human goodness and divine goodness are not the same. The Puritans believed that God was glorified in the damnation of some people. They sometimes affirmed their willingness to be damned for the glory of God. Sermons like Jonathan Edwards's "Sinners in the Hands of an Angry God" came close to stating that God enjoyed inflicting torture on those who departed from the approved ways of behaving. The Puritans wanted to believe in both the unlimited power of God and the unlimited goodness of God, but they were so anxious to preserve the monarchical power of divinity that they were willing to diminish the goodness of God.

A second way to explain evil by appeal to the nature of God is to claim that God is less powerful than is commonly supposed. A common form of this theodicy is to argue that God is in conflict with a power of evil. The classic dualistic religion is Zoroastrianism, with its conflict between Ahura-Mazda, the god of good symbolized by light, and Angra-Mainyu, the god of evil symbolized by darkness. The presence of a superhuman evil personality is part of the Hebrew myth of the Garden of Eden, but it is in Zachariah 3:2 that the word *Satan* first appears. The early followers of Jesus believed implicitly in the malignant activities of a devil, but they were confident that the evil one would eventually be overthrown. Gnostic Christianity was usually dualistic in its theology. During the Dark Ages European Christians commonly regarded evil events as the work of the devil and his league of demons. Dante's *Divine Comedy* and Milton's *Paradise Lost* stimulated imaginative people to believe in the existence of a cosmic evil force. Hindu and Buddhist mythology contain evil deities, for example, Rudra (the god of destruction) and Yama (the god of death).

Theodicies that argue from human nature point out that the human being is a finite agent with free will. Freedom of choice would be meaningless were there no evil to be chosen. So evil is required as an alternative to good, or human freedom would be meaningless. One variation of this thesis is that evil is necessary to stimulate sluggish humans to do good works. The Christian Chrysippus argued that bedbugs are divine stimuli to arouse men and women into action at the break of day!

The third rationale for evil is the contention that evil is a necessary opposition to good. Evil is part of the chiaroscuro that makes good obvious. Augustine wrote, "For as the beauty of a picture is increased by well-managed shadows, so, to the eye that has skill to discern it, the universe is beautified even by sinners, though, considered by themselves, their deformity is a sad blemish."[96] Another argument is that the consciousness of evil is a stage in human evolutionary development. Lower animals have no sense of sin. As humanity evolves more and more out of animality human beings might also evolve out of the present stage in which good and evil loom so large in the human perspective. For example, a level may evolve in which what today seems immoral will be regarded as unaesthetic.

A third variation of a theodicy from the nature of evil is the view that evil is a matter of perspective. That which is evil from one point of view is not evil from another point of view. A town in which no one has decaying teeth would be a bad town for dentists. Almost everyone has had an experience that at the time seemed unremittingly evil, but which later came to be regarded as a blessing in disguise. A fourth variation is the contention that evil is merely an illusion. Augustine and John Scotus Erigena bordered on this view when they insisted that there is no evil since evil is merely the absence of good.

The nontheist can point out to the theist that the problem of evil is his own making. The theist expects human life to be better because of the notion that a deity is in control. Perhaps the final defense of the theist is that the nontheist may be in error in supposing that the world is rational. The solution to the problem of evil may not be an intellectual solution. Peter Ilich Tchaikovsky said one should work until inspiration takes over. The resolution may be found in action rather than thought. Katherine Mansfield, a gifted author who died in 1922 at the age of thirty-four after a long struggle with disease, wrote in her journal: "There is no limit to human suffering. When one thinks: 'Now I have touched the bottom of the sea—now I can go no deeper,' one goes deeper. . . . I do not want to die without leaving a record of my belief that suffering can be overcome. For I do believe it. What must one do? . . . Do not resist. Take it. Be overwhelmed. Accept it fully. Make it part of life. Everything in life that we really accept undergoes a change. So suffering must become Love."[97]

Beyond God and Evil

What is the future of religion? Is it a passing phase or a permanent feature of the human condition? August Comte (1798–1857) is sometimes cited as one who prophesied the end of religion. Each body of knowledge, he said, passes through two stages in development—a theological and a metaphysical—before reaching the proper stage—the scientific. In the theological stage all phenomena are explained by supernatural factors; in the metaphysical stage phenomena are thought to be the result of unobserved causes said to lie beneath the surface of events; in the positive or scientific stage only natural causes are sought. But rather than reject religion, Comte turned science into a religion of humanity. Nietzsche engaged in bitter vituperations against the Christianity of his day, but he did not believe in nor recommend the terminus of religion. Rather, he was anxious to tear down the worship of humility ("slave worship") that men might worship strength and follow the morality of the masters. There are also those who do not predict the demise of religion, but who recommend it; Max Otto wrote that humans must "accept the stern condition of being psychically alone in all the reach of space and time."[98]

Others argue from the fact that religion in some form has been found in all societies that it will continue to characterize humanity. For example, Harris F. Rall has written, "The persistence of religion is one of the most striking facts in human history. Religion belongs to every race and age. With advancing knowledge it has had to alter its ideas. Its institutions and practices have been modified with social change. Particular religions have passed away. Yet religion persists. Bread and love and religion have been the three great impelling interests of man."[99]

At a much more sophisticated level others have argued that the human animal may evolve from its present finitude to a level of being in which religion as we now know it will be passé; Teilhard de Chardin in *The Phenomenon of Man* foresaw a time when humanity will converge at the "Omega Point," and Sri Aurobindo in *The Life Divine* predicted a similar convergence of "Gnostic Being" in *Saccidānanda*. Religion may be a roundabout road the human animal is taking to find the self by way of the symbol of God. Historically, the divine, not the human, has been the mystery.

Theology may be miscued anthropology. Ludwig Feuerbach held that the next task for Christianity is the humanization of God and that Christian theology must be transformed into anthropology. Karl Barth, a leading Christian theologian of the twentieth century, after insisting for many years on the transcendence of God, in the late 1920s, referring to his "well-known false start," wrote on "the humanity of God."[100] Human beings may have erred in seeking God for themselves rather than in themselves. In so doing they may have damned their own nature and their expectations of what they can accomplish. Teilhard described a journey of hominization and Aurobindo a journey of Brahmanization, and both pointed to a posttheistic goal. Or could it be that the gods are silent because that is their nature? "When the gods are dumb, when the 'godhead' is silent, this is ultimately not so much because they have been put to silence, but rather because their eternal silence has been exposed to a us as their most essential, their 'mystical' characteristic."[101]

There may be another reason why God is silent. One argument is that human beings have created God, and then have reified their creation into an entity. God belongs in the category of art, poetry, and imagination. But unimaginative scientists, philosophers, and theologians have placed God in the order of beings. Religious thinkers often give the wrong answers because they ask the wrong questions. "Does God exist?" suggests that existence is a proper attribute for divinity. "What is God?" implies that the answer will be "God is a being . . . a thing . . . an object . . . a spirit . . . a person." In other words, the question intimates that God is a member of a class of objects with attributes that distinguish God from other members of the class. Christians and Jews have not given sufficient attention to some of the intellectuals in their traditions. Harry Wolfson in his study of Philo (c. 25 B.C.–A.D. 45) reported that Philo said God is "the most generic" (*tó genikṓtaton*). This means, wrote Wolfson, "that God, being the highest genus, has within Him no distinction of genus and species, for only that which is between the highest genus and the ultimate species that has within it the distinction of genus and species, being the genus of that which is below it and the species of that which is above it. But since God is the highest genus He has no distinction of genus and species, that is, He belongs to no class and hence we do not know what He is."[102] Bertrand Russell quoted John Scotus Erigena (810–877) as having written, "God does not know himself, what He is, because He is not a *what*."[103] According to Martin Buber, "God is not an object besides objects and hence cannot be reached by renunciation of objects. God, indeed, is not the cosmos, but far less is the Being minus cosmos. He is not to be found by subtraction and not to be loved by reduction."[104]

Charles Hartshorne contended that Augustine, Anselm, Aquinas, and Leibniz agree in the classical theistic view of God as "eternal consciousness that knows but excludes the world." However, Augustine does not fit that classification. He wrote with respect to God,

> If we say Eternal, immortal, incorruptible, unchangeable, living, wise, powerful, beautiful, righteous, good, blessed, spirit; only the last of this list as it were seems to signify substance, but the rest to signify qualities of that substance; but it is not so in that ineffable and simple nature. For whatever seems to be predicated therein according to quality, is to be understood according to substance or essence. For far be it from us to predicate spirit of God according to substance, and good according to quality; but both according to substance.[105]

Each of the apparent qualities are substances. So God according to Augustine is eternity, immortality, incorruptibility, unchangeableness, life, wisdom, power, beauty, righteousness, goodness, blessedness, and spirituality. There is no word expressing substance, nature, essence, thatness, quiddity, or species, that can be stated as a class of which God is a member. God has no individuality, uniqueness, particularity, singularity, independent nature, distinction, specificity, thusness, or haecceity such that God can be a being in a class of beings. The Christian God is not a spirit, not a person, not even a god. In other places in his work *On the Trinity* Augustine made similar observations: "God the Father is not wise . . . being wisdom itself."[106] God is "the essence of the truth [reality] itself."[107] God is "the good itself."[108] "God, therefore, does not live, unless by the life which he is to Himself."[109] If thou "canst discern the good in itself, thou will have discerned God."[110] "God is not good by a good that is other than Himself, but the good of all good."[111] "It is not one thing to God to be, and another to be great or to be good."[112] "But in God to be is the same as to be strong, or to be just, or to be wise, or whatever is said of that simple multiplicity, or multifold simplicity, whereby to signify his substance."[113] Hence, for Augustine God is not good, God is Goodness; God is not beautiful, God is Beauty; God is not truthful, God is Truth; God is not lovely, God is Love; God is not real, God is Reality; and God does not exist, God is Existence.

Paul Tillich said that the question "What is God?" forces human speculation into supernaturalism, that is, a way of thinking that divides things into two classes: (1) natural beings, such as trees, houses, butterflies, rocks, and human beings; and (2) supernatural beings, of which there may be only one, namely, God. There are two undesirable results from this style of thinking. One is negative theology. If God is a being, then he is a sort of being very different from other beings. They are finite; he is infinite. They change; he is changeless. They are mortal; he is immortal. They are evil; he is good. The second undesirable result is that the terms used to describe things cannot be applied to God-as-a-being as they are applied to beings other than God.

God is said to see, to hear, to know, and to love, and a human being is also said to see, to hear, to know, and to love. But these activities are not the same. The human needs eyes, ears, a brain, and other physical organs for these activities. Both divine and human beings are said to be angry, jealous, fearful, and kind, but not in the same manner or in the same way. So theologians have defended what is called the language of analogy. God is a "father," yet not a father in the human sense. God is a "person," yet not like a human person. The undesirable result is that meaning is drained from terminology appropriate to the human self. But this could be helpful were it understood that activities, attitudes, emotions, thoughts, values, and qualities assigned to the deity is the language of devotion rather than the language of philosophy and science. God is a "what" in the order of myth. Philosophy must demythologize the myth to comprehend the nature of reality yet recognize the role of myth in the full lives of human beings.

The Advaita Vedāntic interpretation of the insights of the *Upaniṣads* point the way. Brahman is not a god. "Brahman" is synonymous with the Absolute or Totality. All things and all values are manifestations or appearances of Brahman. Brahman is the All, the One without a second. Brahman cannot be known nor worshipped for the simple reason that knowing and worshipping require a distinction between knower and known, between worshipper and the object of worship. But no subject-object relationship can be established with respect to Brahman. There is nothing outside Brahman. Brahman is both knower and known, both worshipper and worshipped. Brahman has no qualities. Therefore Brahman is said to be qualityless (*nirguṇa*). This is what Augustine meant when he said that God cannot be a substance with attributes. Brahman is the whatness of whats, the beingness of beings, the objectivity of objects, and the subjectivity of subjects. Advaita Vedāntists realize that, since Brahman is the All, everything affirmed of Brahman must also be denied of Brahman. Nothing can be excluded from Brahman. Brahman is, Brahman is not, Brahman both is and is not, Brahman neither is nor is not! The way of affirmation-negation must be carried to this extreme if one is to discuss the nature of Brahman. This violates the law of noncontradition. Brahman reduces all speech to silence, all thought to no thought, all worship to no worship. Yet the seers of the *Upaniṣads* and the

Vedāntic interpreters did in fact write and speak about Brahman. How can this be? The answer is that there are two modes of dealing with Brahman: *nirguṇa* (without qualities) and *saguṇa* (with qualities). Although the *Upaniṣads* refer to both Nirguṇa Brahman and Saguṇa Brahman, there is only one Brahman. Nirguṇa is Brahman as it is. Saguṇa is Brahman insofar as it can be talked about, thought about, and worshipped. Nirguṇa is Brahman in reality; Saguṇa is Brahman in appearance. Nirguṇa is Brahman as unknowable; Saguṇa is Brahman as knowable. Nirguṇa cannot be worshipped; Saguṇa is an object of worship. Nirguṇa is the Absolute; Saguṇa is Īśvara (the Lord). Both modes are legitimate. Nirguṇa presents Brahman as it is, Saguṇa as it can be known.

Advaita Vedāntism clarifies the problems inherent in the question "What is God?" by reminding us that the question is in the mode of religious worship, and therefore should not be answered as if it were a question about the Absolute. Tillich wrote, "The being of God is being-itself. The being of God cannot be understood as the existence of being alongside others or above others. . . . Many confusions in the doctrine of God and many apologetic weaknesses could be avoided if God were understood first of all as being-itself or as the ground of being."[114] But Tillich continued to baffle his readers by using the word *God* for both the object of religious worship and the ground of being. In *The Courage to Be*[115] Tillich referred to "the God above god,"[116] "the God above God,"[117] "the God beyond God,"[118] "the God above the God of theism,"[119] and "the God who transcends the God of the religions."[120]

The Advaita Vedāntists carefully distinguish Nirguṇa Brahman, the Absolute or Totality, from Saguṇa Brahman, God or the Lord. The former are in the mode of absolutism; the latter are in the mode of relativism. The former are necessary for philosophy, the latter for worship. "What is God?" is a proper question to ask when dealing with the ultimate object of worship, and the answer should refer to a being with qualities. But "What is God?" is not a proper question when asking about the Absolute. God is how reality must be limited in order to be known and worshipped. When Tillich wrote "God does not exist. He is being-itself beyond essence and existence"[121] and when Augustine denied that God is a substance, they were using *nirguṇa* language—and they should have used a term like *Brahman* rather than *God*. "What is God?" is a question about the devotional aspects of man's life. "What is Brahman?" is a question best answered by silence.

The danger of not demythologizing the conception of a personal god, that is, of not understanding that *God* is a mythological way of symbolizing Totality, has been clearly and forcefully stated by Nalini Kanta Brahma in his summary of the teaching of the *Bhagavad Gītā*:

> It does not matter whether we call it realisation of God or of the Absolute, of the Personal or of the Impersonal, but if we miss the infinitude and expansion, then everything is lost. The *Gītā* had anticipated the degeneration of the

worship of the Personal God and had warned us against that contingency. The worship of the limited gods or smaller divinities, the *Gītā* tells us, produces fruits speedily; but as it is not the worship of the Infinite God, who is the Lord of all the worlds, it is of temporary value. This is the danger of the worship of the Personal God,—it soon degenerates into the worship of a limited Power having a fixed shape and form. Although all divinities are forms of the One God and have their source in Him, still as they are limited manifestations and are worshipped as such without full knowledge of their Infinite substratum, emancipation from finitude cannot result from them. Thus, while the *Gītā* strongly advocates the worship of the Personal God and regards the Bhakti line of *Sādhanā* as the easiest method of attaining the highest end, it, at the same time, repeatedly declares that as soon as the Personal God ceases to be regarded as the Infinite and becomes worshipped as a limited divinity, all hope of attaining liberation (*mokṣa*) is lost.[122]

Postlude

Fifty years. A second in geological history. A minute in cultural history. A considerable length of time in personal history. That is approximately the portion of my life that I have devoted to the study of the relationships of Eastern and Western philosophical and religious thought. What have I learned? What are my conclusions? The time has arrived to depart from the objectivity of the scholar's study and to summarize what I have come to believe.

The journey has been worthwhile. My horizons have been expanded. My appreciations have been enriched. I have not found the Holy Grail. Perhaps the pursuit itself is the Grail.

I began slowly and simply. I was blessed with loving and supportive parents. By age twenty-one I had traveled fewer than two hundred miles from the place of my birth. But I had learned to use eye, ear, nose, tongue, and hand to explore the natural world, mind to criticize my narrow social world, and heart to appreciate the limited aesthetic world and conservative religious world of my upbringing.

The years of my youth happen to have been the years that I believe future historians will describe as the period in which human beings began to realize that self-consciousness is not only the apex of cosmic evolution but also the necessary condition of the survival of life on this planet. It was the time when the self-aware animal first glimpsed the awesome fact that the future existence of all forms of life—"grass, and herb yielding seed after his kind, and the tree yielding fruit . . . great whales, and every living creature that moveth . . . cattle, and creeping thing, and the beast of the earth after his kind . . . and man in his own image"[1]—depend on human consciousness. Humans became the determiners of their own destiny. Humanity became its own god—creator, preserver, destroyer.

My liberal arts education in Western languages, Western literature, Western arts, and Western sciences conditioned me to assume the real world lay between a mysterious holy land in the east known as "Palestine" and a rich and sinful place in the west called "California." Somewhere on the other side of the globe were benighted peoples—Indians, Chinese, Japanese, Koreans—waiting to be converted to Christianity and Western culture.

Upon graduation from college I entered a Protestant theological seminary to prepare myself to become one of the "Soldiers of the Cross" who would take the true religion to the heathen. Before I had completed theological training I decided the ministry was not for me. The questions raised in the seminary were interesting. The answers offered were often pedestrian. Friends with whom I argued sometimes referred to me scathingly as "the philosopher." I, taking the appellation as a compliment, began to make plans to study philosophy after seminary graduation.

In graduate school I continued the study of literary criticism, religion, and classical Greek philosophy. I profited, more than I had anticipated, from exposure to logical positivism, analytic philosophy, and philosophy of language. In retrospect, my seven years in formal theological and philosophical studies were largely years of conflict between science and religion. More accurately, I struggled between commitment to the scientific quest for truth and commitment to the values traditionally associated with Christianity. I sometimes felt I was being pressured to choose between being vaguely right as a Christian and precisely wrong as a philosopher. I wanted to be precisely right.

After settling into my first teaching position I discovered the existentialists. I began to suspect there is something lacking in philosophical traditions that require existential protests. I decided Western philosophies have been too essentialistic. Thinking is not enough. Western philosophers from Socrates to Russell tend to deal with the human being from the chin up. I reasoned that there must have been philosophers, somewhere and sometime, concerned about human beings in their totality. I began to study Eastern thought, hoping I might find philosophies that deal with human life in its completeness.[2]

My pilgrimage has included four encompassments of the earth, five long study periods in India, including two Fulbrights and two visiting professorships, several trips to Europe, months of research in the British Library in London and the Indian National Library in Calcutta, two summers at East-West Philosophers' Conferences in Hawaii, the writing of many papers and books on Eastern philosophy, forty-five years teaching philosophy, and countless hours discussing religious and philosophical topics with colleagues. On the nonacademic side of the ledger are forty years of a marriage that produced two children and that ended with the tragic death of my wife, a happy remarriage, and a secondary career in long-distance running.

My philosophical quest, no matter where I began, has always included study of the self. The Socratic injunction *gnōthe sauton* (know yourself!) has been primary in my *sādhanā* (quest for fulfillment). George F. Kennan put the issue excellently in the Blashfield Foundation address delivered at a meeting of the American Academy of Arts and Letters on 21 May 1986 when he asked, "In this bewildering and dangerous age, when the very preservation of civilization has been placed, as though by some angry and impatient deity, in the week and trembling human hands that have so long abused it, what greater cause, what nobler commitment, could there be than to help people see themselves as they really are?"[3] My first book, after the publication of my doctoral dissertation, was titled *The Examined Life*[4] and my first book in Eastern philosophy was *The Self in Indian Philosophy*.[5]

I have chosen to present my philosophy by indicating my indebtedness to cross-cultural studies. This I wish to do by commenting briefly on twelve ideas that have influenced my thinking and living. The twelve ideas and their sources are the following: (1) *lógos* (Greek philosophy), (2) clarity (analytic philosophy), (3) *ṣedek* (Judaism), (4) *falāh* (Islam), (5) *jen* (Confucianism), (6) *ahiṁsa* (Jainism), (7) *agápē* (Christianity), (8) *hon'i* (Zen), (9) *bodhi* (Buddhism), (10) *mārgas* (Hinduism), (11) *yin-yang* (Taoism), (12) *Saccidānanda* (Indian philosophy).

Lógos

The *Metaphysics* of Aristotle opens with a sentence that has become one of the most widely known propositions in Greek philosophy: "*Pántes ánthrōpoi toû eidénai orégontai phúsei.*" W. D. Ross translated this as "All men by nature desire to know."[6] John Herman Randall, Jr. has suggested that the sentence should have been in the optative mood, "Would that all desire to know." Randall's own words are "I am not at all sure that is literally true: Aristotle never had the privilege of teaching in an American university. Had he had that chance to observe human nature, he might not have been so rash."[7] The Ross translation does not do justice to the rich meaning of the Greek text. Aristotle used the word *ánthrōpos* (human being) rather than *anḗr* (male). There are many terms he might have used to express "to know." He selected the one that means "to be assured by appeal to sense experience." *Phúsei* means that which is the case because of its essential nature, that which must necessarily be included in a definition. The curious word *orégontai* was originally a term in horsemanship meaning "to go at full gallop." Here it could mean "to lunge," "to stretch out," "to extend one's self," or "to crave." A full and accurate translation of this wonderful affirmation might be "All human beings by reason of their nature as human beings zealously seek to be assured of the truth of their opinions by appealing to sense experience."

Although *lógos* means "word," it also denotes knowledge that can be expressed in words. Such terms as *wisdom*, *reasoning*, *rational thought*, and *understood information* may be appropriate translations in different contexts.

My study of Greek philosophy led me to prize knowledge—and above all, self-knowledge. I regard self-knowledge as the distinguishing feature of human beings. The more one treasures knowledge the more human one is.

The manificent beginning of the Fourth Gospel—"In the beginning was the Logos"—strikes me as a curious mixing of Hebrew and Greek ideas. I cannot square the concept of an eternal plan of an omniscient mind with the facts of evolution. If there was a logos at the beginning, it certainly was not a mind that followed the three laws of thought descerned by Aristotle.

The only *lógos* I recognize is the slow and plodding process by which human minds solve problems. Insights may come in the knowing process, but dependable information must be intersubjectively testable and expressible. This, however, is not to deny that human beings may have noncognitive experiences that defy accurate verbalization.[8]

Clarity

My first awareness of the need for clarity of thought and expression arose when I began as a child to question expressions I found in the Bible: "Does God actually see, hear, and speak, and do floods clap their hands, do valleys shout for joy, and can hills be joyful?" The fundamentalist preacher in the church my family attended claimed the Bible is "literally true from cover to cover." But I began to suspect it contains much poetry, and that poetry is not "literally true." In my college and seminary years I received some help in thinking my way through to a solution of the problem of Biblical interpretation, but it was not until graduate school that I began to see how to resolve the issue.

The classification of statements by the logical positivists into the factual and the nonfactual—with the nonfactual further classified into the emotional, pictorial, and motivational—made sense to me. However, the Oxford analytic philosophers convinced me that this classification is far too simple. For one thing, factual statements have emotional, pictorial, and motivational connotations in different contexts. For another, there are far more uses of language than those indicated by the positivistic classification. I began the study of words as signs. I concluded that signs have three dimensions: (1) they express the symptoms of senders; (2) they appeal as signals to receivers; (3) they as symbols denote referents, designate aspects of referents, and connote effective attitudes toward referents.

I recognized the importance of being clear, precise, and accurate in the use of words, but I also realized that some experiences break the back of words; Charles Chaplin, whom I regard as a quasiphilosopher, has written that "perfect love is the most beautiful of all frustrations because it is more than one can express."[9] I felt I had to go beyond the criteria of empirical meaningfulness and semantic accuracy if I were to convey my reaction to what seemed to me to be real, true, good, and beautiful. The signs of the poet, the musician, and the lover are sometimes more meaningful than the propositions of the scientist.[10]

Ṣedek

From my study of Judaism I have gleaned the conception of justice. The ancient prophets may have been unpleasant men with stern faces, loud voices, and bad tempers, but they were on fire with the desire to promote social justice. The rights of the poor, the oppressed, and the downtrodden were defended by these courageous critics. Justice for them was no abstract principle to be discussed impassionately in law courts or classrooms. Justice was a practical relationship that ought to be manifest throughout the community. The term *community* for them denoted two types of relationships: those among human beings and those between human beings and God.[11] The Hebrew word for justice or righteousness is *ṣedek*. It designates a relationship in which each partner is an individual having rights and obligations. Closely related terms are *mishpāṭ* (the decision of a judge) and *hesed* (loyalty to one's community obligations). According to the ancient Hebrew seers the community and its members are healthy, wholesome, and in harmony with other peoples when justice subsists among humans and between humans and God.

Plato in *The Republic* helped me to see another dimension of justice, namely, justice as a principle of hierarchy. It is the principle by which the parts are properly related, each doing that which belongs to it: the rulers rule, the soldiers defend the state, and the workers work. Also in the principle of hierarchy there is subordination of the less qualified to the more qualified. In this connection I have both in India and in the United States defended some features of the Hindu caste system. I have always indicated that the caste system is not necessarily a form of social organization in which the Brahmins, Kṣatriyas, and Vaiśyas dominate the Śudras and outcastes. I prefer an honest caste system to the structuring of groups that has plagued America. Attitudes and actions against Jews, Blacks, American Indians, and women are as unjust as some of the expressions of caste in India. Justice is a social value that requires constant vigilence.[12]

Falāh

There is much in Islam I do not like. I do not care for its strict montheism, its dogmatism, its rigid doctrines, its attitude toward women, its defense of holy warfare. But I do approve of its concept of *falāh*, its rigorous discipline. So many people do not realize their potentialities because of lack of self-discipline. I have been impressed in my travels by Moslems praying on street corners, in railway stations, and in public parks. They do these acts, not to be seen, but to faithfully fulfill the obligation of prayer at specified times.

Falāh is variously translated: "do your duty," "pursue your welfare," "seek well-being," "be good." *Falāh* is in the imperative mood: " You! I mean *you* as a single individual. Get to work. Straighten out your life. Be rigorous about achieving the fullness of humanity within the Muslim community. Your social responsibilities are religious and your religious responsibilities are social. Act in accord with your belief. Be a true Muslim."

These admonitions have struck me as important. How often we excuse ourselves rather than exert ourselves. I fault Islam as a theory when it advises intolerance with respect to the non-Muslim; but my observation is that Muslims often express kindness, charity, and good will far beyond that which I have found advised in the *Koran.*[13]

Jen

Jen is the supreme moral virtue in Confucianism. This Chinese character is composed of the symbol for man and the symbol for two. Thus *jen* means two human beings living in harmony. Before Confucius *jen* meant the harmony of ruler and subjects, but Confucius generalized the concept to symbolize the harmony of any two people. Translations of *jen* include "goodness," "virtue," "benevolence," and "love." However, better translations are "true manhood," "human-heartedness," "humanity," "humanness," "man-to-man-ness," "humanhood as its best," and "hominity."

Jen is an active principle, a way of doing. It is the act-qua-motivation. Confucius stated the principle negatively: "Do not do to another what you would not desire yourself." The negative form is significant. "Do not . . ." is a warning against manipulating people. A positive principle such as the Christian Golden Rule assumes one knows what is another's good. The negative principle recommends letting others alone. Let each work out his own salvation. *Jen* advises respect for the actions, opinions, evaluations, and motivations of others.

Jen is the moral principle that makes distinctions. I despise a democracy that assumes all are equal and a Christianity that commands me to love everyone. I cherish the opportunity to be unequal to the "average person." I want the privilege to hate those who in my opinion dishonor the human condition.[14]

Ahiṁsā

Nonviolence is the virtue associated with Mahatma Gandhi and Martin Luther King, Jr. While *ahiṁsā* is a Hindu moral principle, it has been developed most fully in Jainism. The negative prefix indicates that it is a principle of avoidance. *Hiṁsā* means harm. Hence, *ahiṁsā* is best understood as harmlessness. It singles out doing harm as a heinous vice: "Do not injure another!"

Ahiṁsā in Jainism is linked with the hylozoism of the religion. "Do not harm any entity that has the capacity to be aware of pain" is perhaps the best formulation of the principle in Jainism. But according to Jainism all objects are sentient. Objects in the natural world are classified according to the number of senses they possess, ranging from one (the sense of touch) to five. A Jain monk ceremonially sweeps the path before him as he walks lest he step on an insect. He also wears a nose mask—not to avoid hurting an insect, as is commonly supposed, but to avoid hurting the air by violently squeezing it as he breaths. Similarly, he avoids clapping his hands or stamping his feet. The Jain pacific modes of behavior are perhaps best interpreted as metaphors of respect for the natural environment. The principle of harmlessness is a reminder that human beings must cease destroying the balance of nature, exhausting sources of natural energy, polluting rivers, decimating species of animal life, eroding the topsoil, destroying the ozone layer, and in additional ways committing genocide.

The situation on this planet has become so serious we must rigorously and violently control some aspects of human behavior. We must commit *hiṁsā* to create a world safe for *ahiṁsā*. I have argued, for example, that our current methods of population control are inadequate and that we may need to perform vasectomies on unwilling males and sterilize most infants at birth.[15] This proposal goes counter to my impulse to be tolerant, but the alternatives of allowing unlimited human reproduction or of continuing the existing modes of control endanger the quality of life for everyone.

Agapē

I claim no novelty in selecting love as the Christian concept that has most affected my life and thought. However, love has been interpreted so diversely both in the New Testament and in subsequent Christian thought and practice that one has difficulty distilling a definition. What is the common denominator of an individual's love for self, children, parents, spouse, the oppressed, the poor, riches, fame, possessions, reputation, food, sex, sleep, literature, art, music, church, community, nation, and God? The problem becomes more complex when it is a group rather than an individual that is said to love. And when love is reified, as in "God is love," how can any common feature be found?

Efforts to classify the Christian conception of love into three divisions in accord with three Greek words—*agápē*, *phília*, and *érōs*—have not been fully successful. Love as self-giving to others, love as friendship, and sexual love tend to merge. They are not three distinct kinds of love.

Christian love has often been identified as good will, charity, benevolence, and self-sacrifice for others. One of the problems is that Christians have usually not sufficiently recognized the centrality of self-love. One must *have* something and *be* something before one can contribute to the welfare of others. Good intentions are not enough. Only that person who loves himself or herself enough to devote time and energy to self-knowledge and self-development has a base from which to do good to another.[16] I despise the do-gooders whose desire to help others far exceeds their talents. Door-to-door peddlers of religion get short shrift at my door! The gift of an ungifted giver is poor indeed. Jesus' admonition "Love your neighbor as yourself" obviously impressed the authors of the synoptic Gospels, since all three quote it.[17] In my opinion Christian love begins with proper love of self and moves out from that base to love of others.[18] In the language of Hinduism, one starts with the *jīva* and moves to the realization that the *jīva* is a manifestation of the *Ātman* (the Universal Self).

Hon'i

Karl Barth said human beings should seek both salvation and significance. I claim that significance is a part of salvation—and especially those forms of significance that can be classified under the rubric "the beautiful." I have many memories of experiences of beauty. I have stood only one gorge away from the glaciers of the Jungfrau. I have seen the Matterhorn in moonlight, the peak of Everest and the twin peaks of Kanchenjunga at dawn, the range of the Rockies from the top of Longs Peak, Mt. McKinley white in winter snow, and the Scottish highlands aflame with heather. I have seen the Parthenon, the Pyramids, the Taj Mahal, and tiny gardens in unexpected places in Japan. I have stood in awe before the Mona Lisa in the Louvre, the Turner paintings at the Tate, Giotto's tower in Florence, and the wats in Bangkok. I have heard Lily Pons sing the "Bell Song" in *Lakmé*, the London Symphony at Royal Festival Hall, Bāul singers in West Bengal villages, and Alpine horns across meadows in Switzerland. I have read and reread the *Bhagavad Gītā*, *Laṅkāvatāra Sūtra*, the poems of Sappho, *The Odyssey*, *Aeneid*, *Divine Comedy*, *Faust*, *Hamlet*, *Leaves of Grass*, and hundreds of other literary masterpieces. The joys of eating, sleeping, talking, reading, writing, walking, jogging, of getting well after illness, of sharing ideas with friends, of making love, and of remembering such experiences—are these joys I experience, or am I the joys themselves? Would loss of memories be loss of self?

My preference for height, light, cold, dryness, action, ascent, roughness, circles, arcs, low pitches, and salinity over depths, darkness, heat, wetness, quiescence, descent, smoothness, squares, straight lines, high pitches, and sweetness may be rooted in "memories" antecedent to my conception and birth. That is, some of these preferences may be based on molecular memories—behavioral sequences manifested in biochemical energy. Others are clearly based on atomic memories—recollections of an individual consciousness. I remember, therefore I am. I am what I remember. Can self and memory be identified?

The answer—if there be an answer—I have found in the study of Zen. Zen masters sometimes use the Japanses word *hon'i* to express the unity of the aesthetic experience and the experiencer. *Hon'i* designates both grasping and expressing the reality and mystery of things. *Hon'i* is often translated as "intuition," but this does not do justice to the term, since *hon'i* designates untiring and persevering activity rather than passive waiting for insight. In Japanese drama *hon'i* is the unity of the actor with the character portrayed on the stage. The aim of the artist is to reveal in a chosen medium an experience that bridges the gap between what the object is and what the subject senses, between the external world and the self. This is what popular books on Zen try to state.[19] But—to paraphrase Louis Armstrong's remark about the meaning of his music: "Man, if you got to ask, you'll never know!"—if one has to state it, one will never grasp its full significance. *Hon'i* denotes an existential empathy in which one becomes identical with the aesthetic object.

Hon'i brings its own credentials. I once asked D. T. Suzuki how one could know when *satori* (the goal of Zen) is reached. He paused several moments, staring at me, perhaps in amazement at my stupid question. Then he shouted, "You'll know!"[20]

Bodhi

According to Buddhist legends the Hindu heretic Siddhartha Gautama left his royal home, deserted his wife and infant son, gave his clothes to a beggar, and joined a band of monks in his efforts to find meaning in life. When asceticism failed, he sat under a tree to meditate. Finally, he experienced illumination. This is known as *bodhi*. He became the Buddha (the Enlightened One). His *bodhi* consisted of four insights: (1) to live is to suffer; (2) suffering has a cause; (3) the cause is clinging; (4) there is an eightfold path for the removal of clinging, and this path leads to *Nirvāṇa*.

The Buddhist way of salvation is a rational way, but the goal transcends reason. Reason takes one to the gate. But reason cannot enter. Insight goes beyond the rational. As Plato wrote to Dionysius in his *Seventh Letter*, "a leaping spark" (*eklámpsis*) must carry the student beyond the instruction of the teacher.[21]

While I do not claim to have had a mystical ecstasy, I affirm that I have had many moments of insight. I have learned from Buddhism and from personal experience that enlightenment comes effortlessly following effort. When life fell apart after the suicide of my wife, I resolved that if I collapsed it would be despite the struggle to put things back in order. I organized my mourning, disciplined my eating and sleeping habits, programmed my teaching, studying, writing, jogging—and *bodhi* came. There was no opening of the heavens, no celestial voice, no flashing light; I came to the realization that life and love can go on, that suffering belongs, that there is a way though sorrow to significance, wholeness, fulfillment, happiness. Life became meaningful once more.

Mārgas

When I began to suspect that Western religions and philosophies are insufficient guides to life and thought, I first turned to Buddhism. But I soon had doubts that I could find in this process philosophy what I sought. I began the study of the metaphysics that emerged from the *Upaniṣads*. I have found so much of value in Hinduism that I have difficulty in selecting a single idea as the one that has been most valuable to me. Upon reflection I conclude that the premier idea from Hinduism is the plurality of the ways of life.[22] I find "the straight path"[23] of Islam and the "narrow" way[24] of Christianity constraining. I much prefer Hinduism with its four *mārgas*: (1) *karma mārga*, the way of an active life of helpfulness to others; (2) *jñāna mārga*, the way of thought that leads to the solution of existential problems; (3) *bhakti mārga*, the way of devotion to a chosen deity; (4) *yoga mārga*, the way of physical and psychological disciplines leading to a life of rich meaningfulness. The *mārgas*, as I understand them, are inclusive in the sense that any one, pursued faithfully, will encompass the values of the others. The notion that there is only one way to salvation seems to me an intolerably limited conception of the manifold potentialities of the human being. William James once said that most people live like cats asleep in a great library, unaware of the richness around them. I recall that when life began to unfold for me in college I wrote in my diary

I want to do and do and do things:
To write a thousand poems;
To drink a thousand pots of beer;
And kiss a thousand girls.

My youthful enthusiasm exceeded my talents and capacity. But the tone was right. Unreached goals my be prognostic of further opportunities in this life and in the life or lives to come. Perhaps in other times and places each *mārgayatin* (one on the path) can explore them all.

Yin-yang

The aspect of Taoism that has been most important for me is the nondestructive dualism known as *yin-yang*. Some students refer to the two principles as *yin* and *yang*, or *yin* or *yang*, or *yin* versus *yang*. Such formulations are seriously erroneous. *Yin* and *yang* are the two oxymoronic components of the totality known as *Tao*. They are contrasting-complementing, conflicting-converging, contrasting-harmonizing. The participial form is important, for they are active components. The position of *yin* (submission) is prior to *yang* (aggression) since Taoism is essentially a feminine philosophy.

Yin-yang is the chiaroscuro of both reality and value. One is impossible without the other. The list of *yin-yang* subprinciples is seemingly endless: female-male, earthly-celestial, dark-bright, cool-warm, wet-dry, passive-active, conceiving-procreating, rest-motion, wrong-right, negative-positive, rain-shine, soft-hard, evil-good, black-white, sorrow-joy, punishment-reward, death-life, retreat-advance. In the natural world the north side of a hill and the south side of a river are *yin* whereas the south side of a hill and the north side of a river are *yang*. In a painting the sea represents *yin* and the mountain represents *yang*.

One of the most interesting problems in Christianity—the problem of evil—would never have been a problem had Christianity developed a *yin-yang* conception. In Christianity, because of this deficiency, the curious figure of the devil has entered. God is responsible for all that is good. Yet evil and death seem very real. If God were fully good and fully in control, there would be no evil. Hence a quasideity has been created to account for evil.

Hinduism has no *problem* of evil, for evil is in the Godhead. The *Trimūrti* is composed of Brahmā (Creation), Viṣṇu (Preservation) and Śiva (Destruction). Taoism avoids the problem by having no gods.

The *yin-yang* polarity has many applications, perhaps none more relevant than in the sexual context. The male without the female is not male, and the female without the male is not female. Domination of one over the other is a form of suicide. A man is male only in a man-woman relationship, and a woman is female only in a woman-man relationship. Usually this implies marriage, but there are many other arrangements in which the sexual polarity may be expressed and developed.

Yin-yang is a reminder that during most of the human experiment on the surface of this planet only one half of the members of the human race have been permitted to contribute to cultural evolution. Male domination has been the usual pattern. The subjugation of females is an ancient evil that is being righted in the twentieth century. As I look over the indexes of *Philosophy and the Self: East and West* and *The Self in its Worlds: East and West* I notice how few women are listed. This is in no way a reflection on the abilities of women. Rather it is a reminder of the stupidity of men in assuming, as Aristotle did in *De Generatione Animalium* that a woman is "an impotent male." I celebrate the liberation of women.[25]

Saccidānanda

At a very tender age I began putting questions about God to my Sunday School teachers. "How can God be everywhere at once?" "Does God know now what I'll do tomorrow?" "Could I fool God and do something different?" "Can God change what happened yesterday?" I read the Bible from Genesis to Revelation when I was twelve years of age. I had been told that God himself is the author. I was surprised how much nonsense the Bible contains. I asked myself, "Who cares about those lists of patriarchs or about those so-called miracles that obviously could not have taken place? Who believes that the world was created in six days, that the sun can stand still, that the Jordan River once flowed backwards, that mountains skipped like rams and hills like young sheep, that the Red Sea parted, that a fish swallowed a man, that angels sing in the sky, that God sits in the heavens? And who believes that pi is 3.0 as did the author of I Kings 7:23?" I had discovered myth, metaphor, and allegory, but I did not have the intellectual tools to handle them. I know now that a religious institution turns its memories into myths to justify its existence, and that it selects from its folklore that which can be used to justify the institution's existence. But I did not know this at age twelve. When I compared stories about Adam, Noah, Moses, Daniel, and Jesus with stories about Santa Claus, Paul Bunyan, Joe Magarac, and Pecos Bill, I received no encouragement from parents or teachers. When I indicated that I found the Old Testament more interesting than the New, I was cautioned that this evaluation was not proper for a Christian. At age fourteen, despite my protests, I was forced to join the church.

During college years I surmised that the God of Christianity is a cultural divinity much like Osiris, Zeus, Neptune, Jupiter, Odin, and other gods. I began to refer to God as "the god concept." Not until I studied Hinduism did I find a solution to the problem that made sense to me.

Paul Tillich's conception that he first expressed as "The God Beyond God" and later as "The Ground of Being" prepared me for the conception of reality transcendent to that symbolized by the term *God*. Śaṅkara's distinction between the reality that can be symbolized, namely, Saguṇa Brahman, and the Reality that cannot be symbolized, namely, Nirguṇa Brahman, reminded me of the epistemic gap between any term and that which the term symbolizes. But it was the conception of *Saccidānanda* that finally clarified the notion of deity for me. *Saccidānanda* (Being-Consciousness-Value), particularly as developed by Śaṅkara and Aurobindo, represents the integral foundation of all that is, all that cognizes, and all that values and is valued. *Saccidānanda* is the Reality that cannot exist, for it is the ground of existence; that cannot be known, for it is the ground of knowledge; and that cannot be valued, for it is the ground of value. God is a mythical figure that makes *Saccidānanda* available for worship and thought. The term *God* designates important relationships of human beings to Reality. It does not denote an existent being.

If I were asked to itemize the basic realities, fundamental elements, existent parts, or building blocks of the universe, I might first refer historically to an ancient Greek division—solids, liquids, and vapors—or to an ancient Chinese classification—earth, air, fire, water, and wood—and then I would speak seriously of chemical elements such as atoms, electrons, neutrons, and positrons. Never would I include angels, ghosts, witches, devils, gods, or God. To refer to water, for example, as hydrogen plus oxygen plus God would be grotesque. There are contexts in which the concept of God is relevant, significant, and meaningful, but ontology is not one of them.[26]

These are twelve ideas that have shaped my life and thought. I am still learning, growing, changing. My *sādhanā* is incomplete. Perhaps that is the nature of *sādhanā*. To be human is to be not yet. The human being is a becoming. Intention is more important than attainment. The reach should exceed the grasp. Will *tat tvam asi* become a universal discovery? Will Plato's Form of the Good be actualized in time and space? Will self-consciousness evolve into what Teilhard de Chardin called the Omega Point? Will the condition that the Apostle Paul symbolized as "all are one in Christ" ever be realized?[27] When I am tempted to hold these and other "impossible dreams" such as a world of love without strife, or a Plotinian return to the One, or a Marxian classless society, I am constrained by the polarity of the real and the ideal. Perfection is a vision of a Never-Never Land. Utopia is indeed nowhere. I try to earn my daily bread by making a few melioristic contributions. I seek for no more. I hope for no less. I pray with an ancient Vedic *ṛiṣi*

Asato mā sad gamaya.
Tamaso mā jyotir gamaya.
Mṛtyor mā mrtam gamaya.
Śānti. Śānti. Śānti.

Lead me from ignorance to knowledge.
Lead me from darkness to light.
Lead me from death to immortality.
Peace. Peace. Peace.

Notes

Preface

1. This term was coined by Jakob Johann von Uexküll (1864–1944), who is considered to be the father of the science of ethology, which J. S. Mill defined as "the science of character."

Chapter 1. The Self in the Natural World—Theories of Reality

1. *Philosophy: A to Z*, ed. James Gutmann (New York: Grossett and Dunlap, 1963), p. 66.
2. Ed. Dagobert D. Runes (Ames, Iowa: Littlefield, Adams, 1955), p. 137.
3. *The Principles of Human Knowledge*, pt. 1, sec. 1–2.
4. Ibid., sec. 28, 29. Italics are mine.
5. Ibid., sec. 90.
6. Ibid., sec. 29.
7. Ibid., sec. 68.
8. Ibid.
9. *Three Dialogues between Hylas and Philonous*, ed. Colin M. Turbayne (Indianapolis, Ind.: Bobbs-Merrill, 1954), p. 41.
10. Ibid., p. 42.
11. Ibid.
12. See e.g., John O. Nelson, "Does Physics Lead to Berkeley?" *Philosophy* 57, no. 219 (January 1982): 91–103.
13. *Indian Philosophy* (New York: Macmillan, 1951), 2:625–26.
14. *Laṅkavatāra*, chap. 5. in *A Buddhist Bible*, ed. Dwight Goddard. (New York: E. P. Dutton, 1952), p. 306. All quotations from the *Laṅkavatāra* are from the translation of D. T. Suzuki and Dwight Goddard.
15. *Principles of Human Knowledge*, sec. 94.
16. Goddard, *Buddhist Bible*, p. 306.
17. Ibid.
18. Ibid., pp. 306–7.
19. Goddard, *Buddhist Bible*, p. 260.
20. Ibid., p. 294.
21. *Laṅkavatāra*, chap. 1, in Goddard, *Buddhist Bible*, pp. 280–81.
22. Sec. 1–3, in Mary Morris, trans., *Leibniz: Philosophical Writings* (New York: Dutton, 1968), p. 3.
23. Sec. 4–7, in ibid., pp. 3–4.
24. Ruth Lydia Saw, *Leibniz* (Harmondsworth: Penguin, 1954), p. 233.
25. Ibid., p. 50.
26. *The Monadology*, sec. 87, in *Leibniz: Philosophical Writings*, p. 19.

27. Ibid.
28. Sec. 18, in ibid., p. 6.
29. *The Principles of Nature and of Grace, Based on Reason*, sec. 3, in Morris, trans., *Leibniz*, p. 22.
30. *Outlines of Indian Philosophy* (London: George Allen and Unwin, 1952), p. 173.
31. *On Generation and Corruption* (trans. Harold H. Joachim) 325 a 28–34.
32. *Metaphysics* (trans. W. D. Ross) 985 b 5–9. Italics are mine.
33. *On Democritus* as quoted by Simplicius in *De Caelo* 295, in David Ross, ed. and trans., *The Works of Aristotle Translated into English* (Oxford: Clarendon, 1952), 12:148–49.
34. Plutarch, *Adv. Coloten* 4, p. 1108.
35. *God in Greek Philosophy* (Princeton: Princeton University Press, 1931), p. 132.
36. *Early Greek Philosophy* (London: Black, 1908), p. 337.
37. *Letter to Herodotus* (trans. C. Bailey) in *The Stoic and Epicurean Philosophers*, ed. Whitney J. Oates (New York: Random, 1940), p. 5.
38. Ibid., p. 10.
39. *De Rerum Natura*, bk. 1 (trans. H. A. J. Munro) in ibid., p. 70.
40. *De Rerum Natura*, bk. 2, in ibid., p. 93.
41. Ibid., p. 95.
42. See A. L. Basham, *History and Doctrine of the Ajivikas: A Vanished Indian Religion* (London: Luzac, 1951).
43. *A Source Book in Indian Philosophy*, ed. Sarvepalli Radhakrishnan and Charles A. Moore. (Princeton: Princeton University Press, 1957), p. 227.
44. Ibid., p. 233.
45. Ibid., p. 234.
46. Ibid., p. 230.
47. Ibid., p. 235.
48. Ibid., p. 229.
49. Ibid., p. 235.
50. *The Principles of Philosophy*, pt. 4, sec. 13. All the selections from Descartes in this section are from John Veitch, trans., *Descartes* (New York: Dutton, 1937).
51. *The Revolt Against Dualism* (New York: Norton, 1930), p. 27.
52. Med. 6, in Veitch, trans., *Descartes*, p. 130.
53. Pt. 2, sec. 1, ibid., p. 199.
54. Med. 6, in ibid., pp. 132–33.
55. Ibid., p. 135.
56. Pt. 4, sec. 2, ibid., p. 214.
57. Pt. 1, ibid., p. 9.
58. Pt. 4, sec. 20, ibid., p. 228.
59. *The Sāṁkhya System* (Calcutta: Y.M.C.A., 1949), p. 7.
60. 1. 4. 2, 3 (trans. Robert Ernest Hume).
61. 6. 2.
62. *The Secret of the Sacred Books of the Hindus* (Delhi: Bharati Research Institute, 1953), p. xliv. See Troy Organ, "Polarity: A Neglected Insight in Indian Philosophy" *Philosophy East and West* 26, no. 1 (January 1976): 33–39, in which I argue that Sāṁkhya needs to be reconsidered by contemporary Indian philosophers.
63. Trans. S. S. Suryanarayana Sastri, in Radhakrishnan and Moore, eds., *Source Book in Indian Philosophy*, p. 426.
64. *The Sāṁkhya Kārikā* xii (trans. Ganganatha Jha) in ibid., p. 429.
65. Ibid., xix, in ibid., p. 432.
66. Ibid., xx, in ibid., p. 433.
67. Ibid., xv, in ibid., p. 430.
68. Ibid., xvii (trans. S. S. Suryanarayana Sastri), ibid., pp. 431–32.
69. *Critique of Pure Reason*, A 51, B 75, in Norman Kemp Smith, trans., *Immanuel Kant's Critique of Pure Reason* (London: Macmillan, 1950), p. 93.
70. Ibid., B xvi–B xvii, in ibid., pp. 22–23.
71. S. Kroner, *Kant* (Harmondsworth: Penguin, 1955), p. 91.
72. *Fundamental Principles of the Metaphysic of Morals*, trans. T. K. Abbott (London: Longmans Green, 1937), p. 18.

73. *Encyclopedia of Religion and Ethics*, ed. James Hastings (New York: Scribners, 1922), 12:597.
74. *Indian Philosophy*, 2:430.
75. "Prof. J. F. Butler's Comment on 'Philosophy of Life'—A Reply" *The Philosophical Quarterly* 38, no. 4 (January 1966): 271.
76. Trans. George Thibaut, in *Source Book in Indian Philosophy*, p. 510. All quotations from Śaṅkara are from the Thibaut translation.
77. *The Vedānta Sūtras with the Commentary by Śaṅkarākarya*, 1. 1. 1, in ibid., p. 510–11.
78. Ibid., in ibid., p. 511.
79. Ibid., 1. 1. 2, in ibid.
80. These direct attacks on his opponents put the lie to the oft-repeated statement about the tolerance of Indian thought, as when in his comments on *Brahma Sūtra* 2. 2. 32 Śaṅkara made the following attack on the Buddha:

> Moreover, Buddha by propounding the three mutually contradictory systems, teaching respectively the reality of the external world, the reality of ideas only, and general nothingness, has himself made if clear either that he was a man given to make incoherent assertions, or else that hatred of all beings induced him to propound absurd doctrines by accepting which they would become thoroughly confused. So that—and this the *Sūtra* means to indicate—Budha's doctrine has to be entirely disregarded by all those who have a regard for their own happiness.

In reading Śaṅkara one should always keep in mind that his dialectic was usually that of denial rather than affirmation; his system is not monism, but nondualism.
81. Ibid., 2. 1. 6, in ibid., p. 522.
82. Ibid.
83. Ibid.
84. Ibid., 2. 1. 11, in ibid., p. 524.
85. Ibid., 1. 1. 4, in ibid., p. 512.
86. Ibid., 1. 1. 11, in ibid., p. 513.
87. *India: A Wounded Civilization* (New York: Penguin Books, 1979), p. 101.
88. *The Central Philosophy of Buddhism* (London: George Allen and Unwin, 1955).
89. *Psychotherapy East and West* (New York: Pantheon, 1961), p. 64.
90. *Mūlamadhyamakakārikās* 24. 8–10 (trans. Frederick J. Streng). See Frederick J. Streng, *Emptiness: A Study in Religious Meaning* (Nashville: Abingdon Press, 1967), p. 213.
91. *An Introduction to Indian Philosophy* (Calcutta: University of Calcutta, 1948), p. 164.
92. *A History of Indian Philosophy* (Cambridge: Cambridge University Press, 1957), 1:140–41.
93. *Outlines of Indian Philosophy*, p. 221.
94. Ibid., p. 222.
95. "The Swami and the Dragon: A Synthesis of Indian and Chinese Thought in Sung Paintings," *Art Journal* (Spring 1969), p. 282.
96. *Introduction to Indian Philosophy*, p. 165.
97. Junijiro Takakusu, *The Essentials of Buddhistic Philosophy*, ed. W. T. Chan and Charles A. Moore (Honolulu: University of Hawaii, 1947), p. 106.
98. The Jewel in the Lotus (London: Sidgwick and Jackson, 1948), p. 167.
99. *The Philosophers of China* (New York: Citadel, 1962), p. 125.
100. P. 349.
101. Ibid., p. 126.
102. Ibid., p. 160.
103. *Indian Philosophy*, 1:663–64.
104. *Psychotheraphy East and West*, p. 19.
105. *Emptiness*, p. 149.
106. Ibid., p. 169.
107. *The Tantric Tradition* (London: Rider, 1965), p. 26.
108. Ibid., p. 51.
107. *Mūlamadhyamakakārikās* 13. 8; 15. 1–6 (trans. Frederick J. Streng), in Streng, *Emptiness*. pp. 198–99.
110. James Legge, *The Texts of Taoism* (New York: Julian, 1959), p. 13.
111. *The Way of Lao Tzu*. (Indianapolis, Indiana: Bobbs-Merrill, 1963), p. 97.

112. E.g., *Tao Teh Ching*, chap. 39, in Chan, *Way of Lao Tzu*, p. 170.
113. Ibid., chap. 1, in ibid., p. 97.
114. Trans. Wing-tsit Chan, in ibid., p. 173.
115. *The Spirit of Chinese Philosophy*, trans. E. R. Hughes (Boston: Beacon Press, 1962), p. 62.
116. Chan, *Way of Lao Tzu*, p. 8.
117. *Tao Teh Ching*, chap. 45.
118. Ibid., chap. 56, trans. Wing-tsit Chan, in Chan, *Way of Lao Tzu*, p. 199.

Chapter 2. The Self in the Natural World—Causality

1. No one except philosophers who love to redefine words! Moritz Schlick in "Causality in Everyday Life and in Recent Science," *University of California Publications in Philosophy* 15 (1932), argues that when *day* and *night* are analyzed into the series of natural events they signify they are a good example of causal connection.
2. *Space, Time, and Deity* (New York: Dover, 1966), 1:8–9. First published in 1920.
3. *Mysticism and Logic and other Essays* (London: Longmans, Green, 1921), p. 180. In a letter dated 29 April 1959 he wrote that cause is "a concept which belongs to a quite outmoded view" (Barry Feinberg and Ronald Kasrils, eds., *Dear Bertrand Russell*. . . [Boston: Houghton Mifflin, 1969], p. 100).
4. *The Fundamental Questions of Philosophy* (London: Routledge and Kegan Paul, 1951), p. 159.
5. "The Dilemma of Determinism," in *The Will to Believe and Other Essays in Popular Philosophy* (New York: Longmans, Green, 1897), p. 177.
6. *A Treatise of Human Nature*, ed. Ernest Rhys (New York: Dutton, 1939). Most material on causality is found in 1, pt. 1, sec. 4, 5; bk. 1, pt. 3, sec. 1–6, 14, 15; and bk 1, pt. 4, sec. 4. In the Rhys edition these are 1:19–23, 73–96, 153–72, and 247–58. The first quotation is from p. 251.
7. Ibid., p. 155.
8. Ibid. It is interesting to note which terms Hume preferred. I find that he used the various terms in section 14—twenty-six pages in the Rhy edition—the following number of times: "power" (52), "efficacy" (34), "necessity" (24), "connection" (14), "energy" (11), "force" (10), "productive quality" (3), and "agency" (2).
9. Ibid., p. 11.
10. Ibid., p. 155.
11. *Spinoza's Ethics*, trans. A. Boyle (London: J. M. Dent, 1928), p. 1.
12. *Treatise of Human Nature*, p. 73.
13. Ibid. Notice that Hume uses the word "power" here and often through the *Treatise*. We can guess he does this to fix in the reader's mind that it is the notion of power which he wishes to eliminate.
14. Ibid., p. 78.
15. Ibid.
16. Ibid., p. 79.
17. Ibid.
18. Ibid., p. 80.
19. Ibid.
20. Ibid., pp. 80–81.
21. Ibid., p. 19.
22. Ibid., p. 154.
23. Ibid., p. 250.
24. Ibid., p. 251.
25. Ibid., p. 167.
26. Ibid.
27. Ibid., p. 249.
28. Ibid., p. 250.
29. Ibid.
30. Ibid., p. 252.

31. 4th ed. (London: Parker, 1856), 1:355.
32. Ibid., pp. 357–58.
33. Ibid., p. 358.
34. Ibid.
35. Ibid.
36. Ibid., p. 359.
37. Ibid.
38. Ibid., pp. 359–60.
39. Ibid., p. 362.
40. Ibid., p. 363.
41. Ibid., p. 365.
42. Ibid., p. 370.
43. Ibid., p. 371.
44. Ibid.
45. Ibid., p. 372.
46. Ibid.
47. Ibid., p. 441.
48. Ibid., p. 422.
49. Ibid., p. 423.
50. Ibid., p. 429.
51. Ibid., p. 431.
52. Ibid., p. 435.
53. *The Summa Theologica*, ques. 19, art. 4 (trans. Laurence Shapcote), in *Basic Writings of Saint Thomas Aquinas*, ed. Anton G. Pegis (New York: Random, 1945). All quotations from Aquinas are from this edition. To speak of God as the cause of all things may not be as foolish as one might think at first glance. If "God" is a symbol for the Ground of Being, as Paul Tillich says, and if full causality of any event is all events including this event, then "God" is the cause of all events. Hence, to alter Tennyson, "Flower in the crannied wall, to understand you, root and all, and all in all, I should need to know what God and man is."
54. Ibid., ques. 83, art. 1.
55. Ibid., ques. 19, art. 4.
56. Ibid.
57. Ibid.
58. Ibid.
59. Ibid., ques. 23, art. 1.
60. Ibid., ques. 23, art. 5.
61. Ibid., ques. 83, art. 1.
62. See Romans 9–12.
63. *An Encyclopedia of Religion*, ed. Vergilius Ferm (New York: Philosophical Library, 1945), p. 604.
64. Charles Hartshorne, *Man's Vision of God* (Chicago: University of Chicago Press, 1941), chap. 3.
65. (Cambridge: Cambridge University Press, 1929), p. 293.
66. Ibid.
67. Ibid., p. 294. Italics are Eddington's.
68. Ibid.
69. Ibid., p. 220.
70. Ibid., pp. 294–95.
71. Ibid., p. 350.
72. (Cambridge: Cambridge University Press, 1939), p. 182.
73. Ibid.
74. *Physics and Philosophy* (New York: Harper, 1958), p. 44.
75. Ibid.
76. Ibid., p. 44.
77. Ibid., p. 174.
78. Ibid., p. 186.
79. Ibid., p. 4.

80. Ibid., p. 56.
81. *Philosophy of Science* (Englewood Cliffs, N. J.: Prentice-Hall, 1957), p. 347.
82. *Physics and Philosophy*, pp. 52–53.
83. Ibid., p. 58.
84. Ibid.
85. Fung Yu-lan, *A History of Chinese Philosophy*, trans. Derk Bodde (London: George Allen and Unwin, 1937), 1:258.
86. F. Th. Stcherbatsky, *Buddhist Logic* (New York: Dover Publications, 1962), 1:119.
87. *The Central Philosophy of Buddhism* (London: George Allen and Unwin, 1960), p. 166.
88. *Essentials of Buddhist Philosophy*, p. 33.
89. Stcherbatasky, *Buddhist Logic*, 1:119.
90. Ibid.
91. *Ṛg Veda*, 1. 32. 15 (trans. R. T. H. Griffith).
92. Ibid., 2. 28. 4 (trans. H. H. Wilson).
93. Ibid., 7. 87. 7.
94. Ibid., 1. 25. 12.
95. Ibid., 5. 85. 7.
96. Ibid., 1. 24. 8 (trans. S. Radhakrishnan).
97. Ibid., 1. 123. 8 (trans. R. T. H. Griffith).
98. 1. 1. 1–2 (trans. S. Radhakrishnan).
99. The material presented here on the Indian view of causality comes from my fuller discussion in "Causality: Indian and Greek," in *Philosophy East and West: Essays in Honour of Dr. T. M. P. Mahadevan*, ed. H. D. Lewis (Bombay: Blackie, 1974), pp. 48–67, and in Troy Organ, *Western Approaches to Eastern Philosophy* (Athens: Ohio University Press, 1975), pp. 199–222.
100. (London: George Allen and Unwin, 1968), 1:529.
101. *The Religion of India* (New York: Free Press, 1958), p. 118.
102. *Indian Theism from the Vedic to the Mohammedan Period* (London: Oxford University Press, 1915), p. 231.
103. *Religions in Ancient India* (London: Athlone, 1953), p. 68.
104. *Foundations of Indian Philosophy* (Port Washington N.Y.: Kennikat, 1971), p. 201.
105. I state that *karma* refers only to human action even though this creates the interesting problem of how a *jīva* locked into a subhuman body can rise to the level of a human birth. Despite the problems inherent in limiting *karma* to human acts, it is preferable to refer to *karma* only with respect to the acts of man.
106. *The Life Divine* (New York: Greystone Press, 1949), p. 186.
107. See e.g. "*Punarmṛtyu* attains he who thinks he sees manifoldness in this world." *Bṛhad-Āraṇyaka Upaniṣad* 4. 4. 22.
108. E.g., *Mahābhārata*, *Udyoga Parva*, sec. 40.
109. The doctrines of *karma* and *saṁsāra* have sometimes been put to strange uses in India, as when Gandhi wrote forty years after his marriage at age thirteen that in the matter of sexual relations in marriage, "no coaching is really necessary in such matters. The impressions of the former birth are potent enough to make all coaching superfluous" (Louis Fischer, *Gandhi: His Life and Message for the World* [New York: New American Library of World Literature, 1954], p. 8). The view that a thirteen-year-old boy understands his own sexuality and female sexuality, and knows how to perform the sex act in a meaningful manner by reason of his previous incarnation, is absurd.

Chapter 3. The Self in the Natural World—Time

1. *The Voices of Times*, 2d ed., ed. J. T. Fraser (Amherst: University of Massachusetts Press, 1981), p. xvii. In accord with this conviction Fraser in 1966 founded the International Society for the Study of Time. The meetings and publications of the society have confirmed the founder's suspicion that views on the nature of time held by individual scientists and scholars tend to be dogmatic and often contradictory. The papers of the conferences have been published in J. T. Fraser

et al, eds. *The Study of Time*, 4 vols. New York and Heidelberg: Springer Verlag, 1972–81.

2. Ibid., p. xviii.
3. *The Letters of Charles Lamb*, vol. 2, ed. E. V. Lucas (London: Dent, 1935), p. 90.
4. *Hebrew Thought Compared with Greek* (Philadelphia: Westminster, 1960), p. 169.
5. *Concept of Nature* (Cambridge: Cambridge University Press, 1920), p. 73.
6. Fraser, ed., *Voices of Time*, p. 29.
7. *The Confessions* XI, 14 (trans. J. G. Pilkington).
8. *A History of Philosophy* (Garden City, N.Y.: Image, 1963), 4:311.
9. *The Structure of the Universe* (London: Hutchinson's, 1949), p. 42.
10. *Space, Time, and Deity*, 1:35.
11. Fraser, ed., *Voices of Time*, p. xxviii.
12. *Encyclopedia of Religion and Ethics*, ed. James Hastings (New York: Scribners, 1922), 12:334.
13. The following news item is dated 30 June 1981:

PARIS (UPI)—Time waits for no man, but on Tuesday the world's clocks will stand still for exactly one second to give the earth a chance to catch up.

The Paris-based International Time Bureau ordered the 'leap second' for precisely midnight Tuesday Universal Coordinated Time—a new-fangled name for Greenwich Mean Time—which is 8 p.m. EST.

The extra second will allow the earth's rotation to get back in phase with the precise atomic clocks that run the world these days, said ITB Director Bernard Guinot.

Guinot said the earth's spin rate—supposedly once every 24 hours—really falls behind because of the moon's tidal pull on oceans, and other factors, such as earthquakes, that makes bulges in the earth's crust.

"As rotation is not totally consistent, time must be adjusted," he says.

The U.S. Naval Observatory calculates that our planet has slowed down so much over the past 80 million years that a day today is about an hour longer than it was when dinosaurs roamed the globe.

Tuesday's is the 10th leap second the ITB has decreed since 1972 under an international scientific agreement defining the second as the basic unit of time, equal to 9,192,631,770 oscillations of an atom of cesium.

The last time the earth figuratively stood still for a second was at midnight Dec. 31, 1979 when most people were busy celebrating New Years.

After Tuesday, when will it happen again? Guinot says it's not possible to say and only time will tell.

14. "Les problèmes psychophysiologiques de la perception du temps," *Annee Psychol.*, 1923, p. 1.
15. Florian Cajori, ed., *Sir Isaac Newton's Mathematical Principles of Natural Philosophy and His System of the World* (Berkeley and Los Angeles: University of California Press, 1934), pp. 6, 8.
16. A. J. Munro, trans., *The Stoic and Epicurean Philosophers*, ed. Whitney J. Oates (New York: Random House, 1940), p. 77.
17. Cajori, *Newton's Mathematical Principles*, p. 6.
18. *De Principiis* II, III, (trans. Frederick K. Crombie) in Alexander Roberts and James Donaldson, eds., *The Ante-Nicene Fathers* (Buffalo, N.Y.: Christian Literature Publishing Co., 1885), 4:272.
19. E. Panofsky, *Studies in Iconology* (New York: Oxford University Press, 1939), p. 92.
20. *Timaeus* 38C. (trans. Benjamin Jowett).
21. Ibid., 38.
22. *Physics* 218 a 2. (trans. R. P. Hardie and R. K. Gaye).
23. Ibid., 219 b 2–7.
24. Ibid., 220 a 25.
25. Ibid., 223 a 22, 25.
26. Ibid., 223 b 29.
27. *The Confessions* XI, 12 (trans. J. G. Pilkington). All the selections from *The Confessions* are taken from this translation.
28. Ibid.
29. Ibid., chap. 13.
30. Ibid.

31. Ibid., chap. 14.
32. Ibid., chap. 15.
33. Ibid., chap. 26.
34. Ibid., chap. 27.
35. Ibid., chap. 28.
36. Ibid., chap. 30.
37. Ibid., chap. 31.
38. Ibid., chap. 20.
39. Ibid., chap. 24.
40. *Critique of Pure Reason*, Transcendental Aesthetic, sec. 2, subsec. 4 (trans. Norman Kemp Smith).
41. Ibid., subsec. 7.
42. *Space, Time, and Deity*, 2:38.
43. *Duration and Simultaneity*, trans. Leon Jacobson (Indianapolis: The Library of Liberal Arts, Bobbs-Merrill, 1965), p. 73. Originally published as *Durée et Simultanéité*, 1922.
44. *Caste and Outcast* (London: Dent, 1923), p. 75.
45. *The Autobiography of an Unknown Indian* (London: Macmillan, 1951), p. 426.
46. *Śantapatha Brāhmaṇa* 8. 4. 1. 14.
47. Ibid., 8. 7. 1. 1.
48. *The Mahābhārata, Anusanana Parva*, sec. 1, 10:5.
49. "Time in Indian and Japanese Thought." in Fraser, ed., *Voices of Time*, p. 77.
50. Ibid., p. 81.
51. *Ṛg Veda* 3. 62. 10.
52. "Synthesis in Chinese Metaphysics", in *Essays in East-West Philosophy*, ed. Charles A. Moore (Honolulu: University of Hawaii Press, 1951), p. 163.
53. See Joseph Needham, "Time and Knowledge in China and the West," in Fraser, ed., *Voices of Time*, p. 94.
54. *Buddhist Philosophy and Its Effect on the Life and Thought of the Japanese People* (Tokyo: Kokusai Bunka Shinkōkai, 1936), p. 28.
55. Ibid.
56. Ibid., p. 29.
57. Trans. Hajime Nakamura, in Nakamura, "Time in Indian and Japanese Thought," p. 86.
86. Consider Alice's experiences with time in *Alice's Adventures in Wonderland:*

> Alice sighed wearily. "I think you might do something better with the time," she said, "than wasting it in asking riddles that have no answers."
> "If you knew Time as well as I do," said the Hatter, "you wouldn't talk about wasting *it*. It's *him*."
> "I don't know what you mean," said Alice.
> "Of course you don't!" the Hatter said, tossing his head contemptuously. "I dare say you never even spoke to Time."
> "Perhaps not," Alice cautiously replied; "but I know I have to beat time when I learn music."
> "Ah! That accounts for it," said the Hatter. "He won't stand beating. Now, if you only kept on good terms with him, he'd do almost anything you liked with the clock. For instance, suppose it were nine-o'clock in the morning, just time to begin lessons: you'd only have to whisper a hint to Time, and round goes the clock in a twinkling! Half-past one, time for dinner!" (*The Complete Works of Lewis Carroll* [New York: The Modern Library, n.d.], p. 78)

Chapter 4. The Self in the Social World

1. 368 (trans. Francis MacDonald Cornford).
2. Ibid.
3. Ibid., 369.
4. Ibid. The Greek state excluded women and slaves.

5. *Politics* 1253 a 25 (trans. Benjamin Jowett).
6. Ibid., 1253 a 26.
7. Ibid., 1252 b 13.
8. Ibid., 1252 b 16.
9. Ibid., 1252 b 29.
10. Ibid., 1253 a 18.
11. Ibid., 1253 a 20–21.
12. Ibid., 1253 a 2.
13. Ibid., 1252 b 32.
14. Ibid., 1252 b 33.
15. Ibid., 1252 b 34.
16. Ibid., 1252 a 27.
17. Ibid., 1252 a 30.
18. Ibid. Aristotle included women in the state, although as subjects.
19. Ibid.
20. Ibid., 1253 a 29. He meant all human beings—both men and women.
21. Ibid., 1252 b 13.
22. Ibid.
23. Ibid., 1252 b 16.
24. Ibid., 1252 b 15–16.
25. Ibid., 1252 b 27– 28.
26. Ibid., 1252 b 29.
27. Ibid.
28. Ibid., 1281 a 2.
29. Ibid., 1280 a 33.
30. Ibid., 1280 b 30–34, 1281 a 2–4.
31. Ibid., 1253 a 9.
32. Ibid., 1253 a 28.
33. Ibid., 1284 a 3–14.
34. *Nicomachean Ethics* 1125 a 35 (trans. W. D. Ross). Aristotle probably could not imagine a great-souled woman, although he had a higher opinion of women than did most Greeks of his time.
35. Ibid., 1125 a 1.
36. Ibid., 1125 b 9.
37. Ibid., 1125 b 18.
38. *Politics* 1253 a 31.
39. Ibid., 1252 a 3–6 (trans. Benjamin Jowett).
40. Ephesians 6:1, Colossians 3:20.
41. Colossians 3:22.
42. I Timothy 2:2.
43. *Monarchy*, trans. Donald Nicholl (New York: Noonday, 1954), p. 11.
44. Ibid., pp. 92– 94.
45. *The First Treatise of Government*, pars. 56, 57. See *Two Treatises of Government*, ed. Peter Laslett (Cambridge: University Press), 1967.
46. *Leviathan*, pt. 1, chap. 13.
47. Ibid.
48. Ibid., chap. 14.
49. Ibid., pt. 2, chap. 17.
50. *The Second Treatise of Government*, sec. 1.
51. Ibid., sec. 4.
52. Ibid., sec. 7.
53. Ibid., sec. 6.
54. Ibid.
55. Ibid.
56. Ibid., sec. 7.
57. Ibid., sec. 8.
58. Ibid.
59. Ibid., sec. 12.

60. Ibid., sec. 13.
61. Ibid.
62. Ibid., sec. 95.
63. Ibid., sec. 96.
64. Ibid., sec. 97.
65. Ibid., sec. 123.
66. Ibid.
67. Ibid., sec. 124, 125, 126.
68. Ibid., sec. 127.
69. *On the Eternal in Man*, trans. Bernard Noble (New York: Harper, 1961), p. 376.
70. Ibid., p. 373.
71. Ibid., p. 374.
72. Ibid., p. 375.
73. Ibid., p. 376.
74. Ibid.
75. I. 164. 20 (trans. H. H. Wilson). The poem is repeated in *Muṇḍaka Upaniṣad* 3. 1. 1. and *Śvetāśatara Upaniṣad* 4. 6.
76. *The Dance of Shiva* (New York: Noonday, 1957), p. 4.
77. *Source Book of Indian Philosophy*, p. 355.
78. K. M. Panikkar, *Caste and Democracy* (London: Hogarth, 1933), p. 33.
79. See *United Church News*, August 1964, p. 171.
80. The material presented on Confucianism comes from my article "Confucian Ethics," *Listening* 14, no. 1 (Winter, 1979): 44–53.
81. *Confucius and the Chinese Way* (New York: Harper, 1949), p. 125.
82. *Analects* 13:18 (trans. James R. Ware).
83. Ibid.
84. *Hsiao Ching I.* See Laurence G. Thompson, *Chinese Religion: An Introduction* (Belmont, California: Dickenson, 1969), p. 39.
85. *Analects* 3:16 (trans. James R. Ware).
86. Wing-tsit Chan, "The Evolution of the Confucian Concept of Jen," *Philosophy East and West*, January 1955, p. 296. The most significant uses of *jen* may be found in *Analects* 1:2, 3, 6; 3:3; 4:2–6; 6:20, 21, 28; 7:6, 29; 8:7; 12:1, 2, 22; 13:19, 27; 14:30; 15:8, 32, 35; 17:6, 8; 19:6.
87. *Analects* 7:30 (trans. James R. Ware).
88. *The Philosophy of Wang Yang-ming*, trans. F. G. Henke (Chicago: Open Court, 1916), p. 206.
89. *Analects* 12:2 (trans. James R. Ware).
90. 557 (trans. W. H. D. Rouse).
91. *Politics* 1280 a 1–2 (trans. Benjamin Jowett).
92. In creating the words "pluralocracy" and "pantocracy" I follow the leads of Plato who created "timocracy" and "timarchy" and Aristotle who created "polity."
93. *The Two Sources of Morality and Religion*, trans. R. Ashley Audra and Cloudesley Prereton (New York: Holt, 1935), pp. 270–71.
94. *The Republic* 555 (trans. W. H. D. Rouse).
95. Ibid., 557.
96. Ibid.
97. Ibid., 558.
98. Ibid. (trans. Benjamin Jowett).
99. Ibid., 563 (trans. W. H. D. Rouse).
100. Ibid.
101. Ibid. This is strange, as equality of opportunity is later offered to both men and women in the ideal state.
102. Ibid.
103. *Politics* 1301 a 29–33 (trans. Benjamin Jowett).
104. Ibid., 1284 a 20.
105. Ibid., 1317 a 40, b 7–11.
106. Ibid., 1310 a 25.
107. Ibid., 1310 a 26–36.
108. Ibid., 1318 a 5–10.

109. Ibid., 1284 a 16, fn. 1.
110. Ibid., 1282 b 18.
111. Ibid., 1282 b 22–30.
112. Ibid., 1282 b 22.
113. Ibid., 1280 a 10–14.
114. Gilbert Ryle called Plato's blueprint for the ideal state in *The Republic* "a fairyland model rather than a plan." *The Encyclopedia of Philosophy*, ed. Paul Edwards (New York: Macmillan, 1967), 6:332.
115. *Politics* 1301 a 29–31 (trans. Benjamin Jowett).
116. Ibid., 1302 a 5.
117. Ibid., 1302 a 9.
118. Ibid., 1291 b 30–1292 a 6.
119. Ibid., 1301 b 29–35.
120. Ibid., 1283 a 28.
121. Ibid., 1302 a 8.
122. Ibid., 1318 a 33–b 5.
123. Ibid., 1318 a 37.
124. Ibid., 1318 b 1– 5.
125. Ibid., 1307 a 18.
126. Ibid., 1307 a 26.
127. Ibid., 1308 a 5.
128. Ibid., 1308 a 10.
129. Ibid., 1308 a 11.
130. Ibid., 1308 a 20.
131. Ibid., 1308 b 18.
132. Ibid., 1308 b 20.
133. Ibid., 1308 b 30.
134. John Stuart Mill, *On Liberty*, ed. Currin V. Shields (Indianapolis: Liberal Arts, 1956), p. 3. All quotations are from this edition.
135. Ibid.
136. Ibid.
137. Ibid., p. 7.
138. Ibid.
139. Ibid., p. 13.
140. Ibid., p. 16.
141. Ibid., p. 64.
142. Ibid., p. 21.
143. Ibid., p. 41.
144. Ibid., p. 68.
145. Ibid., p. 70.
146. Ibid., p. 72.
147. Ibid., p. 114.
148. The development of democracy in the West can be traced through such documents as the Magna Carta (1215), the Petition of Right (1628), the Bill of Rights (1689) the Declaration of Independence (1776), the Declaration of the Rights of Man (1789), and the Universal Declaration of Human Rights (1948). The Manifesto of the Communist Party (1848) is the document that has most radically challenged the democratic principle.
149. Luke 6:20.
150. Luke 18:25.
151. Matthew 10:34.
152. Marx wrote in his *Theses on Feuerbach*, "The philosophers have only *interpreted* the world differently, the point is, to *change* it." (See Karl Marx and Friedrich Engels, *The German Ideology, Parts I and III*, ed. R. Pascel [New York: International Publishers, 1963], p. 199.)
153. *Early Writings*, trans. E. B. Bottomore (New York: McGraw-Hill, 1964), p. 37.
154. Ibid.
155. Ibid., p. 124.
156. Ibid., p. 125.

157. "Confucius" is the Latinized name of K'ung Ch'iu or K'ung Tzu. In 1986 a Chinese graduate student at Ohio University, who had recently come from mainland China, was asked what she thought of Confucius. Her reply was "I never heard of him. Who is he?"

158. *A Short History of Confucian Philosophy* (Harmondsworth: Penguin, 1955), pp. 190–91.

159. Trans. George Bull (Harmondsworth: Penguin, 1961), pp. 134–35, 138.

160. *Perpetual Peace*, 1, 3 (trans. Lewis White Beck).

161. *Patriotism Without Flags* (New York: Norton, 1974), p. 13.

162. Ibid., p. 16.

163. *The Revolt of the Masses* (New York: W. W. Norton, 1932), p. 162.

164. *New Hopes for a Changing World* (New York: Simon and Schuster, 1952), p. 64. Dwight D. Eisenhower, commander in chief of the Allied forces in World War II and president of the United States from 1953 to 1961, turned against war as a national policy. He made the following statement before the American Society of Newspaper Editors in April 1953:

> Every gun that is made, every warship launched, every rocket fired signifies, in the final sense, a theft from those who hunger and are not fed, those who are cold and are not clothed. This world in arms is not spending money alone. It is spending the sweat of its laborers, the genius of its scientists, the hopes of its children. . . . This is not a way of life at all in any true sense. Under the cloud of war, it is humanity hanging on a cross of iron.

165. *The Lives of a Cell: Notes of a Biology Watcher* (New York: Penguin, 1978), p. 110.

166. *Sources of Indian Tradition*, ed. William Theodore De Barry (New York and London: Columbia University Press, 1958), 2:239–240.

Christopher Isherwood, writing at the time India was separating itself from British control, wrote, "The Indian nation never will be a powerful, conquering people—never. They will never be a great political power; that is not their business, that is not the note India has to play in the great harmony of nations. But what has she to play? God, and God alone" (*Vedanta for the Western World* [London: George Allen and Unwin, 1948], p. 229).

More recently V. S. Naipaul has observed, "India is without an ideology. . . . Its people have no idea of the state, and none of the attitudes that go with such an idea: no historical sense of the past, no identity beyond the tenuous ecumenism of Hindu beliefs, and in spite of the racial excesses of the British period, not even the beginning of a racial sense" (*India: A Wounded Civilization*, pp. 168–69). India, according to Naipaul, is "a wounded old civilization that has at last become aware of its inadequacies and is without the intellectual means to move ahead" (Ibid., p. 18). Nirad C. Chaudhuri thinks Hinduism is "the true nationalism" of India, yet he doubts that this is a sound base for nationhood since Hinduism "has shown anarchy can be as authoritarian as any totalitarian state" (*Hinduism: A Religion to Live By* [Oxford: Oxford University Press, 1979], pp. 24, 121).

167. Ed. H. H. Dodwell (Cambridge: Cambridge University Press, 1934), p. 728.

168. *A Tagore Reader*, ed. Amiya Chakravarty (New York: Macmillan, 1961), p. 200.

169. Ibid., p. 199.

170. "The Call of Truth," *Modern Review* 30, no. 4 (1922): 433.

171. *Creative Unity* (London: Macmillan, 1922), p. 139.

172. Ibid., p. 140.

173. Ibid., p. 142.

174. Ibid., p. 144.

175. Ibid. Mahatma Gandhi thought that although no people have yet gone beyond the national ideal, Indians have been historically trained to think beyond the nation. Gandhi wrote on 15 April 1919, "In modern times, in no part of the earth have people gone beyond the nation stage in the application of satyagraha [truth force]. . . . In India we have been trained from ages past in this teaching and hence it is that we are taught to consider the whole universe as one family" (*Gandhi: Essential Writings*, ed. V. V. Ramana Murti [New Delhi: Gandhi Peace Foundation, 1970], p. 23). Today in many parts of the world groups of people resist being members of a nation; for example, in the western prairies of Canada and the United States are about 25,000 Anabaptist Christians known as Hutterites. They refer to themselves as "God's holy people, chosen by Him out of the whole of the earth, summoned by Him out of all the nations." Their refusal to serve in the military forces and to support national wars has often caused friction with the nations of which they are unwillingly a part. See, for example, Michael Holzach, "The Christian Communists of Canada." *GEO*, November 1979, pp. 126–54.

176. Sisirkumar Mitra, *The Liberator* (Delhi, Bombay, and Calcutta: Jaico, 1954), p. 190.
177. See *The Challenge of Man's Future* (London: Secker and Warburg, 1954).
178. *How to Think about War and Peace* (New York: Simon and Schuster, 1944), pp. 157–58.
179. *The Scientific Outlook* (New York: Norton, 1931), p. 213.
180. *Posthistoric Man* (Chapel Hill: University of North Carolina Press, 1950), p. 70.
181. "Crisis in Civilization," In *Faith of a Poet*, ed. Sisirkumar Ghose (Bombay: Bharatiya Vidya Bhavan, 1964), p. 55.

Chapter 5. The Self and Values

1. *Philosophy in a New Key* (New York: The New American Library, Mentor, 1954), p. 166.
2. *Philosophy and Culture: East and West*, ed. Charles A. Moore (Honolulu: University of Hawaii Press, 1962), p. 342. Cf. "This is an aesthetic rather than a scientific objection, but it may be worth adding that scientists are more concerned with aesthetics than is commonly supposed!" (Fred Hoyle, "When Time Began," in *Adventures of the Mind*, ed. Richard Thruelsen and John Kobler [New York: Knopf, 1959], p. 172).
3. *Art Experience* (Mysore: Kavyalaya, 1954), p. 43.
4. *Principia Ethica* (Cambridge: Cambridge University Press, 1965), pp. 83–84.
5. *Matter, Life and Value* (London: Oxford University Press, 1929), p. 274.
6. *Principia Ethica*, p. 6.
7. Ibid., p. 8.
8. Ibid.
9. *An Introduction to the Principles of Morals and Legislation*, ed. J. H. Burns and H. L. A. Hart (London: Athlone, 1970), p. 12.
10. Ibid., p. 17n.
11. (Cambridge: Harvard University Press, 1926), p. 124.
12. Ibid., p. 611.
13. Ibid., p. 125.
14. *The Nature of Goodness* (Boston: Houghton Mifflin, 1903), p. 11.
15. Ibid., p. 18.
16. Genesis 25:29–34.
17. *Art, the Critics, and You* (New York: Priest, 1944), p. 90.
18. *Aesthetic Quality: A Contextualistic Theory of Beauty* (New York: Scribners, 1938), p. 227.
19. *A Handbook of Marxism*, ed. Emile Burns (London: Victor Gollancz, 1937), pp. 984–86.
20. "High Culture in a Leisure Society," *National Forum* 62, no. 3 (Summer 1982): 4.
21. Ibid., p. 5. See also Kanto's *Leisure and Popular Culture in Transition* (St. Louis, Mo.: Mosby, 1980).
22. *Nicomachean Ethics* 1094 a 4 (trans. W. D. Ross).
23. (Philadelphia: Lippincott, 1941), p. 305.
24. *Meditations* 4, 49 (trans. G. Long) in *The Stoic and Epicurean Philosophers*, ed. Oates, p. 515.
25. (Trans. C. Bailey) in Ibid., p. 36.
26. *Nicomachean Ethics* 1169 a 27 (trans. W. D. Ross).
27. *Emile*, trans. Barbara Foxley (New York: Dutton, 1948), p. 10.
28. "Let Me Live Out My Years."
29. "Rabbi Ben Ezra."
30. *Confessions* 8, 7.
31. Shakespeare, *Henry III*, act 3, scene 1, line 31.
32. (Trans. C. Bailey) in *Stoic and Epicurean Philosophers*, pp. 49, 48.
33. (New York: Macmillan, 1934).
34. (New York: Doubleday, Page, 1917), p. 81. David Grayson is a pseudonym of Roy Stannard Baker.
35. *The Republic* 357 (trans. W. H. D. Rouse).
36. *Nicomachean Ethics* 1094 a 18–22 (trans. W. D. Ross).
37. Ibid., 1096 a 6.

Chapter 6. The Self in the Aesthetic World

1. *Philosophy in a New Key*, p. 166.
2. *A Modern Book of Esthetics*, rev. ed. (New York: Holt, 1952), p. xxxv.
3. *The Principles of Aesthetics* 2d ed. (New York: Crofts, 1946), p. 2.
4. *Art* (New York: Putnam's, 1958), p. 15.
5. Ed. James Gutmann (New York: Grossett and Dunlap, 1963), p. 15.
6. *The Republic* 597 (trans. W. H. D. Rouse). "God made" must not be taken in a theological sense. The translation "we would say God made" is an excellent reminder that, although the forms are not made by God, one can avoid much sophisticated reasoning by merely stating "we would say God made it." Similarly, I have noticed in discussions with Hindus and Jains that they are accustomed to qualify statements about their religions that conflict with modern thought with face-saving phrases such as "so we say," "so we are told," "so we believe," and "so our history tells us"; for example, "Mahāvīra was able to transport his body instantly to any part of the world—so we say," "A part of the body of Kālī fell to earth at this spot . . . so we are told," "My guru can see happenings in Delhi while standing in Calcutta—so we believe."
7. Ibid.
8. Ibid. Jowett translated this as "thrice removed from the king and the truth."
9. Ibid., 598.
10. Ibid., 601.
11. Ibid., 603.
12. Ibid., 607.
13. Ibid.
14. *Art*, pp. 17–18. Bell may have borrowed the term "Significant Form" from a lecture entitled "Poetry for Poetry's Sake" delivered by A. C. Bradley in 1901.
15. (New Haven: Yale University Press, 1926).
16. Ibid., p. 36.
17. Ibid., p. 42.
18. Ibid., pp. 47–48.
19. *The Concept of Expression* (Princeton: Princeton University Press, 1971), p. 97.
20. *A Modern Book of Esthetics* (New York: Holt, 1935), p. xi. The phrase "implicitly if not explicitly" is a reminder that one of the definitions of philosophy is "the study which makes the implicit explicit."
21. Ibid., p. xiii.
22. *Art and Human Values* (Englewood Cliffs, N.J.: Prentice-Hall, 1976), pp. 143–44.
23. *Modern Book of Esthetics*, p. xiv.
24. Ibid., pp. xv, xxvii.
25. Ibid., p. xxvi.
26. Melvin Rader, *A Modern Book of Esthetics*, rev. ed. (New York: Holt, 1952), pp. xv–xvi.
27. Ibid., p. xix.
28. Pp. xxxiv–xxxv.
29. (New York: Rinehart and Winston, 1979), p. 1.
30. *Art*, p. 20.
31. Ibid., p. 27. Consider the sonnet by Edna St. Vincent Millay, "Euclid alone had looked on beauty bare."
32. Ibid., p. 19.
33. *Bonsai* (New York: Van Nostrand, 1955), p. 9. For fuller analysis of the relation of nature and art in Japan see Langdon Warner, *The Enduring Art of Japan* (Cambridge: Harvard University Press, 1965), chap. 8. See also A. K. Coomaraswamy, *The Transformation of Nature in Art* (New York: Dover, 1937).
34. *Bonsai*, p. 9.
35. Ibid., p. 1. Hajime Nakamura agrees: "The love of nature, in the case of the Japanese, is tied up with their tendencies to cherish minute things and treasure delicate things. Contrast the Japanese love of individual flowers, birds, grass, and trees with the British enjoyment of the spacious view of the sea, the Dover Cliffs, and the countryside" (*Ways of Thinking of Eastern Peoples: India-China-Tibet-Japan* [Honolulu: East-West Center Press, 1964], p. 356).

Nakamura also says the Japanese prefer the simple and compact to the distant and boundless that the Chinese prefer. As evidence he calls attention to the Chinese poet Wu-men Hui-k'ai who when he writes of autumn thinks of the moon and of summer thinks of the cool wind, while the Japanese poet thinks of cuckoos in the summer and maple leaves in the autumn (ibid., p. 357).

36. *Bonsai*, p. 2.
37. Ibid., pp. 2–3.
38. *Zen and Oriental Art* (Rutland, Vt.: Tuttle, 1965), pp. 27–28.
39. *Mysticism, Christian and Buddhist* (New York: Harper, 1957), p. 32.
40. 3:26 (trans. James R. Ware).
41. *Analects* 2:5, 1:11.
42. Ibid., 3:12.
43. Ibid., 3:17.
44. Ibid., 10:1.
45. Ibid.
46. Ibid., 8:8.
47. Ibid., 17:9.
48. *Maps of the Mind* (New York: Macmillan, 1981), p. 20.
49. See *Tao Teh Ching*, chaps. 15, 19, 28, 37, 57.
50. *A Source Book of Chinese Philosophy*, trans. Wing-tsit Chan (Princeton: Princeton University Press, 1963), p. 210.
51. Lin Yutang, *The Chinese Theory of Art* (New York: Putnam's, 1967), p. 142.
52. Ibid., p. 143.
53. Ibid., p. 140.
54. Ibid.
55. Ibid., pp. 145–46.
56. Ibid., p. 57.
57. Ibid., p. 181.
58. Ibid., p. 109n.
59. Ibid., p. 109.
60. Ibid., p. 121.
61. Ibid., pp. 43–44.
62. This material is adapted from my article "Indian Aesthetics: Its Techniques and Assumptions," *The Journal of Aesthetic Education* 9, no. 1 (January 1975): 11–27. The article also appears in my book *Western Approaches to Eastern Philosophy*, pp. 254–74.
63. *Introduction to Indian Art* (Delhi: Munishiram Manoharlal, 1969), introduction.
64. *The Elephant and the Lotus* (Bombay: Asia Publishing House, 1965), p. 210.
65. *The Heritage of Indian Art* (New Delhi: Ministry of Information and Broadcasting, 1964), p. 7.
66. *The Flowering of Indian Art* (New York: Asia Publishing House, 1964), p. 12.
67. "Essentials of Hindustani Music," *Diogenes* 45 (Spring 1964), p. 1.
68. (New York: Bollingen, 1960), 1:3.
69. *Heritage of Indian Art*, p. 7.
70. *The Mind and Spirit of India* (Delhi: Motilal Banarsidass, 1967), pp. 2–3.
71. (Boston: Beacon, 1936), p. 1.
72. Ibid., p. 242.
73. Ibid., pp. 242, 249.
74. *The Tantric Tradition*, p. 11.
75. *The Life Divine*, p. 527.
76. *The Art of Indian Asia*, ed. Joseph Campbell (New York: Random House, Pantheon Books, 1955), 1:236.
77. *The Life Divine*, p. 308.
78. *Mahābhārata*, *Vana Parva*, sec. 134 (The Pratap Chandra Roy Translation).
79. Ibid., *Adi Parva*, sec. 7.
80. *Taittirīya Upaniṣad* 2. 7. 1 (trans. Robert Ernest Hume).
81. *The Dance of Shiva* (Bombay: Asia Publishing House, 1948), p. 37.
82. *Essays in National Idealism* (Madras: Natesan, 1909), p. 32.
83. *The Art and Architecture of India* (Harmondsworth: Penguin, 1953), pp. 2, 7.
84. *The Republic* 387 (trans. W. H. D. Rouse).

85. Ibid., 605, 606, 608 (trans. Benjamin Jowett).
86. Ibid., 608.
87. See Melvin Reader and Bertram Jessup, *Art and Human Values* (Englewood Cliffs, N.J.: Prentice-Hall, 1976), chap. 9.
88. *The Civilization of the Renaissance in Italy*, trans. S. G. C. Middlemore, ed. Irene Gordon (New York: New American, 1960), p. 218.
89. Ibid., p. 225.
90. *Oration on the Dignity of Man*, trans. A. Robert Caponigri (South Bend, Ind.: Regnery/ Gateway, 1956), pp. 6–7.
91. Leo N. Tolstoy, *What is Art?*, trans. Aylmer Maude (New York: Liberal Arts, 1960), pp. 10, 14–15.
92. *The Dehumanization of Art and Other Writings on Art and Culture* (Garden City, N.Y.: Doubleday, 1956), pp. 37, 41, 48.
93. Ibid., p. 50.
94. *Art*, p. 28.
95. Ibid., p. 29.
96. *Art and Human Values*, p. 234.

Chapter 7. The Self in the Religious World

1. Nicholas Berdyaev in *The Russian Revolution* (Ann Arbor: University of Michigan Press, 1961) argues that Russian communism contends communism is a new religion in which the proletariat are the chosen people and capitalistic exploitation is the original sin.
2. (New York: Macmillan, 1912), app., pp. 339–61.
3. Ibid., p. 339.
4. *Encyclopedia of Philosophy*, ed. Edwards, 7:141.
5. Ibid., pp. 141–42.
6. Ibid., p. 142.
7. F. T. Fann, ed., *Ludwig Wittgenstein: The Man and His Philosophy* (New York: Dell, 1967), p. 11. This observation is made by the editor. All the quotations concerning Wittgenstein are selected from this collection of essays.
8. D. A. T. Gasking and A. C. Jackson, "Wittgenstein as a Teacher," in Fann, ed., *Wittgenstein*, p. 53.
9. Wolfe Mays, "Recollections of Wittgenstein," in Fann, ed., *Wittgenstein*, p. 82.
10. "Memoirs of Wittgenstein," in Fann, ed., *Wittgenstein*, p. 34.
11. Ibid., p. 35.
12. "Recollections of Wittgenstein," in Fann, ed., *Wittgenstein*, p. 80.
13. "Assessments of the Man and the Philosopher," in Fann, ed., *Wittgenstein*, p. 74.
14. Ibid., p. 71.
15. Ibid.
16. "A Biographical Sketch," in Fann, ed., *Wittgenstein*, p. 26.
17. Ibid., p. 27.
18. "Assessments of the Man and the Philosopher," in Fann, ed., *Wittgenstein*, p. 71.
19. Ibid., p. 73.
20. "Wittgenstein as a Teacher," in Fann, ed., *Wittgenstein*, p. 53.
21. Ibid.
22. Ibid., p. 55.
23. (New Haven: Yale University Press, 1934), p. 3.
24. Ibid., p. 10.
25. Ibid., p. 14.
26. Ibid., pp. 13–14.
27. Ibid., p. 25.
28. Ibid., p. 27.
29. Ibid., p. 2.

30. Ibid., p. 28.
31. Ibid., p. 29.
32. *Types of Religious Experience* (Chicago: University of Chicago Press, 1951), pp. 32–34.
33. *Systematic Theology* (Chicago: University of Chicago Press, 1963), 3:403.
34. *The Natural History of Religion*, ed. H. E. Root (Stanford, Calif.: Stanford University Press, 1957), p. 27.
35. *Magic, Science, and Religion* (Garden City, N.Y.: Doubleday, 1954), p. 17.
36. (Philadelphia: Presbyterian Board of Christian Education, 1888), p. 330.
37. Evariste Regis Huc, *Souvenirs d'un voyage dans la Tartarie, le Thibet, et la Chine* (Paris, 1850). Henry Lord, an English clergyman, concluded his book *A Discoverie of the Sects of the Banians* (1630), the first book on Hinduism written by a European, by noting that Hinduism illustrates how "Sathan leadeth those that are out of the church, a round, in the maze of errour and gentilisme." See Nirad C. Chaudhuri, *Hinduism* (Oxford: Oxford University Press, 1979), p. 110.
38. F. Max Müller, *India: What Can It Teach Us?* (New York: Funk and Wagnalls, 1883), p. 31.
39. *Magic and Religion* (New York: Philosophical Library, 1958), p. 4. E. Washburn Hopkins classified the theories into animism, naturalism, and collectivism in *Origin and Evolution of Religion* (New Haven: Yale University Press, 1925), pp. 3–5.
40. *Magic and Religion*, pp. 5–7. The thirty-two theories are Vetter's, but I have taken the liberty of rephrasing them.
41. *The Study of Religion* (New York: Scribners, 1901), p. 196.
42. *The Psychology of Religion* (Chicago: University of Chicago Press, 1916), pp. 92–93.
43. *The Psychology of Religious Experience* (Boston: Houghton Mifflin, 1910), p. 168.
44. *Eastern Religions and Western Thought*, 2d ed. (London: Oxford University Press, 1975), p. 21.
45. *An Historian's Approach to Religion*, 2d ed. (London: Oxford University Press, 1979), pp. 139–41.
46. *Systematic Theology*, 2:87.
47. *The New Being* (London: SCM Press, 1956), pp. 24, 18–19.
48. II Corinthians 5:17.
49. *Systematic Theology*, 2:89.
50. Ibid., 2:88, 89.
51. Ibid., 2:88.
52. Ibid., 2:80.
53. Ibid., 2:85.
54. Ibid., 2:86.
55. Ibid.
56. Nalini Kanta Brahma, *Philosophy of Hindu Sādhanā* (London: Kegan Paul, Trench, Trubner, 1932), p. 293.
57. *Source Book in Indian Philosophy*, ed. Radhakrishnan and Moore, p. 101.
58. 11:55. My translation.
59. 18:63. My translation.
60. 4:11. My translation.
61. See Raymond Bernard Blakney, *Meister Eckhart* (New York: Harper, 1941), p. 250.
62. *Philosophy of Hindu Sādhanā*, pp. 293, 294. Arnold Toynbee has written:

> There may or may not be only one single absolute truth and only one single way of salvation. We do not know. But we do know that there are more approaches to truth than one, and more means of salvation than one. This is a fortunate fact, because human nature is not entirely uniform. There are variations on our common human nature—a "spectrum" of different "psychological types"—and individuals with different spiritual constitutions find different approaches to truth and different means of salvation specially efficacious for themselves. This spiritual variety of human nature needs the variety of religious aid that the historical religions provide for them.

Toynbee added,

> This is a hard saying for adherents of the higher religions of the Judaic family (Judaism, Christianity, and Islam), but it is a truism for Hinduism. The spirit of mutual good-will, esteem, and veritable love that is stirring today among the adherents of all the religions is the traditional spirit

of the religions of the Indian family. This is one of India's gifts to the world. No gift could be greater and none is more timely in the Atomic Age.

(Preface to John Cogley's "The Many Faces of Religion," *Britannica Perspectives* [Chicago: Encyclopedia Britannica, 1968], 3:456.)

63. *The Gītā: A Synthetic Interpretation* (Calcutta: Sadharan Brahmo Samaj, 1964), p. 7.

64. *Orpheus: A History of Religion*, trans. Florence Simmonds (New York: Liveright, 1929), p. 3.

65. Trans. John W. Harvey (London: Oxford University Press, 1923). The subtitle of the book is "An Inquiry into the non-rational factor in the idea of the divine and its relation to the rational."

66. *The Idea of the Holy*, trans. John W. Harvey (London: Oxford University Press, 1928), p. vii.

67. Ibid., p. 8.

68. Ibid., p. 4.

69. Adapted from the definition in *Webster's New Collegiate Dictionary*.

70. *Idea of the Holy*, p. 10.

71. Isaiah 9:6.

72. Isaiah 11:6.

73. Micah 4:3.

74. John 14:27.

75. *The Teachings of the Compassionate Buddha*, ed. E. A. Burtt (New York: New American Library, Mentor Religious Classic, 1955), pp. 46–47. Burtt writes, "The following selection from the Sutta-Nipata is a hymn to love, expressed in the form of a universal benediction. It is the Buddhist 'Thirteenth Chapter of First Corinthians.'"

76. *Documents of the Christian Church*, ed. Henry Bettenson (New York: Oxford University Press, 1947), p. 49.

77. *The Four Great Heresies* (London: Mowbray, 1955), p. 139.

78. Trans. Nicol Macnicol, in Nicol Macnicol, *Psalms of the Marāṭhā Saints* (Calcutta: Association Press, 1919), p. 66. Viṭṭhal is one of the names of Kṛṣṇa.

79. G. S. Kirk and J. E. Raven, *The Pre-Socratic Philosophers* (Cambridge: Cambridge University Press, 1960), pp. 168–69.

80. Ibid., p. 168.

81. Ibid., pp. 169–70.

82. Trithelsm is not to be confused with the Christian Trinity, which is "three in one," nor with the Hindu Trimurti, which is God in three forms, Brahmā, Viṣṇu, and Śiva.

83. Charles Hartshorne and William L. Reese, *Philosophers Speak of God* (Chicago: University of Chicago Press, 1953), p. 17.

84. *Summa Theologica*, pt. 1, ques. 2, art. 3 (trans. Lawrence Shapcote), in *Basic Writings of Saint Thomas Aquinas*, ed. Anton C. Pegis (New York: Random House, 1944), 1:23.

85. William James, *The Will to Believe and Other Essays in Popular Philosophy* (New York: Longmans, Green, 1897), pp. 1–2.

86. Ibid., p. 2.

87. Ibid.

88. Ibid.

89. Ibid., p. 11.

90. Ibid., pp. 5–6.

91. Ibid., p. 6.

92. Ibid.

93. Ibid., p. 29.

94. (Trans. Mary Francis McDonald) in *The Fathers of the Church*. (Washington, D.C.: Catholic University of America Press, 1965), 54:92–93.

95. Matthew 5:27–28.

96. *The City of God*, bk. 11, chap. 23 (trans. M. Dode), in *Basic Writings of St. Augustine*, ed. Whitney J. Oates (New York: Random, 1948), 2:165.

97. Eugene William Lyman, *The Meaning and Truth of Religion* (New York: Scribners, 1933), p. 412.

98. *Things and Ideals* (New York: Holt, 1924), p. 290.

99. *Christianity* (New York: Scribners, 1940), p. 3.

100. *The Humanity of God*, trans. Thomas Weiser and John N. Thomas (Atlanta: John Knox, 1960).

101. Kornelis H. Miskotte, *When the Gods are Silent*, trans. John W. Doberstein (London: Collins, 1967), p. 11.
102. *Philo* (Cambridge: Harvard University Press, 1948), 2:109–10.
103. *A History of Western Philosophy* (New York: Simon and Schuster, 1945), p. 405.
104. *Between Man and Man* (London: Fontana, 1961), p. 80.
105. *On the Trinity*, bk. 15, chap. 5 (trans. A. W. Haddan, rev. W. G. T. Shedd) in *Basic Writings of Saint Augustine*, ed. Anton C. Pegis, 2:836.
106. Ibid., bk. 6, chap. 1, in ibid., p. 761.
107. Ibid., bk. 8, chap. 2, in ibid., p. 774.
108. Ibid., bk. 8, chap. 3, in ibid., p. 775.
109. Ibid., bk. 15, chap. 5, in ibid., p. 835.
110. Ibid., bk. 8, chap. 3, in ibid., p. 776.
111. Ibid., in ibid., p. 775.
112. Ibid., bk. 6, chap. 5, in ibid., p. 765.
113. Ibid., bk. 6, chap. 4, in ibid., p. 764.
114. *Systematic Theory*, 2:235.
115. (New Haven: Yale University Press, 1952).
116. Ibid., p. 15.
117. Ibid., pp. 182, 186.
118. Ibid., p. 188.
119. Ibid., pp. 186, 187, 188, 189, 190.
120. Ibid., p. 188.
121. *Systematic Theology*, 1:205.
122. *Philosophy of Hindu Sādhanā*, p. 316.

Postlude

1. Genesis 1:11, 21, 24, 27.
2. According to William Ernest Hocking, "A race of people who could beget so jejune a scheme of thought as logical positivism, which declares metaphysical problems meaningless, has every reason to listen quietly to the mind of the Orient" ("Comparative Study of Philosophy" in *Philosophy—East and West*, ed. Charles A. Moore [Princeton: Princeton University Press, 1946], p. 5).
3. *International Herald Tribune*. 5–6 June 1986, p. 8.
4. (Boston: Houghton Mifflin, 1956).
5. (The Hague: Mouton, 1964). Some of my other studies of Indian philosophy are the following:

"The Quest for Self-Knowledge in the West and in India," *Darshana International* 2, no. 1 (January 1962): 80–87.
"The Status of the Self in Aurobindo's Metaphysics—and Some Questions," *Philosophy: East and West* 12, no. 2 (July 1962): 135–151.
"The Self as Creation and Discovery in Western and Indian Philosophy," in *East-West Studies on the Problem of the Self*, ed. P. T. Raju and Alburey Castell. (The Hague: Martinus Myhoff, 1968), pp. 163–76.
"What is an Individual?" *International Philosophical Quarterly* 5, no. 4 (December 1965), pp. 666–75.
The Hindu Quest for the Perfection of Man (Athens: Ohio University Press, 1970), 1980.
"The Hindu Images of Man," in *Third Eye Philosophy* (Athens: Ohio University Press, 1987, pp. 126–36.

The following publications are also related to my concern about the self and its development:

"Philosophy as Integrator of General Education," *Journal of Higher Education* 21, no. 9 (December 1950): 476–78.

"Integration in Higher Education," *Journal of Higher Education* 26, no. 4 (April 1955): 180–87.
"Universities and the Educated Man," *Phi Kappa Phi Journal* 37, no. 3 (Fall 1958): 27–32.
"Humanism in Neo-Vedāntism," in *Being Human in a Technological Age*, ed. Donald M. Borchert and David Stewart (Athens: Ohio University Press, 1979), pp. 127–64.
"The Philosophical Bases for Integration," in *The Integration of Educational Experiences*, ed. Nelson B. Henry (Chicago: University of Chicago Press, 1958), pp. 26–42.
"The Use of the Humanities," *Darshana International* 5, no. 3 (July 1965): 1–9.
"On Being Philosophical," in *Philosophy: Theory and Practice*, ed. T. M. P. Mahadevan (Madras: University of Madras, 1974), pp. 298–301.
"Some Humanistic Reflections on the Twenty-first Century," *National Forum* 69, no. 3 (Summer 1979): 42– 48.

6. *Metaphysics* 980 a 21, in *The Works of Aristotle*, 2d ed. trans. W. D. Ross (Oxford: Clarendon Press, 1940).
7. *Aristotle* (New York: Columbia University Press, 1960), p. 1.
8. Some of my publications relevant to *lógos* are the following:

An Index to Aristotle (Princeton: Princeton University Press, 1949; rprt. New York: Gordian Press, 1966).
"Reason and Experience in Mahayana Buddhism," *The Journal of Bible and Religion* 20, no. 2 (April 1952): 78–83.
"Aristotle on the Educated Man," *Basic College Quarterly* (Michigan State University) 3, no. 2 (Winter 1958): 26–29.
"The Excellence of Socrates," *Darshana International* 17, no. 65 (January 1977): 27–34.

9. *My Autobiography* (Harmondsworth: Penguin, 1966), p. 477.
10. Publications of mine relevant to the problem of clarity are the following:

"The Silence of the Buddha," *Philosophy: East & West* 4, no. 2 (July 1954): 125–40.
"The Language of Mysticism," *The Monist* 47, no. 3 (Spring 1963): 417–43.
The Art of Critical Thinking (Boston: Houghton Mifflin, 1965).
"Postmanship," *The Christian Century* 85, no. 4 (24 January 1968): 106–8.
"God-Talk and Beyond," *Quest* 67 (October–December 1970): 39–46.
"Three Platonic Silences," in *Third Eye*, pp. 152–61.

11. This is the significance of the titles of two books by Martin Buber: *Between Man and Man* (1947) and *I and Thou* (1937). This duality was also the mark of Athenian democracy: the citizen was obligated to participate in the government of the city-state and also to worship Pallas Athene.
12. My following publications are related to the problem of justice:

"The Intellectual Obligation to be Moral," *The Humanist* 16, no. 6 (November–December 1956): 273–77.
"Democracy and Caste," *Darshana International* 9, no. 4 (October 1969): 51–60.
"The Bondage of Nationalism," *Cohesion* 3, no. 1 (January–June 1972): 2–8.

13. I have not written on Islam, but I have published an article on the problem of tolerance: "Two Forms of Tolerance," *The Visvabharati Quarterly* 26, no. 1 (Autumn 1960): 162–69.
14. See my article "Confucian Ethics," *Listening: A Journal of Religion and Culture* 14, no. 1 (Winter 1979): 44–53.
15. "The Anatomy of Violence," *The Personalist* 51, no. 4 (Autumn 1970): 417–33.
16. See my article "On Doing Some Good," *The University College Quarterly* (Michigan State University) 22 (November 1976): 3–16. Reprinted in *The Ohio Association of Two Year College Journal* 5 (Fall 1979): 44–48.
17. Matthew 19:19. Mark 12–31. Luke 10:27.
18. Lionel Trilling said of Sigmund Freud: "His own egoism led him to recognize and respect the egoism of others" (*The Life and Work of Sigmund Freud* [Garden Day, N.Y.: Doubleday, 1963], p. xiv).

19. The number of these books—and the variety of titles—is amazing: *Zen in the Art of Archery; Zen and the Art of Calligraphy; Zen and the Art of Flower Arrangement; Zen in the Art of Helping; Zen in the Art of Self-Help; Zen Art for Meditation; Zen and the Art of Motorcycle Maintenance; Zen in the Martial Arts; The Zen Way to the Martial Arts; Zen Combat; Zen and Confucianism in the Art of Swordsmanship; Zen in the Art of Photography; Zen and the Art of Writing; Zen Macrobiotic Cooking; Zen Tastes in Japanese Cooking: "Kaiseki"; Zen Gardens; Zen Gardening; Games Zen Masters Play; Zen and the Cross Country Skier; Zen Running; Zen of Running; Zen and Creative Management; The Zen of Seeing; Zen Shiastsu: How to Harmonize Yin and Yang for Better Health; Zen and Reality: An Approach to Sanity and Happiness on a Nonsectarian Basis; How to Practice Zen; On Zen Practice: Body, Breath and Mind; Zen Action—Zen Person; Zen for Americans; The Zen Connection; Zen Concept & Etc.; The Zen Life; Zen: A Way of Life; Zen, The Turn Towards Life; The Zen Environment; Zen Comics; Zen Telegrams; Beat Zen, Square Zen and Zen; Spelling Water by the River: A Manual of Zen Training; Zest for Zen; Zen: Zest, Zip Zap and Zing; Zen Inklings; Zen Keys; Zen Catholicism; Zen and the Cosmic Spirit; Zen Diary; Zen Edge; Zen Action/Zen Person; Zen and Hasidism.*

20. I have written nothing on Zen aesthetics. Zen is a philosophy in which those who speak do not understand and those who understand do not speak. I have, however, written on Indian aesthetics: "Indian Aesthetics: Its Techniques and Assumptions," *The Journal of Aesthetic Education* 9 (January 1975): 11–27.

21. "For this knowledge is not something that can be put into words like other sciences; but after long-continued intercourse between teacher and pupil, in joint pursuit of the subject, suddenly, like light flashing forth when a fire is kindled, it is born in the soul and straightway nourishes itself" (*Epistle VII*, 341 C [trans. Glenn R. Morrow]).

22. Some of my publications relevant to the view that there are many ways to salvation are the following:

"Pluralistic Christianity," *The Review of Religion* 9, no. 4 (May 1945): 361–65.
"Spirituality—Indian and American," *The Philosophical Quarterly* 26, no. 1 (Autumn 1960): 162–69.
"Liberalism in Religion," *Quest* 35 (October–December 1962): 13–18.
"Hinduism as *Sādhanā*," *Ohio University Review* 9 (1967): 44–52.
"The Yogic Man," *Darshana International* 10, no. 3 (July 1970): 14–18.
"A Cosmological Christology," *The Christian Century* 88 (3 November 1971): 1293–95.
"Some Contributions of Hinduism to Christianity," *Religion in Life* 47, no. 4 (Winter 1978): 450–59. Also in *Christianity and the Religions of the East*, ed. Richard W. Rousseau (Scranton, Penn.: Ridgerow Press, 1979), pp. 17–26.

23. *Sūrah* 1:5.

24. Matthew 7:13.

25. As I review my publications I am surprised by the number of articles that refer to dualism. Here are a few of them:

"The Fascination of the Terrible," *Religion in Life* 10, no. 3 (Summer 1941): 272–79.
"Browning's Message for Dark Days," *College English* 5, no. 1 (October 1943): 13–18.
"Paul Elmer More and Platonic Dualism," *Visvabharati Quarterly* 33, nos. 1, 2 (1967–68): 1–28.
"Alternation in the Spiritual Life," *Seven* (Patna, India) (1 April 1968): 7.
"An Interpretation of *Māyā*," *Visva Bharati Journal of Philosophy* 6, no. 2 (February 1970): 51–56.
"Three into Four in Hinduism," *Ohio Journal of Religious Studies* 1, no. 2 (1973): 7–13.
"*Phusis* and *Aphusis* in Aristotle," *Thomist* 39, no. 3 (July 1975): 575–601.
"Polarity: A Neglected Insight in Indian Philosophy," *Philosophy East and West* 23, no. 1 (January 1976): 33–39.
"Time and Polarity in Hinduism," in *Third Eye Philosophy*, pp. 137–51.
"Oxymorons as Theological Symbols," in *Third Eye Philosophy*, pp. 1–14.

26. My following publications are related to *Saccidānanda*:

"Proving the Existence of God," *Presbyterian Tribune* (October 1948): 13–15.
"The Philosophy of India," *Ohio University Review* 1 (1959): 59–72.
"Is God a What?" *Philosophy in Context* (Fall 1978): 30–36. Also in *Third Eye Philosophy*, pp. 35–45.

"Oxymorons as Theological Symbols," *Christian Century* (November 1984): 1128–30. Also in *Third Eye Philosophy*, pp. 1–14.

27. Galatians 3:28. A similar monism is found in the Fourth Gospel. The author of this Gospel reports that Jesus affirmed his unity with God: "I am in the Father, and the Father in me" (14:11), "the Father is in me, and I in him" (10:38), "I and the Father are one" (10:30). Jesus seemed to have anticipated a union of all human beings with God: "That they also may be one: as thou Father, art in me, and I in thee, that they may be one with us" (17:21). Teilhard de Chardin's favorite verse in the Bible was a portion of I Corinthians 15:28, which in the Vulgate translation appears as "*En pasi panta Theos*." Teilhard translated it as "That God may be all in all" and interpreted it to imply an ultimate pantheism.

Recommended Readings

Chapter 1. The Self in the Natural World—Theories of Reality

Chan, Wing-tsit. "Synthesis in Chinese Metaphysics." In *Essays in East-West Philosophy*, edited by Charles A. Moore, pp. 163–77. Honolulu: University of Hawaii Press, 1951.

———. *A Source Book in Chinese Philosophy*, pp. 10, 14, 40, 292, 516, 522, 574, 595, 752, 763. Princeton: Princeton University Press, 1963.

Conger, George P. "Eastern and Western Metaphysics." In *Philosophy—East and West*, edited by Charles A. Moore, pp. 235–47. Princeton: Princeton University Press, 1946.

Kramrisch, Stella. "Natural Science and Technology in Relation to Cultural Patterns and Social Practices in India." In *Philosophy and Culture—East and West*, edited by Charles A. Moore, pp. 156–71. Honolulu: University of Hawaii Press, 1962.

Leshan, Lawrence, and Henry Margenau. *Einstein's Space and Van Gogh's Sky*. New York: Macmillan, 1982.

Malalasekara, G. P. "Some Aspects of Reality as Taught by Theravāda Buddhism." In *Essays in East-West Philosophy*, edited by Charles A. Moore, pp. 178–95. Honolulu: University of Hawaii Press, 1951.

Moore, Charles A. "Metaphysics and Ethics in East and West." In *Essays in East-West Philosophy*, edited by Charles A. Moore, pp. 398–424. Honolulu: University of Hawaii Press, 1951.

Nikhilananda. "The Nature of Brahman in the Upaniṣads—The Advaita View." In *Essays in East-West Philosophy*, edited by Charles A. Moore, pp. 234–48. Honolulu: University of Hawaii Press, 1951.

Radhakrishnan, S., and Charles A. Moore, eds. *A Source Book in Indian Philosophy*, pp. 386–452, 506–43. Princeton: Princeton University Press, 1957.

Raju, P. T. "Metaphysical Theories in Indian Philosophy." In *Essays in East-West Philosophy*, edited by Charles A. Moore, pp. 211–33. Honolulu: University of Hawaii Press, 1951.

Sheldon, W. H. "Main Contrasts Between Eastern and Western Philosophy." In *Essays in East-West Philosophy*, edited by Charles A. Moore, pp. 288–97. Honolulu: University of Hawaii Press, 1951.

Takakusu, Junjiro. "Buddhism as a Philosophy of 'Thusness.'" In *Philosophy—East and West*, edited by Charles A. Moore, pp. 69–108. Princeton: Princeton University Press, 1946.

———. "*The Essentials of Buddhist Philosophy*, pp. 29–56. Honolulu: University of Hawaii Press, 1947.

Thompson, Laurence G. *Chinese Religion: An Introduction*, chap. 1. Belmont, Calif.: Dickenson, 1969.

Weiss, Paul. *Nature and Man*. New York: Holt, 1947.

Whitehead, A. N. *The Concept of Nature*, chap. 1. Cambridge: Cambridge University Press, 1920.

———. *Science and the Modern World*, chap. 1. New York: Macmillan, 1925.

Wild, John. "Certain Basic Concepts of Western Realism and Their Relation to Oriental Thought." *Essays in East-West Philosophy*, edited by Charles A. Moore, pp. 249–70. Honolulu: University of Hawaii Press, 1951.

Chapter 2. The Self in the Natural World—Causality

Aristotle. *Physics*, bk. 2.

Aquinas, Thomas. *Summa Theologica*, pt. 1, ques. 83, 116.

Boethius. *The Consolation of Philosophy*, book 5.

Conze, Edward. *Buddhist Thought in India*, pp. 144–58. Ann Arbor: The University of Michigan Press, 1967.

Eddington, A. S. *The Nature of the Physical World*, chap. 14. Cambridge: Cambridge University Press, 1929.

Frank, Philipp. *Philosophy of Science*, chaps. 10–12. Englewood Cliffs, N.J.: Prentice-Hall, 1957.

Harris, N. G. E. "Causes and Events." *Philosophy and Phenomenological Research* 42, no. 2 (December 1981): 236–53.

Head, Joseph, and S. L. Cranston. *Reincarnation in World Thought*. New York: Julian, 1967.

Hook, Sidney, (ed.) *Determinism and Freedom*. New York: Macmillan, 1969.

Hume, David. *A Treatise of Human Nature*, bk. 1, pt. 1, sec. 4, 5; bk. 1, pt. 3, sec. 1–6, 14, 15; bk. 1, pt. 4, sec. 4.

Kalupahana, David J. *Causality. The Central Philosophy of Buddhism*. Honolulu: University of Hawaii Press, 1975.

Mill, John Stuart. *A System of Logic*, bk. 3, chaps. 5–10.

Organ, Troy. "Causality: Indian and Greek." In *Western Approaches to Eastern Philosophy*, pp. 199–222. Athens: Ohio University Press, 1975.

———. "Radhakrishnan and Teleology." In *Dr. S. Radhakrishnan Souvenir Volume*, pp. 323–30. Moradabad, India: Darshana International, 1964.

Russell, Bertrand. *Mysticism and Logic*, chap. 9. New York: W. W. Norton, 1929.

Stcherbatsky, F. Th. *Buddhist Logic*, vol. 1, pt. 3, chap. 2. New York: Dover Publications, 1962.

Chapter 3. The Self in the Natural World—Time

Alexander, S. *Space, Time, and Deity*, vol. 1, bk. 1. New York: Dover Publications, 1966.

Aquinas, Thomas. *Summa Theologica*, pt. 1, ques. 65–74.

Aristotle. *Physics*, 217 b 29–224 a 15.

Augustine. *Confessions*, bk. 11, chaps. 10–31.

———. *On the Immortality of the Soul.*

Bergson, Henri. *Duration and Simultaneity*. Translated by Leon Jackson. New York: Bobbs-Merrill, 1965.

Boman, Thorlief. *Hebrew Thought Compared with Greek*. Translated by Jules L. Moreau, chap. 3. Philadelphia: Westminster, 1960.

Broad, C. D. "Time." In *Encyclopedia of Religion and Ethics*, edited by James Hastings, 12: 334–45. New York: Scribners, 1922.

Callahan, John F. *Four Views of Time in Ancient Philosophy*. Cambridge: Harvard University Press, 1948.

Cassirer, Ernst. *An Essay on Man*, chap. 4. New Haven: Yale University Press, 1944.

Cleugh, Mary. *Time and Its Importance in Modern Thought*. New York: Russell, 1970.

Conze, Edward. *Buddhist Thought in India*, pp. 134–44. Ann Arbor: The University of Michigan Press, 1967.

Cottle, Thomas J. *Perceiving Time*. New York: Wiley, 1976.

Danto, Arthur, and Sidney Morgenbesser, eds. *Philosophy of Science*, pt. 3. Cleveland and New York: World, 1960.

Eddington, A. S. *The Nature of the Physical World*, chap. 3. New York: Macmillan, 1928.

Fraisse, P. *The Psychology of Time*. New York: Harper and Row, 1963.

Fraser, J. T. *Time as Conflict: A Scientific and Humanistic Study*. Brookfield, Vt.: Renouf, 1978.

Fraser, J. T., ed. *The Voices of Time*. New York: Braziller, 1966.

Freeman, Eugene, and Wilfred Sellars, eds. *Basic Issues in the Philosophy of Time*. LaSalle, Ill.: Open Court, 1971.

Gale, Richard M., ed. *The Philosophy of Time*. London: Macmillan, 1968.

Gold, Thomas, and D. L. Schumacher, eds. *Nature of Time*. Ithaca, N.Y.: Cornell University Press, 1967.

Gombrich, R. F. "Ancient Indian Cosmology." In *Ancient Cosmologies*, edited by Carmen Blacker and Michael Loewe, pp. 110–42. London: George Allen and Unwin, 1975.

Grunbaum, A. *Philosophical Problems of Space and Time*. New York: Knopf, 1963.

Gunn, J. A. *The Problem of Time*. London: George Allen and Unwin, 1929.

Inge, W. R. *Mysticism in Religion*, chap. 5. London: Hutchinson, 1947.

Kant, Immanuel. *Critique of Pure Reason*, pt. 1, sec. 2.

Kaufmann, Walter. *Time is an Artist*. New York: McGraw-Hill, 1978.

Korzybski, Alfred. *Manhood of Humanity*, pp. 209–64. New York: E. P. Dutton, 1921.

Mahadevan, T. M. P. *Time and the Timeless*. Madras: Upanishad Vihar, 1953.

Munitz, Milton K. *Space, Time and Creation*. Glencoe, Ill.: Free Press, 1957.

Newton-Smith, W. H. *The Structure of Time*. Boston: Routledge and Kegan Paul, 1980.

Ornstein, Robert E. *On the Experience of Time*. Harmondsworth: Penguin, 1969.

Patrides, C. A. *Aspects of Time*. Toronto: University of Toronto Press, 1976.

Poulet, Georges. *Studies in Human Time*. Translated by Elliott Coleman. Baltimore: Johns Hopkins University Press, 1956.

Prigogine, Ilya. *From Being to Becoming: Time and Complexity in the Physical Sciences*. San Francisco: Freeman, 1980.

Priestly, J. B. *Man and Time*. London: Aldus, 1964.

Prior, Arthur N. *Past, Present and Future*. Oxford: Clarendon, 1967.

Reyna, Ruth. "Metaphysics of Time in Indian Philosophy and Its Relevance to Particle Science." In *Time in Science and Philosophy*, edited by Jiri Zeman, pp. 227–39. Amsterdam: Elsevier, 1971.

Smith, Huston. "Evolution and Evolutionism." *Christian Century*, 7–14 July 1982, pp. 75–57.

Starr, Chester G. "Historical and Philosophical Time." In *History and the Concept of Time*, pp. 24–35. Middleton, Conn.: Wesleyan University Press, 1966.

Toulmin, S. E. *The Discovery of Time*. New York: Harper and Row, 1965.

UNESCO. *Cultures and Time*. Paris: UNESCO, 1976.

Van Fraassen, Bas C. *An Introduction to the Philosophy of Time and Space*, chaps. 2, 3. New York: Random, 1970.

Zwart, P. J. *About Time: A Philosophical Inquiry into the Origin and Nature of Time*. Amsterdam: Elsevier, 1976.

Chapter 4. The Self in the Social World

Anshen, Ruth N., ed. *Freedom: Its Meaning*. New York: Harcourt, Brace, 1940.

Aronson, Eliot. *The Social Animal*. San Francisco: W. H. Freeman, 1972.

Berle, Adolf A. "Steps Toward World Unity." In *An Outline of Man's Knowledge of the Modern World*, edited by Lyman Bryson, pp. 505–23. New York: McGraw-Hill, 1960.

Brown, Norman O. *Life Against Death*. St. Paul. Minn.: Vintage, 1959.

Burridge, Kenelm. *Someone, No One*. Princeton: Princeton University Press, 1979.

Carpenter, Edward. *Civilisation: Its Cause and Cure and Other Essays*, pp. 1–56. New York: Scribners, 1900.

Cassirer, Ernst. *An Essay on Man*, chaps. 6, 10. New Haven: Yale University Press, 1944.

Chan, Wing-tsit. "Chinese Theory and Practice, with Special Reference to Humanism." In *Philosophy and Culture—East and West*, edited by Charles A. Moore, pp. 81–96. Honolulu: University of Hawaii Press, 1962.

———. "The Humanism of Confucius." In *A Source Book in Chinese Philosophy*, edited by Wing-tsit Chan, pp. 18–48. Princeton: Princeton University Press, 1963.

Chand, Tara. "The Individual in the Legal and Political Thought and Institutions of India." In *The Status of the Individual in East and West*, edited by Charles A. Moore, pp. 411–27. Honolulu: University of Hawaii Press, 1968.

Copleston, Frederick C. *Philosophies and Cultures*, chap. 6. New York: Oxford University Press, 1980.

Dasgupta, Surama. "The Individual in Indian Ethics." In *The Status of the Individual in East and West*, edited by Charles A. Moore, pp. 285–99. Honolulu: University of Hawaii Press, 1968.

Datta, D. M. "Political, Legal, and Economic Thought in Indian Perspective." In *Philosophy and Culture—East and West*, edited by Charles A. Moore, pp. 569–93. Honolulu: University of Hawaii Press, 1962.

Eliade, Mircea. *The Myth of the Eternal Return, or Cosmos and History*. Princeton: Princeton University Press, 1954.

Fromm, Erich. *Marx's Conception of Man*. New York: Frederick Unger, 1961.

———. *The Sane Society*. New York: Holt, Rinehart and Winston, 1955.

Holland, Ray. *Self and Social Context*. London: Macmillan, 1977.

Hook, Sidney. "Philosophy and Human Culture." In *Philosophy and Culture—East and West*, edited by Charles A. Moore, pp. 15–32. Honolulu: University of Hawaii Press, 1962.

Hsieh Yu-Wei. "Filial Piety and Chinese Society." In *Philosophy and Culture—East and West*, edited by Charles A. Moore, pp. 411–27. Honolulu: University of Hawaii Press, 1962.

Hsü, Lang-Kuang. *Aspects of Culture and Personality*, edited by Francis L. K. Hsü. New York: Abelard-Schuman, 1954.

Hume, David. *An Enquiry Concerning the Principles of Morals*, app. 2.

Lakoff, Sanford A. *Equality in Political Philosophy*. Cambridge: Harvard University Press, 1964.

Loiskandi, Helmut H., "Japanese Ethics: Its Sources and Values." *Listening* 14, no. 1 (Winter 1979): 73–83.

Mahadevan, T. M. P. "Indian Ethics and Social Practice." In *Philosophy and Culture—East and West*, edited by Charles A. Moore, pp. 476–93. Princeton: Princeton University Press, 1962.

———. "Social, Ethical, and Spiritual Values in Indian Philosophy." In *Essays in East-West Philosophy*, edited by Charles A. Moore, pp. 317–35. Honolulu: University of Hawaii Press, 1951.

Marx, Karl, and Frederick Engels. *Communist Manifesto*. Translated by Paul M. Sweezy and Leo Huberman. New York: Monthly Review Press, 1964.

Masaaki, Kosaka. "The Status and Role of the Individual in Japanese Society." In *The Status of the Individual in East and West*, edited by Charles A. Moore, pp. 361–72. Honolulu: University of Hawaii Press, 1968.

Mead, George H. "The Social Self." *The Journal of Philosophy, Psychology, and Social Methods* 10 (1913): 374–80.

Mei, Y. P. "The Basis of Social, Ethical, and Spiritual Values in Chinese Philosophy." In *Essays in East-West Philosophy*, edited by Charles A. Moore, pp. 301–16. Honolulu: University of Hawaii Press, 1951.

———. "The Status of the Individual in Chinese Social Thought and Practice." In *The Status of the Individual in East and West*, edited by Charles A. Moore, pp. 333–46. Honolulu: University of Hawaii Press, 1968.

Moore, Charles A. "Metaphysics and Ethics in East and West." In *Essays in the East-West Philosophy*, edited by Charles A. Moore, pp. 398–424. Honolulu: University of Hawaii Press, 1951.

Myers, H. A. *Are Men Equal?* Ithaca, N.Y.: Great Seal Books, 1955.

Nakamura, Hajime. *Ways of Thinking of Eastern Peoples: India-China-Tibet-Japan*, chaps. 9, 13, 18, 24. Honolulu: East-West Center Press, 1964.

Nikhilananda. "The Realistic Aspects of Indian Spirituality." In *Philosophy and Culture—East and West*, edited by Charles A. Moore, pp. 494–517. Honolulu: University of Hawaii Press, 1962.

Organ, Troy. "Confucian Ethics." *Listening* 4, no. 1 (Winter 1979): 44–53.

———. "The Anatomy of Violence." In *Western Approaches to Eastern Philosophy*, pp. 119–34. Athens: Ohio University Press, 1975.

———. "The Bondage of Nationalism." In *Western Approaches to Eastern Philosophy*, pp. 108–18. Athens: Ohio University Press, 1975.

———. "Democracy and Varṇa." In *Western Approaches to Eastern Philosophy*, pp. 93–103. Athens: Ohio University Press, 1975.

Pappu, S. S. Rama Rao. "Human Rights and Human Obligations. An East-West Perspective." *Philosophy and Social Action*, 8, no. 4 (October–November–December 1982): 15–28.

Pennock, J. Roland, and John W. Chapman, eds. *Equality*. New York: Atherton, 1967.

Ramaswami Aiyar, C. P. "The Philosophical Basis of Indian Legal and Social Systems." In *Essays in East-West Philosophy*, edited by Charles A. Moore, pp. 336–52. Honolulu: University of Hawaii Press, 1951.

Rees, John. *Equality*. New York: Praeger, 1971.

Saksena, S. K. "Relation of Philosophical Theories to the Practical Affairs of Men." In *Philosophy and Culture: East and West*, edited by Charles A. Moore, pp. 19–40. Honolulu: University of Hawaii Press, 1962.

———. "The Individual in Social Thought and Practice in India." In *The Status of the Individual in East and West*, edited by Charles A. Moore, pp. 347–59. Honolulu: University of Hawaii Press, 1968.

Sankamaki, Shunzō. "Shinto: Japanese Ethnocentrism." In *Philosophy—East and West*, edited by Charles A. Moore, pp. 130–136. Honolulu: University of Hawaii Press, 1951.

Stoops, J. D. "The Real Self." *Philosophical Review* 12, no. 1 (1903): 37–46.

Suzuki, D. T. "Basic Thoughts Underlying Eastern Ethical and Social Practice." In *Philosophy and Culture—East and West*, edited by Charles A. Moore, pp. 428–47. Honolulu: University of Hawaii Press, 1962.

Tawney, R. H. *Equality*. London: George Allen and Unwin, 1952.

Tesshi, Furukawa. "The Individual in Japanese Ethics." In *The Status of the Individual in East and West*, edited by Charles A. Moore, pp. 301–13. Honolulu: University of Hawaii Press, 1968.

Tucker, Robert C. *Philosophy and Myth in Karl Marx*. Cambridge: Cambridge University Press, 1961.

Werkmeister, W. H. "The Status of the Person in Western Ethics." In *The Status of the Individual in East and West*, edited by Charles A. Moore, pp. 317–29. Honolulu: University of Hawaii Press, 1968.

Wilson, John. *Equality*. New York: Harcourt, Brace and World, 1966.

Wu, John C. H. "Chinese Legal and Political Philosophy." In *Philosophy and Culture—East and West*, edited by Charles A. Moore, pp. 611–29. Honolulu: University of Hawaii Press, 1962.

———. "The Status of the Individual in the Political and Legal Tradition of Old and New China." In *The Status of the Individual in East and West*, edited by Charles A. Moore, pp. 411–27. Honolulu: University of Hawaii Press, 1968.

Chapter 5. The Self and Values

Abel, Reuben. *Man Is the Measure*, chap. 21. New York: Free Press, 1976.

Hartman, Robert S. *The Structure of Value*. Carbondale: Southern Illinois University Press, 1967.

Laird, John. *The Idea of Value*. Cambridge: Cambridge University Press, 1929.

Lepley, Ray, ed. *Value: A Cooperative Inquiry*. New York: Columbia University Press, 1949.

Osborne, H. *Foundations of the Philosophy of Value*. Cambridge: Cambridge University Press, 1933.

Parker, DeWitt H. *Human Values*. New York: Harper, 1931.

———. *The Philosophy of Value*. Ann Arbor: University of Michigan Press, 1957.

Perry, R. B. "The Definition of Value." *The Journal of Philosophy, Psychology and Scientific Methods* 11, no. 6 (1914): 141–62.

Rescher, Nicholas. *Introduction to Value Theory*, chaps. 1, 2. Englewood Cliffs, N.J.: Prentice-Hall, 1969.

Chapter 6. The Self in the Aesthetic World

Ames, Van Meter. *Introduction to Beauty*, chaps. 1, 2, 3, 16. New York: Harper and Row, 1968.

Anati, Emmanual. "The Origins of Art." *Museum* 33, no. 4 (1981): 200–210.

Cassirer, Ernst. *An Essay on Man*, chap. 9. New Haven: Yale University Press, 1944.

Coomaraswamy, Ananda K. *Introduction to Indian Art*. 2d ed. Delhi: Munshiram Manoharlal, 1969.

Ducasse, C. J. "What Has Beauty to Do With Art?" *The Journal of Philosophy* 25 (1928): 181–86.

Frondizi, Risieri. *What is Value?* LaSalle, Ill.: Open Court, 1971.

Ghose, Aurobindo. *Sri Aurobindo Birth Centenary Library*, 14:196–254. Pondicherry, India: Sri Aurobindo Ashram, 1972.

Langer, Susanne K. *Philosophy in a New Key*, chaps. 8, 9. New York: The New American Library, Mentor, 1942.

Masson, J., and N. Patwardhan. *Aesthetic Rapture*. Poona, India: Deccan College, 1970.

Munsterberg, Hugo. *Zen and Oriental Art*. Rutland, Vt.: Tuttle, 1965.

Nakamura, Hajime. *Ways of Thinking of Eastern Peoples: India-China-Tibet-Japan*, pp. 130–

52, 277–83, 355–72. Honolulu: East-West Center Press, 1964.

Organ, Troy. "Indian Aesthetics: Its Techniques and Assumptions." In *Western Approaches to Eastern Philosophy*, pp. 256–74. Athens: Ohio University Press, 1975.

Rader, Melvin, and Bertram Jessup. *Art and Human Values.* Englewood Cliffs, N.J.: Prentice-Hall, 1976.

Ray, Niharranjan. *Idea and Image in Indian Art.* Delhi: Munshiram Manoharlal, 1973.

Thurston, Carl. "The Principles of Art." *The Journal of Aesthetics and Art Criticism* 4 (1945): 96–100.

Whitehead, A. N. *Adventures of Ideas*, chaps. 17, 18. New York: Macmillan, 1933.

Chapter 7. The Self in the Religious World

Ames, Edward Scribner. "Religious Values and the Practical Absolute." *International Journal of Ethics* 32 (1922): 347–65.

Aquinas, Thomas. *Summa Theologica*, pt. 1, ques. 2.

Boethius. *The Consolation of Philosophy*, bk. 4.

Brightman, Edgar S. "The More-than-Human Values of Religion." *The Journal of Religion* 1 (1921): 362–77.

Cassier, Ernst. *An Essay on Man*, chap. 7. New Haven: Yale University Press, 1944.

Chan, Wing-tsit. "The Individual in Chinese Religions." In *The Status of the Individual in East and West*, edited by Charles A. Moore, pp. 181–98. Honolulu: University of Hawaii Press, 1968.

Hick, John, ed. *Classical and Contemporary Readings in the Philosophy of Religion.* Englewood Cliffs, N.J.: Prentice-Hall, 1964.

Ichiro, Hori. "The Appearance of Individual Self-Consciousness in Japanese Religions and Its Historical Transformations." In *The Status of the Individual in East and West*, edited by Charles A. Moore. Honolulu: University of Hawaii Press, 1968.

James, William. "The Will to Believe." *New World* (June 1896).

Kenny, A. *The God of the Philosophers.* Oxford: Clarendon, 1979.

Murti, T. R. V. "The World and the Individual in Indian Religious Thought." In *The Status of the Individual in East and West*, edited by Charles A. Moore, pp. 199–216. Honolulu: University of Hawaii Press, 1968.

Organ, Troy. "Five Forms of God-Talk and Their Perversions." In *Western Approaches to Eastern Philosophy*, pp. 149–59. Athens: Ohio University Press, 1975.

———. "God-Talk and Beyond." In *Western Approaches to Eastern Philosophy*, pp. 135–48. Athens: Ohio University Press, 1975.

Plantinga, A. *God and Other Minds.* Ithaca: Cornell University Press, 1967.

Raju, P. T. "Religion and Spiritual Values in Indian Thought." In *Philosophy and Culture—East and West*, edited by Charles A. Moore, pp. 263–92. Honolulu: University of Hawaii Press, 1962.

Regamey, Constantin. "The Meaning and Significance of Spirituality in Europe and in India." In *Philosophy and Culture—East and West*, edited by Charles A. Moore, pp. 316–41. Honolulu: University of Hawaii Press, 1962.

Rupp, George. *Beyond Existentialism and Zen.* New York: Oxford University Press, 1979.

Schiller, F. C. S. "Faith, Reason, and Religion." *The Hibbert Journal* 4 (1905–1906): 329–45.

Schneider, Herbert W. "Faith." *The Journal of Philosophy* 21 (1924): 36–40.

Smith, John E. "The Individual and the Judeo-Christian Tradition." In *The Status of the Individual in East and West,* edited by Charles A. Moore, pp. 251–67. Honolulu: University of Hawaii Press, 1968.

Swinburne, Richard. *The Existence of God.* New York: Oxford University Press, 1979.

T'ang Chün-i. "The Development of Ideas of Spiritual Value in Chinese Philosophy." In *Philosophy and Culture—East and West,* edited by Charles A. Moore, pp. 225–44. Honolulu: University of Hawaii Press, 1962.

Index

Adler, Mortimer J., 127
Advaita Vedāntism, 36–40, 197–99
Aesop, 140
Aesthetics, 143–67
Agrawala, Vasudeva S., 156, 157
Ajita, 28
Alexander, Samuel, 48, 78, 87, 88, 188
Alston, William P., 169
Ames, Edward Scribner, 176
Ames, Van Meter, 130
Ananda, 18
Andonicus, 11
Andrews, C. F., 126
Anselm, 188, 196
Aquinas, 58–61, 188, 189, 196
Aristotle, 24, 51–52, 83, 84, 96–98, 99, 111, 114, 115–18, 139, 140, 142, 145, 167, 188, 202
Armstrong, Louis, 208
Art, 129–30, 144–67; in China, 151–55; in India, 156–64; in Japan, 148–51; in the West, 164–67
Aryāsaṅga, 15
Aṣvaghosa, 15
Atomism, 23–27
Augustine, 60, 78, 83, 85, 86, 98, 140, 141, 142, 188, 193, 194, 197, 198
Aurobindo, 75, 123, 126, 157, 158, 161, 195

Bacon, Francis, 34
Bādarāyaṇa, 37
Barth, Karl, 195, 207
Baumgarten, Alexander, 143
Bell, Clive, 144, 145, 149, 166–67
Belvalkar, S. K., 27
Benjamin, A. Cornelius, 77
Bentham, Jeremy, 133
Bergson, Henri, 88–89, 113
Berkeley, George, 12–15, 16, 17, 34
Bharati, Agehananda, 44, 158
Bhattacharyya, K. C., 27
Blofeld, John, 43
Bohr, Niels, 63, 64
Boman, Thorleif, 77
Bose, Subhas Chandra, 71
Brahma, Nalini Kanta, 180, 198–99
Brahman, 37–40, 197–99, 211
Brightman, E. S., 188
Broad, C. D., 78
Brown, Harrison, 127
Browne, Lewis, 175
Browning, Robert, 140
Buber, Martin, 196
Büchner, Karl, 26
Buddha, 17, 18, 41, 68, 106, 208, 215 n. 80
Burckhardt, Jacob, 165
Burnet, John, 25
Burrell, David James, 172
Burtt, E. A., 230 n. 75

Canto, Thomas M., 138
Carnap, Rudolf, 169
Cārvāka, 27–29
Causality, 48–76; Aristotle on, 51–52; Buddhist view of, 67–70; Chinese view of, 66–67; Heisenberg on, 61–66; Hume on, 52–55; Indian view of, 70–76; Mill on, 56–58; Scholastic view of, 58–61
Chan, Wing-tsit, 45, 46, 47, 91
Chang Yen-yüan, 154, 155
Chao Meng-fu, 154–55
Chaplin, Charles, 203
Chatterjee, Satischandra, 42

Chaudhuri, Nirad C., 89, 224 n. 166
Ch'en Tu-hsiu, 123
Chiang Kai-shek, 123
Chidamian, Claude, 149–50
Chi-tsang, 41
Chrysippus, 193
Chuang Tzu, 152
Cicero, 127
Coe, George Albert, 176
Colebrooke, H. T., 27
Comte, August, 194
Confucius, 67, 91, 107–11, 152
Constantine, 142
Coomaraswamy, Ananda K., 156, 164
Copernicus, 35
Copleston, Frederick, 78
Creel, H. G., 107

Dante Alighieri, 99, 130, 193
Dasgupta, Surendranath, 42
Datta, Dhirendramohan, 42
Day, C. B., 43
De Bona, Joseph, 42
de Lemettrie, J. O., 26
Democracy, 111–24; Aristotle on, 115–18; Eastern views of, 122–24; Marx on, 121–22; Mill on, 118–21; Plato on, 114–15
Democritus, 24
Descartes, 12, 26, 29, 30–31, 34
Deussen, Paul, 27, 157
Devaraja, N. K., 157
Dewey, John, 170–71
Dignāga, 15
Diogenes Laertius, 187
Dionysius, 208
Dogen, 92–93, 150
Drury, J. M. O'C, 170
Dubs, Homer H., 47
Ducasse, C. J., 136
Durkheim, Émile, 174

Eddington, A. S., 61, 62, 63, 64
Einstein, Albert, 20, 63, 64, 87, 88
Eisai, 150
Eisenhower, Dwight D., 224 n. 164
Eliade, Mircea, 177
Eliot, T. S., 94
Emerson, R. W., 27
Empedocles, 212
Epicurus, 25, 26, 140, 141, 175

Erigena, John Scotus, 194, 196
Euclid, 19
Euhemerus, 175
Euripides, 115
Evil, 191–99
Ewing, A. C., 50

Fa Hian, 27
Feuerbach, Ludwig, 176, 195
Filmer, Robert, 99–100
Fisher, Louis, 218
Frank, Philipp, 65
Fraser, J. T., 77, 78
Frazer, J. G., 174
Freud, Sigmund, 176
Fry, Roger, 146
Fung Yu-lan, 46, 123

Gandhi, Indira, 105
Gandhi, Mahatma, 71, 135, 158, 205, 218 n. 109, 224 n. 175
Garbe, Richard, 27, 37
Gasking, D. A. T., 170
God, 187–91, 194–99
Gough, A. E., 32
Grayson, David, 141

Hack, R. K., 25
Hampden-Turner, Charles, 152
Hartshorne, Charles, 188
Heisenberg, Werner, 51, 61–66
Heraclitus, 89
Hesiod, 82, 187
Hiriyanna, Mysore, 23, 27, 42, 130
Hobbes, Thomas, 26, 100–101, 103, 125
Hocking, William Ernest, 231 n. 2
Holbach, P. H. T., 26
Homer, 141, 164, 187
Hume, David, 34, 35, 51, 52–55, 56, 58, 172, 175, 216 n.13
Hu Shih, 123

Idealism, 11–23
Isherwood, Christopher, 224 n. 166
Iśvarakṛṣṇa, 31

Jackson, A. C., 170
Jainism, 22–23
James, William, 50, 64, 188, 190–91, 209
Jastrow, Morris, 176
Jefferson, Thomas, 113

Jessup, Bertram, 147, 167
Jesus, 121, 185, 207, 234 n. 27
Jha, Ganganatha, 74
Joad, C. E. M., 131
Jones, William, 27

Kālidāsa, 90
Kamalaśīla, 67
Kant, Immanuel, 34, 36, 55, 86, 87, 125, 183
Karma, 74–76, 218 n. 105
Keith, A. Barriedale, 31
Kempis, Thomas à, 140
Kennan, George F., 201
Keśakambalin, 28
King, Martin Luther, Jr., 205
Ku Ning-yüan, 155

Lactantius, 191
Lamb, Charles, 77
Lang, Daniel, 125
Langer, Susanne K., 129, 130, 143, 146
Lao Tzu, 107
Laplace, Pierre Simon, 50
Leibniz, G. W., 18–21, 34, 82, 188, 196
Lequier, Jules, 188
Leuba, James H., 168
Leucippus, 24, 25
Lincoln, Abraham, 111, 142
Lin Yutang, 153, 155
Lippmann, Walter, 141
Liu Wu-Chi, 123
Locke, John, 12, 16, 34, 100, 101–3
Lokāyata. *See* Cārvāka
Long, Wilbur, 12
Lord, Henry, 229 n. 37
Lovejoy, Arthur O., 29
Lucretius, 26, 81, 175

Machiavelli, Niccolo, 124
Macnicol, Nicol, 74
Madhva, 37
Mādhyamika, 40–45
Mahāvīra, 22
Malcolm, Norman, 170
Malinowski, Bronislaw, 172
Malkani, G. R., 37
Mansfield, Katherine, 194
Mao Tse-tung, 123
Marcus Aurelius, 140
Marx, Karl, 121–22
Materialism, 23–29
Mays, Wolfe, 170
Mei, Y. P., 67
Metaphysical dualism, 29–34
Metaphysics, 11
Mill, J. S., 51, 56–58, 118–21
Milton, John, 172, 193
Minkowski, Eugene, 87
Mirandola, Giovanni Pico Della, 165
Monistic idealism, 12–18
Moore, Charles A., 105, 178
Moore, G. E., 131, 132
Mo Tzu, 67
Mukerjee, Radhakamal, 156
Mukerji, Dahn Gopal, 89
Müller, F. Max, 27, 172, 176
Munsterberg, Hugo, 151
Murti, T. R. V., 40, 43, 67
Murti, V. V. Ramana, 224 n. 175

Nāgārjuna, 40–45
Naipaul, V. S., 40, 224 n. 166
Nakamura, Hajime, 89, 226–27 n.35
Naravana, V. S., 156
Nation, 124–28
Nehru, Jawaharlal, 158
Neihardt, John G., 140
Newton, Isaac, 63, 64, 65, 66, 81, 82
Nietzsche, F. W., 194
Northrop, F. S. C., 65

Origen, 82
Ortega y Gasset, José, 125, 166
Otto, Max, 194
Otto, Rudolf, 182–84

Paley, William, 189
Palmer, George Herbert, 134
Parker, DeWitt H., 144, 146
Parmenides, 23, 24, 25
Pascal, Blaise, 190
Pater, Walter, 147
Paul, 61, 98, 121, 177, 212
Peirce, C. S., 64
Perry, Ralph Barton, 134
Phelps, William Lyon, 139
Philo, 195
Piéron, Henri, 80
Plato, 41, 83, 95, 96, 111, 114–15, 142, 145, 148, 164, 204, 208, 212
Plotinus, 188, 212

Pluralistic idealism, 18–23
Pluralistic materialism, 23–29

Rader, Melvin, 144, 147, 148, 167
Radhakrishnan, S., 16, 27, 37, 43, 105, 158, 177, 178
Rall, Harris F., 195
Rāmānuja, 37, 188
Ranade, R. D., 27
Randall, John Herman, Jr., 202
Reid, L. A., 146
Reinach, Solomon, 182
Religion, 168–97; classifications of, 177–81; nature of, 168–72; origin of, 172–76; values of, 181–87
Renou, Louis, 74
Ross, W. D., 202
Rousseau, Jean Jacques, 140
Rowland, Benjamin, 164
Roy, M. N., 123
Royce, Josiah, 188
Rufinus, 185
Runes, Dagobert D., 49
Russell, Bertrand, 50, 126, 127, 170, 196, 201
Ryle, Gilbert, 223 n. 114

Sāṁkhya, 31–34
Śaṅkara, 7, 27, 32, 36–40, 42, 161, 188, 215 n. 80
Saw, Ruth Lydia, 20
Saxena, Sishil Kumar, 156
Scheler, Max, 103
Schlick, Moritz, 216 n. 1
Schopenhauer, Arthur, 27, 157
Schweitzer, Albert, 157
Seal, Brejendra Nath, 181
Seidenberg, Roderick, 127
Sen-no-Rikyu, 151
Shahn, Ben, 146
Shakespeare, William, 79, 130, 135
Shen Tsung-ch'ien, 154
Shih-t'ao, 153, 154
Sidgwick, Henry, 131
Singh, Bilbir, 73
Snow, C. P., 79, 148
Social state, 94–128; Aristotle on, 96–98; Buddhist view of, 106–7; Chinese view of, 107–11; medieval Christian view of, 98–100; Hindu view of, 103–6; Hobbes on, 100–101; Locke on, 101–3; Plato on, 95; Scheler on, 103
Socinus, Faustus, 188
Socrates, 25, 30, 95, 114, 127, 201
Solipsism, 12
Spencer, Herbert, 175
Spinoza, 18, 34, 53, 141, 188
Stcherbatsky, F. Th., 42, 68
Streng, Frederick J., 44
Suzuki, D. T., 45, 92, 124, 151, 208

Tagore, Rabindranath, 126, 127, 157
Takakusu, Junjiro, 42, 68
Taoism, 45–47, 152, 209–10
Tchaikovsky, Peter Ilich, 194
Teilhard de Chardin, Pierre, 195, 212, 234 n. 27
Thadani, T. V., 32
Thomas, Lewis, 126
Tillich, Paul, 172, 177–78, 197, 198, 211
Time, 77–93; Buddhist view of, 92–93; Chinese view of, 90–92; Indian view of, 89–90; Western theories of, 82–89
Tolstoy, Leo, 166
Tormey, Alan, 147
Toynbee, Arnold, 177, 229 n. 62
Transcendental metaphysics, 34–47
Tukārām, 186
Tylor, E. B., 174

Ullman, James Ramsey, 139

Vājñavalkya, 32
Value, 129–42
Vardhamāna. *See* Mahāvīra
Vetter, George B., 173–74
Vidyabusana, S. C., 27
Vivekananda, 158
von Hartmann, Karl Robert Eduard, 176
von Uexküll, Jakob Johann, 213 n. 1

Wach, Joachim, 171–72
Walker, Benjamin, 74
Ward, J. W. C., 185
Watts, Alan W., 40, 43
Weber, Max, 74
Whitehead, A. N., 77
Whitrow, C. J., 78
Wieman, H. N., 189
Wilkinson, T. S., 106
Wilson, H. H., 27
Wittgenstein, Ludwig, 169, 170

Wolfson, Harry, 195
Wu Tao-tse, 154

Xenophanes, 187

Yardhamāna, 22
Yogācāra, 15–18

Zimmer, Heinrich, 156, 158